INTERNATIONAL BUSINESS LAW

This book provides an accessible introduction to selected new issues in transnational law, and connects them to existing theoretical debates on transnational business regulation. More specifically, (i) it introduces the argument about the evolving character of contemporary international business regulation; (ii) it provides an overview of some of the main fields of law that are currently important for firms that operate across borders; and (iii) it sets out an interpretive framework for making sense of disparate developments occurring across a number of jurisdictions, among which are the form of regulation and style of enforcement, issues of legal certainty, and behavioural aspects of regulation.

The selected topics are indicative of some key issues confronting businesses looking to operate across national borders, as well as policy makers seeking to introduce and enforce meaningful regulatory standards in an increasingly global society. Topics include: consumer law; product liability; warranty law and obsolescence; collective redress; alternative dispute resolution; corporate wrongdoing; corporate governance; and e-commerce.

This timely work offers a novel perspective on transnational business law and examines a range of legal issues that preoccupy companies operating transnationally. This book is intended not only for law students looking for an introduction, overview or commentary on the contemporary state of international business law, but also for anyone looking for an introduction to the regulation of business in a global, inter-connected economy.

International Business Law

Emerging Fields of Regulation

Mark Fenwick and Stefan Wrbka

·H A R T·

OXFORD · LONDON · NEW YORK · NEW DELHI · SYDNEY

HART PUBLISHING

Bloomsbury Publishing Plc

Kemp House, Chawley Park, Cumnor Hill, Oxford, OX2 9PH, UK

HART PUBLISHING, the Hart/Stag logo, BLOOMSBURY and the Diana logo are
trademarks of Bloomsbury Publishing Plc

First published in Great Britain 2018

Copyright © Mark Fenwick and Stefan Wrbka, 2018

A catalogue record for this book is available from the British Library.

Library of Congress Cataloging-in-Publication data

Names: Fenwick, Mark (Law teacher), author. | Wrbka, Stefan, 1976- author.

Title: International business law : emerging fields of regulation / Mark Fenwick and Stefan Wrbka.

Description: Oxford [UK] ; Portland, Oregon : Hart Publishing, 2018. | Includes bibliographical
references and index.

Identifiers: LCCN 2018010205 (print) | LCCN 2018012287 (ebook) |
ISBN 9781509918072 (Epub) | ISBN 9781509918058 (paperback : alk. paper)

Subjects: LCSH: Commercial law. | International business enterprises—Law and legislation. |
Foreign trade regulation.

Classification: LCC K1005 (ebook) | LCC K1005 .F46 2018 (print) | DDC 346.07—dc23

LC record available at https://lccn.loc.gov/2018010205

ISBN: PB: 978-1-50991-805-8
       ePDF: 978-1-50991-806-5
       ePub: 978-1-50991-807-2

Typeset by Compuscript Ltd, Shannon
Printed and bound in Great Britain by CPI Group (UK) Ltd, Croydon CR0 4YY

To find out more about our authors and books visit www.hartpublishing.co.uk.
Here you will find extracts, author information, details of forthcoming events
and the option to sign up for our newsletters.

Preface

This book proceeds from the idea that existing accounts of contemporary international business law could be broader in their coverage. While such accounts have been extremely helpful in developing our understanding of this emerging field, the focus has tended to fall on a fairly narrow range of subjects. The result is that various legal issues that are increasingly important for a business operating internationally or cross-border get neglected or, at least, receive minimal coverage. Fields of law that were at the periphery of international business law have become increasingly central for businesses and the legal profession.

Driving this change is a combination of hyper-competitive global markets and the proliferation of disruptive innovation, most obviously networked technologies. Adapting to the new business realities of a globally connected economy obliges companies to engage with an ever more diverse range of legal risks. Equally, regulators are confronted with a new set of challenges as they attempt to protect important public interests.

This is not to suggest that the issues that previously dominated the discussion are no longer important. Rather, it suggests that other topics need to be given more attention. By doing so, contemporary debates on the scope and meaning of international business regulation can be enriched.

This book aims (i) to introduce this argument about the evolving character of contemporary international business regulation; and (ii) to provide an overview of some of the main fields of law that are currently important for firms that operate across borders. We hope that it will be of interest to anyone concerned with international business law or the regulation of global markets. The unique approach of this book aims to ensure that it is particularly suitable for undergraduate or graduate students looking for an introduction to, overview of or commentary on the contemporary state of transnational business law.

This book would not have been possible without the financial support of Kyushu University's English Education Project. This funding allowed us to host a series of workshops that helped in the development of the idea and content.

Special thanks also go to Hart Publishing, especially to Roberta Bassi, and to the anonymous referees who have accompanied and supported this project from an early stage.

Mark Fenwick
Stefan Wrbka
Fukuoka, Japan/Vienna, Austria
January 2018

Contents

Table of Cases

Table of Legislation

National

International

European Union

Soft Law

List of Abbreviations

ABA	American Bar Association
ABGB	*Allgemeines Bürgerliches Gesetzbuch*; Austrian Civil Code
ACL	Australian Consumer Law
ADP	automatic data processing
ADR	Alternative Dispute Resolution
AECB	ASEAN Economic Community Blueprint 2025
ALI	American Law Institute
AQSIQ	Chinese General Administration of Quality Supervision, Inspection and Quarantine
ASAPCP	ASEAN Strategic Action Plan for Consumer Protection 2016–2025
ASEAN	Association of Southeast Asian Nations
ATA	Asia-Pacific Trustmark Alliance
B2B	business-to-business
B2C	business-to-consumer
BGB	*Bürgerliches Gesetzbuch*; German Civil Code
CC	*Code civil*; French Civil Code
CEO	Chief Executive Officer
CESL	Common European Sales Law (EU)
CISG	United Nations Convention on Contracts for the International Sale of Goods
CJEU	Court of Justice of the European Union
CPEC	Consumer Policy Evaluation Consortium (EU)
CPS	consumer product safety
CRD	Directive on Consumer Rights; Consumer Rights Directive (EU)
CSD	Consumers Sales Directive (EU)
DCFR	Draft Common Frame of Reference on the Principles, Definitions and Model Rules of European Private Law (EU)
DG	Directorate General (EU)
DGCL	Delaware General Corporate Law
DOJ	Department of Justice (US)
DPA	deferred prosecution agreement
DPL	direct producer liability
DRC	development risk clause
DRD	development risk defence
DSM	Digital Single Market (EU)
EC	European Community
ECC	European Consumer Centre
ECC-Net	European Consumer Centres Network
ECJ	European Court of Justice
ECLI	European Case Law Identifier

e-commerce	electronic commerce
EDI	Electronic Data Interchange
EEC	European Economic Community
EEJ-Net	Network for the extra-judicial settlement of consumer disputes
EEN	Enterprise Europe Network
EESC	European Economic and Social Committee
EMOTA	European eCommerce and Omni-Channel Trade Association
ESCP	European Small Claims Procedure
EU	European Union
FCA	Financial Conduct Authority (UK)
FCPA	Foreign and Corrupt Practices Act
FRCP	Federal Rules of Civil Procedure (US)
FSC	Financial Services Council (Australia)
FTC	Federal Trade Commission (US)
FTE	Full-time equivalent
GATT	General Agreement on Tariffs and Trade
GBDe	Global Business Dialogue on e-Society
GDP	gross domestic product
GTA	Global Trustmark Alliance
HCCH	Hague Conference on Private International Law
ICANN	Internet Corporation for Assigned Names and Numbers
ICT	information and communication technology
ILPF	Internet Law & Policy Forum
IP	intellectual property
ISS	Institutional Shareholder Services
KapMuG	*Kapitalanleger-Musterverfahrensgesetz* (German Capital Markets Model Case Act)
KCC	Korean Civil Code
MMWA	Magnuson-Moss Warranty Act (US)
MRA	Mutual Recognition Arrangement
NCCUSL	National Conference of Commissioners on Uniform State Law (US)
NYSE	New York Stock Exchange
OADR	online alternative dispute resolution
ODR	online dispute resolution
OECD	Organization for Economic Cooperation and Development
OI	Optional Instrument
OJ	Official Journal (EU)
PECL	Principles of European Contract Law
PLD	Product Liability Directive (EU)
PLSC	Principles of the Law of Software Contracts (US)
PMS	market surveillance of products
PQL	Product Quality Law (China)
RCRC	Rough Consensus and Running Code
s	section
SEC	Securities & Exchange Commission (US)
SME	small or medium-sized enterprise

SoGA	Sale of Goods Act (UK)
TFEU	Treaty on the Functioning of the European Union
UCC	Uniform Commercial Code (US)
USC	United States Code
UCITA	Uniform Computer Information Transactions Act (US)
UETA	Uniform Electronic Transaction Act (US)
UK	United Kingdom
UN	United Nations
UNCITRAL	United Nations Commission on International Trade Law
UNIDROIT	International Institute for the Unification of Private Law
US/USA	United States of America
WCT	WIPO Copyright Treaty
WIPO	World Intellectual Property Organization
WPPT	WIPO Performances and Phonograms Treaty
WTA	World Trustmark Alliance
WTO	World Trade Organization

Introduction

The aim of this book is to offer an introduction to selected issues in the field of international business law, adopting a comparative and transnational perspective. In this Introduction, we outline the framework that informs the selection of issues and discuss some key themes ('I. Context and Themes'), before reviewing the topics addressed in each of the chapters ('II. Structure and Topics').

I. Context and Themes

This book is based on a particular understanding of the expanding scope and changing character of contemporary business regulation, and in particular the claim that, over the last half century, a series of significant developments have transformed this field of law. More specifically, the book focuses on three developments:

— A greater recognition of consumer interests in business-to-consumer (B2C) transactions has led to a global trend to protect consumers via a combination of substantive and procedural private law.
— A greater awareness of firm misbehaviour has led to a global trend to improve firm organisation and governance via the use of company law and criminal/regulatory law.
— The emergence of new technologies—notably, the invention and proliferation of the Internet—has led to a global trend to adapt the law in order to regulate the novel forms of commercial transaction and corporate organisation that such networked technologies have made possible.

Together, these emerging fields of regulation have transformed the content and reach of contemporary business law.

The broader context of these developments comprises related changes in the global economy that have occurred over the same period. In particular, economic globalisation—ie the opening up of national markets, the expansion of global supply chains, and the resulting growth of cross-border business—means that, in order to be effective, any national regulation in this field needs to be cognisant of the cross-border character of much modern business. At the same time, multiple new transnational actors—at both the regional and international levels—have emerged and now provide important competing sources of authority.

The combined result of these developments? Contemporary international business regulation is a highly complex and rapidly evolving mosaic of overlapping national and transnational norms and procedures covering multiple fields of law and affecting all aspects of business operations.

The effects of this transformation have been profound for consumers, policymakers and—of course—business. Consumers have been empowered to an historically unprecedented degree. Globalisation and new technologies have provided a more diverse range of products and services that are widely accessible. Moreover, consumer interests are afforded greater legal protection via the creation of new substantive rights and procedural mechanisms that facilitate the enforcement of these rights. Particularly important, in a legal context, are the expansion of consumer law, product liability law, warranty law and procedural innovations, for example collective actions and alternative dispute resolution (ADR).

Conversely, these developments have created an enormous challenge for regulators and other policymakers, as they work to put in place meaningful and effective legal standards without compromising business performance and economic growth. Policymakers—whether at the national, regional or international level—struggle to identify and protect important public interests under conditions of economic, technological and legal uncertainty. The realities of regulatory competition—the fact that businesses can relocate to other, more attractive jurisdictions—add to these difficulties.

Arguably, however, perhaps the most significant effect of these developments has been their impact on business. Navigating a highly competitive and uncertain business environment is a major issue for all businesses. Equally, the emergence of a more complex regulatory landscape requires a significant investment in managing legal risk. The rapid growth of compliance—that part or section of a business responsible for the management of legal risk—is one of the most important changes in business organisation over the last three decades, and is directly linked to the expanded scope of regulation.

In putting forward a framework that focuses on these three developments, it is important to stress that the topics discussed in this book are not the only issues that might be considered. Clearly, there are other topics that could have been included, for example developments in environmental law, health and safety law, or labour law. As such, we do not aspire to be comprehensive in coverage, but merely to identify and explore some of the most important and representative legal developments that are shaping this fast-evolving field of law. Our general claim is for a more open and inclusive conception of business law that encompasses diverse fields of national and transnational regulation, and evaluates their impact on all relevant stakeholders.

Before turning to an overview of each chapter, it might be helpful to comment on some of these issues.

A. The Business Challenges of a Global, Innovation-driven Economy

All businesses—but particularly businesses looking to operate in multiple markets—are currently facing a series of challenges without precedent in the history of modern capitalism. Most obviously, the emergence of global markets and digital technologies has resulted in more competition and the constant disruption of existing business models. Firms are obliged to constantly re-examine their products or services, as well as their organisational structures. New commercial realities mean that corporations must exist in a permanent state of innovation. This is a task that is not easily accomplished by over-extended and oftentimes cumbersome organisations that can easily lose the capacity for agile reinvention associated with younger or smaller firms.

In addition, there are significant changes in public attitudes to consumption and work. Much of the discussion on this cultural shift has focused on 'Generation Y' or 'Millennials', ie those born between the early 1980s and 2000, but these social changes cut across generations and national boundaries. The shared experience of belonging to a globally connected community has had a profound effect on how people think about consumption and work.

An obvious example of this transformation is attitudes towards environmental issues. Both in terms of product performance and working environment, individuals now expect firms to act in an environmentally more responsible manner. Understanding these shifting expectations is vital in terms of identifying the kind of products and services that firms need to develop to attract consumers, and the corporate culture that such firms need to offer in order to attract the most responsible investors and the most talented executives, managers and employees.

Lastly, there are a number of likely 'near-future' developments that are already having an impact on the thinking of many companies. Foremost amongst these is the coming automation revolution, in which, it is estimated, up to 50 per cent of jobs will be done by machines (the so-called disappearance of work). Managing the transition to a 'low-work' or 'post-work' society will inevitably have an impact on a firm's relationship with customers, employees and other stakeholders.

Hyper-competitive global markets; disruptive technologies; cultural shifts in expectations regarding consumerism and work; new demands for environmental sustainability; and looming automation represent just some of the issues that businesses are facing today.

Complicating the task of meeting these business challenges is a background of declining public trust in corporations and increased regulatory scrutiny. Confidence in the integrity of the business world has declined, as scandals involving household corporate brands have become a routine feature of everyday life. Previously respected names, such as Enron, Olympus or Volkswagen, have become synonymous with corporate arrogance and greed. Executives and managers are widely regarded as exhibiting an unethical disregard for the consequences of their actions. Under pressure to 'do something', politicians and policymakers respond to such scandals by introducing ever more layers of regulation aimed at improving firm behaviour and offering greater protection to consumers.

Navigating the multiple uncertainties of this new economic and social order is crucial to the long-term prospects of any business. But identifying the most appropriate response to these challenges is not at all obvious and—taken together—they make it extremely difficult for any firm to achieve sustainable growth.

B. The 'Complex' Character of the Contemporary Regulatory Environment

The contemporary regulatory environment is increasingly complex, as the sources of legal norms and the form of regulation have become more diverse. In particular, governance 'beyond' the nation state now co-exists and interacts with traditional forms of state law. The most obvious manifestation of this trend is the range and diversity of regulatory forms that now affect any business that operates transnationally. Consider 'soft' measures, such as codes of conduct, rankings, indicators, statements of best practice, guidelines, etc. In each case, new demands are being made of companies, and legal risks and other costs attach to any decision about how to adapt their behaviour in response to these new demands.

Navigating this increasingly complex regulatory landscape becomes enormously difficult, even for well-resourced businesses with an existing global footprint. The various theoretical issues raised by this transformation in business regulation are matched by practical, real-world decisions for business. Getting these decisions right can represent an existential challenge for many firms.

From the point of view of the law, the key feature of this new transnational regulatory order is that it breaks from many of the fundamental tenets of modern legal and political theory. In large part, this derives from the declining significance of nation states and a settled understanding of the role and function of the nation state in making and enforcing law. Conceptions of democratically legitimate public officials operating within clearly de-limited constitutional powers have been undermined—or at least challenged—by the emergence of a diverse new cast of transnational institutional actors and organisations that are all competing for regulatory supremacy in this new global space.

Whereas business regulation previously comprised relatively settled, clear and binding national rules issued by identifiable and democratically legitimate institutions, the global regulatory landscape now consists of multiple actors (both state and non-state), operating with wide-ranging sources of legitimacy, competing for authority and issuing fluid norms in diverse forms across multiple areas of law.

A particularly important aspect of this new complexity concerns the uncertain legitimacy of transnational regulation. Traditionally, at least in the context of political modernity, the validity of a legal norm derived from the (democratic) authority that issued it, namely a national legislative assembly comprising representatives of the people. In this way, the law was made 'by the people for the people'. In a contemporary transnational context, however, one of the ways in which law has become more diverse is in terms of how the validity of a norm—whatever the form—is established. In some contexts, the legitimacy of transnational regulation derives from the rationality (or, as we shall see below, in some contexts, the common sense) of the adopted regulation. In other situations, the legitimacy is based on the expertise of a particular group of relevant actors who are delegated the task (or assume the task) of identifying appropriate standards and designing a regulatory scheme. In this way, competing conceptions of legitimacy have emerged that challenge the settled narratives of legitimacy in a representative democracy.

The new pluralism of international business regulation also undermines many of our settled distinctions between public and private law, and the regulatory and coordinative functions of law. Traditionally, private law was conceptualised as creating an infrastructure or space that allowed individuals to freely pursue economic goals. In contrast, public law was concerned with regulating how public goods were distributed and utilised. With the emergence of transnational regulation, however, this settled distinction has been disrupted and contemporary regulation takes on a hybrid character.

A final example of how international business regulation disrupts conventional understandings of the law is the impact it has had on conceptions of legal certainty. In the context of legal modernity, the principle of legal certainty—the idea that the law must be sufficiently clear to provide those subject to legal norms with the means to regulate their own conduct and to protect against the arbitrary exercise of public power—has operated as a foundational rule-of-law value. As such, legal certainty played a vital role in determining the space of individual freedom and the scope of state power. In this way, the ideal of legal certainty was central in stabilising normative expectations and in providing a framework for business and economic interactions, as well as defining the limits of individual freedom and political power in modern societies.

Over recent decades, however, legal certainty has come under increasing pressure from a number of competing demands that are made of contemporary law, in particular the demand that the law be more flexible and responsive to an environment characterised by fast-paced economic and technological change. The expectation that the law operates in new transnational contexts and regulates ever-widening spheres of economic life has created a greater degree of uncertainty about the value of legal certainty.

C. The Limits of Compliance and Private Enforcement

A third important theme worthy of brief comment concerns the issue of compliance and enforcement. A potential risk of the expanding scope and reach of contemporary business regulation has been to feed the growth—inside the firm—of an unhealthy corporate culture in which conservative decision making, a short-term perspective or formalistic compliance are over-emphasised. Companies are obliged to spend more time and money on managing the rising costs associated with navigating the thicket of legal rules that now constitutes the regulatory landscape. This is an issue for all firms, but for those larger, publicly listed firms that conduct a significant part of their activities across multiple jurisdictions and in different sectors of the new economy, managing transnational and cross-sectoral legal risk can become a debilitating burden. The risk of regulatory initiatives aimed at requiring—or even simply nudging—'better' behaviour or greater responsibility on the part of firms is that they might not have the intended effects (and benefits).

For example, more regulation might encourage box-ticking behaviour, in which managing the appearance of compliance becomes the primary objective. The focus is on projecting an image of compliance—often recommended by advisors and consultants, who insist that there is a direct correlation between compliance and sustainable performance. Alternatively, there is a risk that policy initiatives can distort incentives and create a more conservative business culture or a focus on short-term, rather than long-term, growth. In each of these scenarios, compliance can eat up resources and distract from other business-related activities, without achieving the underlying goals of the regulation.

Against this background, issues of private enforcement become crucial. In particular, the question of how to incentivise private parties to bring enforcement actions against corporate defendants has to be constantly re-examined in order to ensure that regulatory initiatives have their desired effects.

In addressing this issue, a number of procedural innovations have been introduced across multiple fields of law to facilitate private enforcement. Important examples of this trend are the expansion of collective redress, ADR and online dispute resolution (ODR). In each case, the aim of the procedural reform has been to offer private parties greater opportunities to successfully bring their claims to fruition and—indirectly—to incentivise firms to implement meaningful compliance.

II. Structure and Topics

The book explores the above issues in seven substantive chapters and a conclusion.

Chapter 1 looks at consumer law. Arguably, consumer law is one of the most important legal fields for a business, at least when one considers the number of transactions that are governed by its rules. Moreover, consumer law comprises a diverse selection of legal mechanisms, covering both substantive and procedural law, which have developed over the last half century. Lastly, in a contemporary context, consumer law is increasingly transnational in its formation and operation.

The chapter focuses on the example of the European Union (EU), where consumer law has emerged as one of the most heavily discussed fields of regulation. The tensions between national and supranational policy making become particularly obvious in this context, largely due to the fact that different jurisdictions have distinctive approaches that need to be respected.

Chapters 2 and 3 focus on the closely related fields of product liability and warranty law. In both cases, there has been an expansion in the scope of private law protection for consumers. Chapter 2 adopts a narrow conception of product liability law, focusing on specific tort law questions. The chapter identifies significant differences in national approaches that have important implications for businesses operating in multiple markets. Issues of interest include the question of the liable party, the material scope of product liability law, as well as the remedies offered by different jurisdictions.

Chapter 3 discusses warranty law. Warranty law can be defined as the set of legal provisions that aim to safeguard party autonomy in contracts in which one party promises to transfer a good to another party for value. This is done with the help of certain remedies that can be applied ex post to restore the contractual equilibrium between performance and counter-performance (as negotiated by the parties) if the transferee receives a good that is not in conformity with contractual expectations. Examples include the right to repair, replacement, price reduction and withdrawal from a contract.

The discussion in this chapter summarises key questions of warranty law by explaining some of its most striking features. In addition, it highlights one of the most heavily discussed issues in a contemporary business context, namely, the issue of planned obsolescence (ie the expression of hidden defects). The central question in this context is whether warranty law offers a viable mechanism to combat strategies and techniques of premature product aging applied by producers and sellers with the aim of making end users buy new products faster than they ordinarily would.

As mentioned above, the extended transnational reach of modern business law introduces significant new challenges and complexities for those agencies responsible for enforcement, as well as businesses managing disputes. Modern nation states do not possess the means, authority or resources to police all norms effectively. In large part, this is simply because of the prohibitive administrative costs associated with investigating corporate actions in a transnational setting. In an era of austerity in public finances, it is often not practicable for regulatory agencies to fulfil the new expectations that have arisen in the context of transnational corporate misconduct. This is particularly so when one considers the complex character of corporate behaviour and the sophisticated efforts that are made to cover it up by well-resourced and highly motivated corporations.

Against this background, the question of private enforcement needs to be reconsidered. Chapter 4 explores this issue in the context of collective redress. As a second step this chapter further deals with ADR and ODR, ie non-litigative forms of dispute resolution designed to facilitate private enforcement. In recent times, ADR—formerly used primarily in the US—has become increasingly popular in other jurisdictions. Most notably, the EU adopted an ADR Directive and ODR Regulation in 2013 to offer tailor-made ADR/ODR platforms. Chapter 4 comments on these developments.

Taken together, Chapters 1 through 4 explore the first of the three developments in business regulation identified in section I, namely, the greater protection afforded to the consumer. Chapters 5 and 6 concentrates on the second development, namely, legal efforts that aim to improve firm behaviour via corporate law and criminal law.

Chapter 5 discusses the issue of corporate governance, focusing on larger publicly listed companies. Modern business has benefited enormously from various management-finance principles offered by the corporate form: (i) the corporate form is a legal entity that exists separately and independently from its founders, managers and shareholders; (ii) specialised, professional managers offer improved performance, since managers are better placed to streamline operational processes within a firm; and (iii) limited liability allows a relatively large number of investors to diversify risk and trade their shares publicly. In this way, the corporate form provided the framework by which capital (via investors) was able to combine effectively with the entrepreneurial spirit of manager for economic growth and the benefit of society.

Nevertheless, this 'separation' of ownership from control creates a risk that opportunistic managers can act in their own, and not the company's and investors', best interests. Managing these 'agency risks' has emerged as the central issue in corporate governance over recent decades, and particularly post-2000. Chapter 5 will introduce this topic, focusing on contemporary debates around the board of directors and stewardship codes, as potential mechanisms for minimising agency risk.

Chapter 6 discusses measures adopted in response to corporate wrongdoing and scandals. Recent decades have seen an important shift in public awareness of, and attitudes towards, corporate wrongdoing. This shift in contemporary understandings of what constitutes the crime problem is, no doubt, the result of multiple factors, but the prevalence of corporate scandals and the greater media attention given to the exposure of corporate wrongdoing has been a key element in this change. This chapter introduces some of the main regulatory developments over the last two decades, focusing on the expanded scope of corporate criminal law and procedural innovations, such as deferred prosecution agreements (DPAs).

The final chapter and the conclusion turn to the third of the trends identified in section I, namely, the impact of new technologies—particularly the Internet—on business regulation.

Chapter 7 focuses on the issue of e-commerce. E-commerce law can be understood as the body of law that governs questions relating to transactions concluded electronically over a distance, most commonly via the Internet, and is one of the key areas of law in a modern business environment. Most businesses today are obliged to offer—or at least engage in—some form of e-commerce. With an increasing number of transactions concluded over the Internet, such transactions pose various interesting legal questions. Most notably, questions arise as to how to govern legal transactions concluded over the Internet in the most effective way, and how to enforce rights if the parties are located far away from each other. In both cases the situation can become even more complicated if the parties reside in different jurisdictions.

The chapter outlines the underlying legal complications of e-commerce by focusing on B2C transactions concluded over the Internet. In this context, it critically assesses more recent developments, such as the introduction of a comprehensive online dispute resolution tool in the EU and plans to introduce tailor-made, special legislation to deal with issues that might arise from e-commerce.

The book ends with a shorter concluding chapter examining the possible future direction of business law in the context of further technological evolution and an emerging 'Digital Society'. There is a broad consensus that the on-going process of rapid technological change will further disrupt traditional forms of corporate organisation. All companies are now obliged to engage with emerging technologies. Stated bluntly, every company will need to think like a tech company.

In an age of ever shorter innovation cycles, the next technological development is always looming. Firms already have to engage with the challenges created by near-future technologies, such as robotics, automation and artificial intelligence. The pressures are incessant, and anticipating the next big thing is crucial for maximising a firm's chances of survival.

Designing a regulatory framework that is appropriate for the new constantly shifting realities of a digital economy is by no means easy. Particularly when such a framework needs to ensure the safety of consumers and the public, whilst facilitating the commercial use and consumer enjoyment of disruptive innovation.

1

Consumer Law

I. Outline

Consumer law is arguably one of the most dynamic and—at least in terms of the frequency of applicability—relevant areas of contemporary business law. This might largely be explained with the fact that it potentially affects everybody's life on a regular, if not daily basis, and impacts upon the activities of almost all businesses. Managing the legal risk that consumer law has created constitutes a substantial challenge for all companies.

Consumer law comprises a broad catalogue of legal themes that range from substantive law to procedural law topics, from private law to public law questions. This wide range of differently conceptually embedded, underlying issues makes consumer law difficult to clearly define. Although it might not be possible to conclusively stake out its territory, it is justified to say that consumer law originates from the idea to create a level playing field for (at least) one 'acquiring'/consuming non-professional and (at least) one 'offering' professional stakeholder. Such cases are usually referred to as business-to-consumer (B2C) transactions.

Business-to-consumer transactions have—from time immemorial—been part of our lives. Consumer law, ie a (more or less) systematic body of law that is specifically designed as a framework to apply in B2C cases, is, however, of rather recent origin. This does not mean that consumers had remained without any protection. As, for example, Iris Benöhr explains, even in ancient (Roman) times, purchasers were able to enjoy some special treatment.[1] Such protection has, however, remained quite narrow in the sense that it related only to very few, specific questions.

It was only after the end of World War II that more comprehensive ideas reached the legal policy stage. The economic developments in the post-War years led politicians to conclude that the laissez-faire approach that dominated, in particular, the post-Industrial Revolution period until the mid-twentieth century, had not necessarily proved positive in terms of satisfying both business *and* consumer interests. Consumers were generally considered as possessing less legal knowledge, bargaining power and control over the quality and health standards of goods and services.

---

[1] I Benöhr, *EU Consumer Law and Human Rights* (Oxford, Oxford University Press, 2013) 11.

In an important speech made in 1962, then US President John F Kennedy expressed his wish to comprehensively protect consumers. He opened his argument with the following statement:

> Consumers, by definition, include us all. They are the largest economic group in the economy, affecting and affected by almost every public and private economic decision. ... But they are the only important group in the economy who are not effectively organized, whose views are often not heard.[2]

Kennedy listed four key tasks that he believed had to be resolved to improve the legal situation for consumers.[3] First, goods that had safety issues should be banned from the market (the 'right to safety'). One (time-wise related) example to explain the need for stricter action, was the thalidomide scandal that hit dozens of countries around the globe in the late 1950s and 1960s. It showed that goods potentially create high risks for consumers regardless of their place of residence or societal status.

Second, Kennedy pointed out that information deficits on the consumer side could lead to choices consumers might later regret. Correct and transparent information would ensure that consumers could make rational decisions in their own best interest (the 'right to be informed').

Third, and complementing the right to be informed, one had to guarantee that consumers could either choose from a variety of reasonably priced goods and services or—where market competition was not possible—at least had access to affordable goods and services (the 'right to choose'). This had to be understood as a call to satisfy the basic needs and interests of consumers (in principle) regardless of their financial background.

Lastly, Kennedy identified possible implementation deficits and called for an improved system of rights enforcement (the 'right to be heard'). This should guarantee that justifiable consumer interests would be safeguarded not only in theory, but also in practice.

Approximately one decade after Kennedy had presented his ideas, the consumer law debate hit the European continent.[4] Several European Union (EU) Member States had already autonomously begun to acknowledge consumer law as a particularly important area of law and/or to apply specific consumer legislation in the early 1970s (at the latest).[5] But not only the Member States themselves, the European Economic Community (EEC), the predecessor of the EU, also initiated broader policy debates during the 1970s.[6] The first explicit, more detailed mentioning of the relevance of

---

[2] JF Kennedy, 'Special Message to the Congress on Protecting the Consumer Interest' in *Public Papers of the United States, Public Messages, Speeches and Statements of the President, 1 January to 31 December 1962* (1962) 235, quod.lib.umich.edu/p/ppotpus/4730892.1962.001?view=toc.

[3] For details see ibid.

[4] In this chapter, we focus on the developments in the EU as an illustration of a more general trend to embrace consumer law and to discuss possible tensions that exist between supranational and domestic legislation in this field.

[5] For examples from the UK, see I Ramsay, *Consumer Law and Policy*, 3rd edn (Oxford, Hart Publishing, 2012) 5–7 (with references to some even earlier occasional examples). For German examples, see M Tamm, *Verbraucherschutzrecht* (Tübingen, Mohr, Siebeck, 2011) 184–89 (again with some references to older models). For a discussion from the Austrian perspective, see B Lurger and S Augenhofer, *Österreichisches und Europäisches Konsumentenschutzrecht*, 2nd edn (Vienna, Springer, 2008) 10.

[6] For general comments on the development of EU consumer law, see, eg, S Weatherill, *EU Consumer Law and Policy*, 2nd edn (Cheltenham, Edward Elgar, 2013); S Weatherill, 'Consumer Policy' in P Craig and G de Búrca (eds), *The Evolution of EU Law*, 2nd edn (Oxford, Oxford University Press, 2011) 837–76;

consumer protection was issued in the mid-1970s, when the Council of the European Communities, the predecessor of the Council of the European Union (Council), presented its Resolution on a preliminary programme of the EEC for a consumer protection and information policy[7] and the Preliminary Programme of the EEC for a consumer protection and information policy (1975 Preliminary Programme)[8] annexed to it. Paragraph 9 of the latter document enshrined five 'basic rights'. It differentiated between the rights to 'protection of health and safety', 'protection of economic interests', 'redress', 'information and education' and the 'right of representation (the right to be heard)', with the last one involving the chance to voice one's interests in general—adding an extra layer to Kennedy's four claims.

Taking a slightly closer look at the 1975 Preliminary Programme, one can identify an interesting difference in terms of the underlying ideas behind this policy document and more recent consumer law instruments adopted or proposed at the EU level. Unlike the latter ones—that take a more strongly economic-centred approach and stress the importance of a sound consumer law framework for strengthening the (cross-border and internal) market—the 1975 Preliminary Programme emphasises a more traditional rationale behind consumer law known already at a national level. The European consumer policy expressed in the Programme aimed to improve the overall 'quality of life'[9] that was considered as having been at risk due to an increased power and information imbalance between parties to B2C contracts. Industrial development had—so the 1975 Preliminary Programme argued—not only led to positive trends, such as more advanced technology and a wider choice of goods and services. It also caused some side-effects that proved detrimental to truly satisfying consumer interests. In its section on 'the consumer and the economy', the 1975 Preliminary Programme explained that the business side—largely as a result of having experienced a comparatively large number of transactions—had been able to develop new marketing strategies and to gain profound legal knowledge. That combination, so the Programme concluded, had put the supply side in a stronger, hence better, situation that would pose concerns over the overall fairness of the B2C market.[10] With the 1975 Preliminary Programme the EEC hoped that the five listed basic consumer rights would guide national and European policymakers in efforts to restore a true level playing field in B2C transactions.

Meanwhile, at a more global level, the United Nations (UN) introduced six general consumer policy principles in 1985 (1985 UN consumer resolution). The UN principles comprised the following issues:

(1)   protecting consumers from hazards to their health and safety;
(2)   promoting and protecting consumers' economic interests;

H-W Micklitz and S Weatherill, 'Consumer Policy in the European Community: Before and after Maastricht' (1993) 16 *Journal of Consumer Policy* 285–321; P Nebbia and T Ashkam, *EU Consumer Law* (Oxford, Oxford University Press, 2004); N Reich et al, *European Consumer Law*, 2nd edn (Cambridge, Intersentia, 2014) 1–65.

[7] Council of the European Communities, Resolution on a preliminary programme of the European Economic Community for a consumer protection and information policy, [1975] OJ C92/1.

[8] Council of the European Communities, Preliminary programme of the European Economic Community for a consumer protection and information policy, [1975] OJ C92/2.

[9] See ibid, para 1.

[10] For details see ibid, s I.A.

(3)   enabling consumers to access adequate information;
(4)   educating consumers;
(5)   providing consumers with effective redress mechanisms;
(6)   giving consumers the freedom to form consumer organisations and allowing the latter to participate in policy decision making.[11]

Although not 100 per cent identical, the UN principles—as much as the aforementioned 1975 Preliminary Programme did—followed Kennedy's vision: Principle (1) resembled Kennedy's right to safety; Principles (3) and (4) related to the right to be informed; Principle (2) showed similarities to the right to choose; and principle (5) embodied ideas known from Kennedy's right to be heard. The UN Principle (6)—in a way similar to the 1975 Preliminary Programme with its right of representation (the right to be heard)—motivated countries to invite consumer interest representatives to the national consumer law decision-making processes. The reason for this seemed obvious: it was hoped that consumer organisations could lend greater substance to consumer interests at a legislative level than individual citizens could do.

Looking at the further development of consumer law, the tasks addressed by the Kennedy declaration, the 1975 Preliminary Programme and the 1985 UN consumer resolution can be considered as key early consumer policy documents. Many later legislative decisions can be traced back to one or more of the claims presented by them. In sections II to V, we touch upon some instruments that either have been introduced already to facilitate B2C transactions, or which we consider as being potentially effective to do so. Mainly due to the vibrant developmental process at the EU level and its leading role for many other jurisdictions, the emphasis will be on examples from the EU and some of its Member States. Rather than giving a conclusive overview, the focus will be on selected instruments, mainly relating to contract law. But before that, we take a brief look at some original sources to discuss the rationale behind consumer law in slightly more detail.

II. Background Information with a Focus on EU Consumer Law

A. General Comments on Consumer Law

The original idea behind consumer law is to respond to the perceived existence of an imbalance between professional sellers and non-professional buyers. Such imbalance can show different faces. The most prominent examples, found in both the literature

---

[11] United Nations General Assembly, Resolution on consumer protection, [1985] A/RES/39/248 Annex, s I.

and policy making, relate to consumer information deficits on the one hand and a perceived imbalance in negotiating power on the other.[12] Martijn Hesselink, for example, summarises this twofold view as follows:

Since [1975] the European Commission has produced a long line of policy papers. These papers formulate objectives and announce policies. However, they rarely analyze why consumers should be protected, and never why only they need protection. Often the argument is mainly limited to the idea that consumers should be protected because, in transactions with professionals, they are typically the weaker parties.

The economic analysis of the law has produced a powerful theory of consumer protection. According to this theory the rationale for consumer protection is existence of market failures. Just as the market may not be working perfectly because of the power concentration on the supply side ..., there may also be market failures as a result of lack of information on the demand side, which can be remedied by consumer law, in particular pre-contractual information duties.[13]

Undeniably, imbalances can exist in non-B2C situations as well. A larger enterprise might be in a better position than a smaller one when it comes to legal knowledge and bargaining strength. However, by traditional legal definition, businesses—whatever size they are—would usually not fall under the consumer concept and hence would not be able to enjoy pertinent protection (unless legislators introduced similar standards for potentially unbalanced non-B2C transactions).[14] On the other hand, there might be B2C situations in which there is no or only a little imbalance. If a consumer interacts with a small start-up company, for example, both sides might lack legal knowledge and bargaining power. In fact, one might even face a reversed unbalanced situation. An experienced attorney who buys something at a small shop in the countryside for personal use, ie in a non-professional capacity, might—at least in terms of legal experience—be in a stronger position. However, these B2C examples are rather the exception. In the vast majority of cases consumers are arguably legally less experienced and informed than their professional counterparts.[15] But even if consumers

---

[12] See, eg, SI Becher, 'Asymmetric Information in Consumer Contracts: The Challenge That Is Yet to Be Met' (2008) 45 *American Business Law Journal* 723–74; MW De Hoon, 'Power Imbalances in Contracts: An Interdisciplinary Study on Effects of Intervention' (2007) *TISCO Working Paper Series on Civil and Conflict Resolution Systems*, papers.ssrn.com/sol3/papers.cfm?abstract_id=985875.

[13] M Hesselink, 'SMEs in European Contract Law' in K Boele-Woelki and W Grosheide (eds), *The Future of European Contract Law* (Alphen aan den Rijn, Kluwer Law International, 2007) 349, 358–59. Hesselink adds a third rationale—the 'limited rationality of consumers'—and explains this as follows: 'In addition to this neo-classical analysis, more recently behavioural law & economics has added, as an additional feature, the limited rationality of consumers (ie even fully informed consumers do not always take the decisions that are in their own best interest) which may justify further-reaching intervention by the legislator' (see ibid).

[14] For a more recent representative example from the EU, see, eg, Art 2(1) Consumer Rights Directive (CRD; Directive 2011/83/EU, [2011] OJ L304/64), which reads as follows: '"[C]onsumer" means any *natural* person who, in contracts covered by this Directive, is acting for purposes which are *outside* his trade, business, craft or profession' (emphasis added). For more details from an EU perspective, see J Hedegaard and S Wrbka, 'The Notion of Consumer under EU Legislation between the Poles of Legal Certainty and Flexibility' in M Fenwick and S Wrbka (eds), *Legal Certainty in a Contemporary Context: Private & Criminal Law Perspectives* (Tokyo, Springer, 2016) 69–88 with further references; the contributions in D Leczyliewicy and S Weatherill (eds), *The Images of the Consumer in EU Law: Legislation, Free Movement and Competition Law* (Oxford, Hart Publishing, 2016).

[15] See, eg, the sources above n 12.

possessed a high level of legal knowledge, would they necessarily be in a position to negotiate terms and conditions on an equal footing? This is highly questionable. In particular at a national level, these concerns have been the driving factors behind legislative endeavours to introduce special mechanisms to empower consumers.

Comparative research shows that one can distinguish between different instruments and underlying concepts to support consumers with legal means. One example of a popular tool to remedy the consumers' bargaining power deficit (with respect to the legal framework accompanying a B2C transaction) lies in ensuring certain minimum standards of substantive legal protection. This can range from declaring certain legal provisions (at least one-sided)[16] mandatory in B2C transactions, to tools to monitor terms and conditions and declare unfair clauses void or non-applicable.[17] Similar concerns, ie the wish to empower consumers by stipulating minimum protection standards, had dominated the early discussions with respect to mandatory information at a regional and even the global level, as the EU and UN examples mentioned in section I showed.

However, in more recent years, one can identify alternative—or at least additional—policy ideas in the field of consumer law, in particular at a regional (ie cross-border or transnational) level. The EU can be considered as one of the best examples in this respect. This is an additional reason why the focus in this chapter will be on developments in the EU.

B. Consumer Law in the EU as a Prime Example of Transnational Consumer Law

Having economic integration at the heart of policy making, EU law is very much interested in creating a market in which stakeholders from both sides—professional and non-professional—can easily engage in B2C transactions, regardless of the country or place in which they reside, shop or operate their business. In this context, the central question is not primarily related to reaching the highest possible level of consumer protection. To create a borderless market with businesses offering their goods and services not only at the domestic level, but also at the international/transnational level, policymakers were convinced that there was the need to align consumer protection rules that govern B2C transactions and to introduce new concepts where national mechanisms were either non-existent or existed in only a few Member States. Hence, and unlike at the national level, the underlying idea at the EU level was not necessarily to search for and introduce the highest possible level of protection for domestic consumers, but to establish standardised rules for B2C transactions throughout the EU.

The first generation of EU instruments that exclusively dealt with consumer issues took a relatively narrow approach and focused on specific, primarily contract

---

[16] In this context, 'one-sided' means that the parties to a B2C contract cannot agree on a contractual clause that would put the consumer in a worse situation than what statutory law/case law would allow for, but may very well on a clause more favourable to consumers.

[17] See, eg, the Unfair Contract Terms Directive (Directive 93/13/EEC, [1993] OJ L95/29), in particular its Art 7 and national implementations.

law-related questions. These eight instruments—commonly referred to as the consumer acquis (in a narrow sense)[18]—were adopted over a period of nearly 15 years, with the first one, the Doorstep Selling Directive,[19] having been introduced in 1985.

In the case of this first wave of pan-European consumer legislation, the more traditional rationale behind consumer law, ie ensuring an appropriate framework of legal protection to remedy the perceived imbalance in B2C situations, still enjoyed priority over purely market-facilitating steps. The just mentioned Doorstep Selling Directive, for example, aimed to regulate the special cases of off-premise sales, since in these situations the buyers were believed to have been at a particularly high level of risk of being taken by surprise. The Directive explained that EU legislation was necessary, because 'any disparity between [national doorstep selling] legislation may directly affect the functioning of the common market'.[20] At the same time it pointed out that off-premise B2C sales constituted a situation in which consumers were at comparatively high risk of making ill-informed and hasty economic decisions. The Directive answered with, inter alia, a catalogue of mandatory information to be provided by the seller[21] and a special withdrawal period of seven days for the buyer,[22] to give consumers the chance to rethink their purchase decisions. Comparable and/or alternative special rights were—based on similar arguments of highly risky B2C transactions—offered by some other sectoral consumer acquis directives, namely the Package Travel Directive,[23] the Timeshare Directive[24] and the Distance Selling Directive.[25]

Some of the other substantive first generation directives, in particular the Consumer Sales Directive[26] and the Unfair Contract Terms Directive,[27] covered a more general range of B2C transactions. They again, however, dealt with specific questions—with warranties and guarantees in the first case and contract clauses that (from a consumer fairness perspective) were not appreciated in B2C contracts in the second.

The Injunctions Directive[28] and the Price Indication Directive[29] completed the consumer acquis. While the former introduced special procedural rules to safeguard consumer interests, the latter enshrined rules to improve price transparency with respect to B2C products.

Although the consumer acquis directives did not have much in common from a thematic point of view, they were still conceptually related to one another. First, they all shared the key idea that consumers were in a weaker position than their professional counterparts. Second, the directives established a set of minimum standards that would align national legislation, but at the same time allowed the Member States

---

[18] S Wrbka, *European Consumer Access to Justice Revisited* (Cambridge, Cambridge University Press, 2015) 162 with further references.
[19] Directive 85/577/EEC, [1985] OJ L372/31.
[20] Preamble, Doorstep Selling Directive.
[21] Art 4 Doorstep Selling Directive.
[22] Art 5(1) Doorstep Selling Directive.
[23] Directive 90/314/EEC, [1990] OJ L158/59.
[24] Directive 94/47/EC, [1994] OJ L280/83.
[25] Directive 97/7/EC, [1997] OJ L144/19.
[26] Directive 99/44/EC, [1999] OJ L171/12.
[27] Above n 17.
[28] Directive 98/27/EC, [1998] OJ L166/51.
[29] Directive 98/6/EC, [1998] OJ L80/27.

to maintain or introduce stricter, consumer-friendlier standards (than the minimum level enshrined in the directives; 'minimum harmonisation approach').

In the first decade of the new millennium, scepticism with respect to the actual merits of the consumer acquis had grown. With three policy documents—the 2001 Contract Law Communication,[30] the 2003 Contract Law Action Plan[31] and the 2004 Acquis Communication[32]—the Commission voiced its concerns over the previous narrow and minimum harmonisation-based approach. This led to the introduction of a research group in late 2004, to evaluate the transposition of the consumer acquis directives in the Member States.

The *Consumer Law Compendium*[33]—the outcome of that study— offered an in-depth look into national consumer law making and in principle revealed two things. First, minimum harmonisation had aligned national consumer laws, but not absolutely. Quite frequently, Member States had made use of their legislative freedom to maintain or introduce consumer-friendlier legislation. Second, Member States had applied different techniques to implement the consumer acquis.[34] This largely had to be explained with historical reasons, since Member States had already applied different conceptual frameworks to regulate consumer issues before EU law asked them to implement a supranational law. Hans-Wolfgang Micklitz, for example, differentiates between four basic categories: the common law approach, the German, the Mediterranean, and the Scandinavian models.[35] The common law approach largely relied on self-regulation by the business side. When implementing EU law, the common law legislator had traditionally taken a rather pragmatic approach and—with the help of 'copying out'—tended to narrowly and quite unsystematically implement European legislation as close to its original wording as possible.[36] Germany chose a different path and—with its law of obligations reform of 2001—aimed to structurally order pertinent rules by integrating most of the consumer acquis directly into its Civil Code. Other Member States—Micklitz refers to them as the Mediterranean countries (although it should be pointed out that, for example, Austria also followed this approach) opted for separate consumer legislation that contained most (but not necessarily all) of the consumer acquis. Lastly, the Scandinavian countries stressed the importance of specifically designed authorities—the ombudsman—to facilitate B2C trade and to mediate in conflict cases.

Shortly before the *Consumer Law Compendium* results were presented to the public, the Commission had already taken the next step. With its Consumer Acquis

---

[30] European Commission, Communication on European Contract Law, 11 July 2001, COM(2001) 398 final.

[31] European Commission, A more coherent European contract law—An action plan, 12 February 2003, COM(2003) 68 final.

[32] European Commission, European Contract Law and the revision of the acquis: the way forward, 11 October 2004, COM(2004) 651 final.

[33] H Schulte-Nölke et al (eds), *EC Consumer Law Compendium: The Consumer Acquis and Its Transposition in the Member States* (Munich, Sellier, 2008).

[34] For details, see ibid.

[35] For details, see H-W Micklitz, 'De la nécessité d'une nouvelle conception pour le développement du droit de la consommation dans la Communauté européenne' in J Calay-Auloy (ed), *Liber Amicorum Jean Calais-Auloy: Études de droit de la consommation* (Paris, Dalloz, 2004) 725.

[36] For details, see, eg, P Giliker, 'The Transposition of the Consumer Rights Directive into UK Law: Implementing a Maximum Harmonization Directive' (2015) 23 *European Review of Private Law* 5.

Green Paper,[37] it communicated the wish 'to achieve a real consumer internal market striking the right balance between a high level of consumer protection and the competitiveness of enterprises'.[38] This statement clearly showed the dual policy the Commission tried to force through. Consumer protection—understood in the aforementioned traditional way of genuinely high protection—had to be reconciled with the idea of stimulating (cross-border) competition on the supply side via simplification of the legal framework.

Taking a closer look at the Consumer Acquis Green Paper, one will realise that the Commission approach caused certain tensions with national consumer law making. Discussing the then status quo of consumer legislation in the EU, the Commission expressed its concern that '[d]ifferent [national] rules resulting from minimum harmonisation may have a negative impact on the internal market'.[39] The fear of possible detrimental effects of national consumer protection on cross-border trade caused by domestic protective levels exceeding the EU standard led the Commission to change its basic consumer policy. Although the Consumer Acquis Green Paper did not explicitly show a preference for full harmonisation, the just cited statement, as well as other comments within this policy document on the harmonisation level,[40] indicate that the Commission considered full harmonisation as the more appropriate—if not the only possible—answer.

This view was emphasised again in 2008 when the Commission presented its fully harmonised Proposal for a directive on consumer rights[41] (CRD Proposal), which did not cover all eight consumer acquis directives but did include four of them (and added several not yet regulated issues): the Doorstep Selling Directive, the Unfair Contract Terms Directive, the Distance Selling Directive and the Consumer Sales Directive. Differences of opinion between the Commission, the Council—that strongly opposed the Commission's plan to cut national legislative competences—and the European Parliament—that stood somewhere in the middle between these two institutions—led to a compromise.

In the end—in late 2011—only two directives, the Doorstep Selling Directive and the Distance Selling Directive, were repealed. The other two, the Unfair Contract Terms Directive and the Consumer Sales Directive, were only imperceptibly revised by the addition of one article each (to inform the Commission about steps exceeding the minimum harmonised level of protection at the national level).[42]

Although the CRD[43] eventually followed (in principle) full harmonisation, it did not fully do so. Due to the opposition from the Council (and even—to a certain extent—from within the Parliament), the CRD rather takes a targeted full harmonisation approach. This basically means that the Directive combines both minimum and

---

[37] European Commission, Green Paper on the review of the consumer acquis, 8 February 2007, COM(2006) 744 final (Consumer Acquis Green Paper).

[38] Consumer Acquis Green Paper, 3.

[39] Consumer Acquis Green Paper, 7.

[40] See, eg, Consumer Acquis Green Paper, 10 and 11.

[41] Proposal for a Directive on consumer rights, 8 October 2008, COM(2008) 614 final. For the harmonisation level recommended by the CRD Proposal, see Art 4 CRD Proposal.

[42] Art 8a Unfair Contract Terms Directive and Art 8a Consumer Sales Directive, inserted via Arts 32 and 33 CRD respectively.

[43] Above n 14.

full harmonisation by giving Member States legislative leeway with respect to certain selected questions.[44] More than that, on several occasions the CRD allows Member States to choose between different 'regulatory options' to decrease the risk of causing inconsistency with respect to national models.[45] The most likely reason why the CRD failed to introduce a fully standardised concept is easy to find: Member States were not willing to concede legislative competences comprehensively, in particular with respect to traditional key issues.

Full harmonisation was not off the table, however. Actually, some consumer instruments already adopted before the CRD had taken an exclusively full harmonisation approach.[46] Also, after the adoption of the CRD the Commission did not stop pushing for a greater amount of full harmonisation. In mid-2013, for example, it proposed a revision of the Package Travel Directive (2013 Package Travel Directive Proposal) that—to a great extent—was based on full harmonisation.[47] But—just as with the CRD—the Commission did not entirely succeed in its attempt to revise another part of the consumer acquis in a (nearly exclusively) fully harmonised way. Just like the CRD, the new Package Travel Directive—adopted in 2015—takes a targeted full harmonisation approach.[48]

One of the most recent more comprehensive EU policy developments relates to a core area of consumer law—sales law. In late 2011, the Commission announced its plan to introduce an innovative sales law instrument to cover a broad catalogue of legal questions relating to certain types of cross-border B2C (and even—under certain conditions—to B2B[49]) sales. This project, the CESL Regulation Proposal, aimed to introduce an alternative sales law—the Common European Sales Law (CESL)—as an Optional Instrument (OI) that (in the covered situations) parties should be able to choose as transaction-governing national law instead of traditional national sales laws.

The CESL Regulation Proposal was a preliminary result of decade-long discussions and research that commenced in the late 1980s with the 'Lando Commission', an academic research group on European contract law founded on the initiative of Ole Lando,[50] and—via the research carried out by several successors[51]—resulted in the

---

[44] For a minimum harmonisation example from within the CRD, see, eg, its Art 5(4), which allows Member States to apply additional/stricter information obligations.

[45] For the term 'regulatory option', see Art 29 CRD. For examples, see Arts 6(7), 7(4), 8(6), 9(3) CRD.

[46] See in particular the Unfair Commercial Practices Directive (Directive 2005/29/EC, [2005] OJ L149/22), the Consumer Credit Agreements Directive (Directive 2008/48/EC, [2008] OJ L133/66) and the 2009 Timeshare Directive (Directive 2008/122/EC, [2008] OJ L33/10, replacing the older, minimum harmonised Timeshare Directive).

[47] Art 12(6) 2013 Package Travel Directive Proposal is a prominent exception to the underlying full harmonisation approach.

[48] Regulation (EU) 2302/2015, [2015] OJ L326/1. For the level of harmonisation see its Art 4 (declaring that the Directive principally rests on full harmonisation) and exceptions in its Arts 12(5), 13(1) and 14(4).

[49] For details, see Proposal for a Regulation on a Common European Sales Law, 11 October 2011, COM(2011) 635 final (CESL Regulation Proposal), Art 7.

[50] For details, see O Lando and H Beale (eds), *Principles of European Contract Law—Parts I and II* (The Hague, Kluwer Law International, 2000); and O Lando et al (eds), *European Contract Law—Part III* (The Hague, Kluwer Law International, 2003).

[51] In this context, in particular two later research groups have to be mentioned—the Study Group on a European Civil Code (SGECC) and the European Research Group on Existing EC Private Law (Acquis Group).

Draft Common Frame of Reference on the Principles, Definitions and Model Rules of European Private Law (DCFR).[52] The CESL Proposal intensified the already heated debates on the possible introduction of a comprehensive pan-EU sales law. The Commission and the vast majority of academic contributors to the committees that were involved in the evolutionary process of the CESL were extraordinarily supportive.

Nevertheless, criticism remained strong. Some of the issues revolved around concerns with respect to the true necessity for this instrument, the alleged simplified legal framework, legal certainty, the perceived voluntariness of the CESL, the envisaged protective standard and the relationship with Article 6 of the Rome I Regulation, the core provision to deal with conflict of (substantive) law questions in the area of consumer law.[53]

III. The Current Situation of Consumer Law at the EU Level

As indicated in the previous section, research has confirmed that EU consumer law has shaped the framework of consumer laws of the Member States. This has, however, happened to a lesser extent than EU policymakers had hoped. Three facts in particular can explain this. First, Member States have repeatedly exercised their legislative freedom (left by minimum harmonisation) to implement their own domestic consumer policies. Second, EU consumer law does not regulate every single potential legal issue that can arise in a B2C relationship. Third, and with respect to some core issues, Member States are not willing to let the Union legislator decide on their behalf, if a centralised decision would mean curtailment of national legislative competences (as a result of full harmonisation).

Consequentially, EU consumer law has only been able to develop incrementally in a relatively narrow and not entirely fully harmonised way. This does not mean that EU consumer law making has reached its limits, or that efforts have been in vain. However, instead of realising bigger and more comprehensive projects, the policymakers might have come to realise that—at least when it comes to substantive 'hard law'—the most appropriate (if not only possible) approach (for the time being) is to answer to specific legal questions, and not necessarily always with the help of full harmonisation. The already discussed example of the Commission plan to revise and standardise the consumer acquis to the highest technically possible extent exemplifies this. Eventually, the Commission had to proceed with a sectoral and not absolutely fully harmonised approach. With the exception of the Doorstep Selling Directive

---

[52] C von Bar et al (eds), *Principles, Definitions and Model Rules of European Private Law—Draft Common Frame of Reference (DCFR) Outline Edition* (Munich, Sellier, 2009).
[53] For details on these issues, see Wrbka, n 18, 215–54 with further references.

and the Distance Selling Directive, which were repealed and widely brought into line with each other, revisions were made individually, ie one by one, and—with the exception of the 2009 Timeshare Directive—not in an entirely fully harmonised way.[54] Nevertheless, seven out of the eight consumer acquis directives have (to a greater or lesser extent) been revised and/or repealed, leaving the Price Indication Directive as the 'last one standing'.

Another example that can be used to illustrate the Commission's limited power relates to the CESL. The Commission and academics who were involved in the drafting process of the CESL Regulation Proposal were drumming up business to bring the decade-long research to a fruitful end. However, already the Parliament's first reaction to the CESL Regulation Proposal showed that the promotion activities were not convincing enough. The Parliament declared the project (if not too far-reaching, at least) too ambitious and recommended switching the focus to cross-border distance selling contracts (only).[55] Eventually the Commission had no choice but to give in. In its Work Programme of 2015 (2015 Work Programme)[56] the Commission announced the reduction of the project's scope to distance selling (with the main emphasis on e-commerce).[57]

Looking at the last example in particular, one could get the impression that the Commission—at least in the short and mid-term—might want to focus on B2C e-commerce issues. One quite recent procedural law example seems to prove this assumption correct. In response to concerns that the number of issues that arise out of online B2C transactions might—in terms of proportionality—increase faster than offline sales issues, the EU legislator adopted the Regulation on online dispute resolution for consumer disputes (ODR Regulation) in 2013.[58] Although not being a totally independent instrument—the ODR Regulation is closely linked to the Directive on alternative dispute resolution for consumer disputes (ADR Directive[59]) (of the same day)—the ODR Regulation (unlike the ADR Directive) limits itself to online sales. The Commission's 2015, 2016 and 2017 Work Programmes,[60] as well as a couple of Directive proposals (to a greater or lesser extent) relating to online B2C transactions,[61]

---

[54] See, eg, the CRD, which repealed the Doorstep Selling Directive and the Distance Selling Directive.

[55] For a comparison between the CESL Proposal and the parliamentary CESL resolution, see www.europarl.europa.eu/sides/getDoc.do?type=TA&language=EN&reference=P7-TA-2014-0159.

[56] For details, see the Commission's Work Programme of 2015, c 2 on the Digital Single Market and, in particular Point 60 of its Annex, where the Commission phrases the new focus as follows: 'Modified proposal in order to fully unleash the potential of e-commerce in the Digital Single Market'; the Commission's Work Programme of 2016, c 2 on the Digital Single Market and, in particular Point 6 of its Annex I, where the Commission emphasises the plan to introduce legislation on free data flow; the Commission's Work Programme of 2017, c 2 on the Digital Single Market and Annex 3 Points 5–12, where the Commission addresses pending legislative projects including, inter alia, geo-blocking and digital contracts.

[57] For details, see, eg, the public consultation on contract rules for online purchases of digital content and tangible goods launched by DG Justice in mid-2015, with information available at ec.europa.eu/justice/newsroom/contract/opinion/150609_en.htm.

[58] Regulation (EU) 524/2013, [2013] OJ L165/1.

[59] Directive 2013/11/EU, [2013] OJ L165/63.

[60] For the 2015 Work Programme, see ec.europa.eu/info/publications/work-programme-commission-key-documents-2015_en. The Work Programme of 2016 did not change the direction—for details see ec.europa.eu/commission/work-programme-2016_en. For details on the Digital Single Market (DSM) and the Commission 'Digital Single Market Strategy', see ch 7, 'E-Commerce Law', in this book.

[61] Proposal for a Directive on certain aspects concerning contracts for the supply of digital content, COM(2015) 634 final; Proposal for a Directive on certain aspects concerning contracts for the online and

point in a similar direction and hint that digital sales might dominate legislative discussions in the field of EU consumer law over the next couple of years.

The following section aims to introduce some possible ways in which EU consumer law might be developed further. In this respect, the focus will be on the issue of 'consumer trust', because we believe that increased consumer confidence is the key to facilitating the B2C market—regardless of whether market growth results from online or offline B2C transactions.

IV. Taking Transnational (EU) Consumer Law to the Next Level

To unlock the full potential of the B2C market one needs to establish an environment that is—to the greatest possible extent—free from (unnecessary) B2C transaction barriers. The first question that needs to be answered is thus the question of whether impediments exist and (if they do exist) what they are. In a second step, one would have to look for possible solutions that take both views on B2C transaction obstacles—the business and consumer perspectives—into consideration and reconcile both sides' interests. This section will again put the EU into the spotlight, because it arguably constitutes the most relevant transnational environment to discuss the challenges to, and potential of, consumer law.

With respect to the EU internal market, the Commission published a survey in 2011 that confirmed the existence of B2C transaction barriers in a cross-border setting (as seen from the business perspective). The report, the 2011 B2C Contract Survey,[62] ranked potential cross-border obstacles according to feedback from the business side. Perceived difficulties relating to information on and adapting to foreign contract law ranked high, with overall first and third place mentions. In total 40/38 per cent of respondents said that these issues had at least 'minimal impact' on their decision (not) to sell abroad.[63] Tax regulations came second with 39 per cent. These numbers were basically confirmed by a follow-up evaluation report of 2015 that focused on obstacles to the development of online sales (only).[64] The three issues mentioned

---

other distance sales of goods, COM(2015) 635 final. For details of these two Proposals, see European Commission, 'Commission proposes modern digital contract rules to simplify and promote access to digital content and online sales across the EU' (2015), europa.eu/rapid/press-release_IP-15-6264_en.htm. See, in addition, the more recent e-commerce legislation listed in ch 7, 'E-Commerce Law', in this book.

[62] The Gallup Organization Hungary, 'European Contract Law in Consumer Transactions. Analytical Report' (2011), ec.europa.eu/commfrontoffice/publicopinion/flash/fl_321_en.pdf.

[63] For the concrete results, see ibid, 19.

[64] TNS Political & Social, 'Retailers' attitudes towards cross-border trade and consumer protection. Summary' (2015), ec.europa.eu/COMMFrontOffice/PublicOpinion/index.cfm/ResultDoc/download/DocumentKy/67560.

scored high again—all three with on average roughly 40 per cent.[65] Some concerns that are not necessarily of a legal—at least not directly of a legal—nature also scored quite high in 2011, with language issues ranking close behind in fourth place (36 per cent) and cultural differences kept at a slightly more respectful distance, with 27 per cent of respondents considering them as having at least a 'minimal impact' on their decision (not) to get engaged in cross-border B2C transactions. Unfortunately, the 2015 report omitted these primarily non-legal issues from its catalogue of potential trade barriers.[66] Putting these reports into context, one can nevertheless conclude that various issues—of both a primarily legal and primarily non-legal nature—can complicate cross-border B2C transactions. Addressing a small number of obstacles could improve the situation, but a more holistic approach might be preferable.

Unlike the just mentioned materials on obstacles reported by the business side, an earlier survey of 2002 focused on consumers (2002 B2C Contract Survey)[67] and their viewpoint on B2C transactions. Unlike the 2011 B2C Contract Survey, it did not include the predominantly non-legal issues of language and cultural differences in its catalogue of possible answers. The results are nevertheless useful, because they reveal that the key legal reasons why consumers refrain from shopping abroad relate to rights enforcement and support in the event that something goes wrong.

According to the 2002 B2C Contract Survey, the top three answers were (i) perceived problems with filing complaints, (ii) problems with taking legal action (if initial complaints did not lead to a satisfactory result) and (iii) difficulties in getting support from a public authority/private body representing consumer interests. Differences in national consumer law standards were not considered as having played a similar, important de-motivating role, although problems in finding out about foreign laws and the fear that the protective standard of foreign consumer laws would be lower than under the consumers' home country laws were still popular answers.[68]

Taking a look at the results of the 2002 B2C Contract Survey and other, more recent consumer feedback (which adds insight into predominantly non-legal concerns),[69] one can conclude the following: when it comes to legal issues, the main reason why consumers shop locally rather than cross-border seems to be linked to the alleged lack of legal support and information. In addition, language issues, as well as cultural habits, undeniably play an important role, as one of the authors has already explained in detail elsewhere.[70] Even if the legal framework did not cause a headache, consumers

---

[65] ibid, 13.

[66] Unlike cultural differences (which were excluded from the list in 2015), language-related concerns still remained in the list. However, in 2015 language issues were directly linked to financial barriers, ie additional costs arising from language differences. The fact that language differences as such were no longer listed might be the main reason explaining the decrease from 36% to 27% (of respondents linking language to trade barriers in 2015).

[67] European Opinion Research Group and EOS Gallup Europe, 'Public Opinion in Europe: Views on Business-to-consumer Cross-border Trade' (2002), ec.europa.eu/COMMFrontOffice/PublicOpinion/index. cfm/ResultDoc/download/DocumentKy/54160.

[68] On these issues, see ibid, ch II.1.

[69] See, eg, TNS Political & Social, 'Consumer attitudes towards cross-border trade and consumer protection' (2015) Table 69, which shows that—on average—nearly every second respondent could use only his/her own country's language comfortably when shopping; ec.europa.eu/COMMFrontOffice/PublicOpinion/index.cfm/ResultDoc/download/DocumentKy/69149.

[70] Wrbka, n 18, 277 with further references.

would still refrain from shopping cross-border as a result of not understanding foreign language, or just out of insecurity due to customer prejudice against foreign sellers.[71]

These findings show us that diverse reasons can explain why businesses and consumers do not get involved in cross-border transactions more actively. Some of the reasons, in particular rights enforcement issues, actually can have a negative effect on B2C transactions more generally, ie regardless of whether one faces a cross-border scenario or not. To address the concerns, different mechanisms could be used. Some would be limited to cross-border B2C transactions; others would deal with broader questions and would involve national cases too. Let us briefly take a look at some selected possible instruments.

One way to answer some of the aforementioned concerns, more precisely those revolving around differences in national substantive law, could be by tackling them with the help of an increased amount of full harmonisation, or with a pan-EU OI similar to the CESL. However, putting voiced concerns—in particular the consumer concerns expressed in the pertinent studies—into the proper perspective, one has to say that either move would only address a small number of perceived obstacles, ie those that relate to substantive (contract) law issues. Moreover, instead of addressing the key obstacles, such a move might rather cause more problems than it could resolve. This is mainly due to two reasons. First, procedural questions and questions of consumer and business support would not be answered. (One could, of course, argue that procedural questions are covered by procedural law mechanisms introduced at the EU level. But, as shown on a different occasion, most of them have not had great effect yet.[72] We shall briefly return to this issue later.)

Second, with respect to full harmonisation it should further be noted that it cannot guarantee that the protective standard of all current Member States would be maintained. Compromises would have to be made, which basically means that in Member States with a higher protective level, some existing rights would diminish or (at least) their protective standard would be lowered. With respect to an OI (as known from the CESL), it should be added that such an OI sales law approach would lead to a two-tiered regime of different, parallel national legal frameworks that could, in principle, apply to the same cases. Not only would this cause increased legal uncertainty, but it might also be a physical impossibility for the average consumer to decide which available sales law of one and the same country—the traditional sales law or the newer OI—could offer a higher level of protection.[73] Choosing the 'better' one might generally be difficult, because it can be assumed that neither instrument could trump the other with respect to every single issue that could arise, and that nobody can foresee the issues that might arise in a concrete situation.

Hence, neither full harmonisation nor an OI could successfully answer the concerns listed earlier. Fortunately, these two approaches are not the only possible solutions. In the following we would like to discuss an alternative move that could likely satisfy

---

[71] Regarding the latter, see European Opinion Research Group and EOS Gallup Europe, 'Public Opinion in Europe', ch II.1, where it was shown that the fear of falling victim to fraud or deception by foreign shops or sellers was a big deterrent. Ultimately, this perceived risk somehow connects to the rights-enforcing issues mentioned earlier.

[72] Wrbka, n 18, 40–101.

[73] On these issues in more detail, see ibid, 221–24.

the wish for increased consumer confidence more comprehensively, and which is not limited to substantive law issues and cross-border cases.[74] On a different occasion one of the authors referred to this concept as 'access to justice 2.0', and subdivided it into the 'facilitating intermediaries approach' and the 'legislative approach'.[75]

The idea behind the facilitating intermediaries approach is to empower the parties to a B2C contract with the help of legal information and support. Although this concept predominantly applies to the consumer side, it can be understood as also benefitting businesses (as explained later).

Facilitating intermediaries can generally be defined as third party stakeholders that facilitate B2C transactions without being a party to a B2C contract. Looking at the consumer side, prominent examples are public authorities and private bodies that engage in consumer representation and support. If conceptualised in the right way, facilitating intermediaries could arguably create an atmosphere of mutual trust and support, which would eventually lead to a win-win situation for both consumers and the business side in any given B2C situation.

One cross-border example will be used to highlight the potential and outline the possible future of facilitating intermediaries. In 2005, the Commission established the European Consumer Centres Network (ECC-Net) as a successor to the Network for the extra-judicial settlement of consumer disputes (EEJ-Net) and the Euroguichet Network.[76] The ECC-Net has regional offices (ECCs) in each Member State, as well as in Norway and Iceland. The budget is provided for by the Commission and the national governments, each in principle bearing half the costs.[77]

The work of the ECCs can be categorised into three main pillars that relate to (i) providing consumer information, (ii) assisting in B2C dispute resolution and (iii) representing consumer interests at the legislative level. In the context of the first of these three, ECCs handle consumer information requests that relate to cross-border B2C transactions.[78] They do so either by answering concrete individual requests, or by providing more general information on their websites, in brochures, etc. With respect

---

[74] Thomas Wilhelmsson is one of those commentators who put a comparatively strong focus on consumer confidence in a broad sense. He comments on this issue as follows: '[C]onsumer confidence reasoning appears to have at least some merits. Consumers may indeed be reluctant to acquire goods and services abroad because of a lack of confidence in the protection offered to them in foreign markets. There is some empirical evidence according to which consumers do not buy from other Member States because of difficulties relating to the exchange or repair of the goods or the settlement of disputes. ... However, looking more closely at the reasons offered in studies such as these, they primarily appear to relate to problems of procedure and access—the consumer refrains from shopping abroad because of fear of practical problems related to the access to the other party and problems of access to justice resulting from the fact that the consumer and the seller are located in different countries—rather than lack of confidence in the substantive law.' For details see T Wilhelmsson, 'Conclusions' in G Howells et al (eds), *European Fair Trading Law—The Unfair Commercial Practices Directive* (Farnham, Ashgate, 2006) 241, 244–46.

[75] Wrbka, n 18, 299–301.

[76] While EEJ-Net focused on assisting consumers to settle B2C disputes, the Euroguichet Network concentrated on informing consumers about their rights in a more general way.

[77] The contributions by the Commission generally cover precisely 50% of the respective ECC costs; insignificant exceptions with respect to ECC Austria and ECC UK prove the rule (information provided by the Commission via email on 10 March 2014—on file with the authors).

[78] Elsewhere, one of the authors has referred to this as the 'facilitating intermediary consumer information pillar'. For more details on the facilitating intermediary consumer information pillar, as well as on the other ECC tasks, see, eg, Wrbka, n 18, 306–09 with further references.

to dispute settlement assistance,[79] ECCs may assist consumers at a relatively early stage of a (likely) dispute. This type of consumer request is usually referred to as a 'simple complaint', which principally means that an ECC may inform the consumer about the steps that can be taken to settle a dispute. At an advanced stage, or whenever an ECC thinks it necessary, the ECC can get more directly involved by trying to facilitate amicable solutions between consumers and traders. Ultimately, ECCs could assist consumers with 'stronger' forms of rights enforcement, ie with stronger ADR forms and litigation, if other dispute settlement attempts fail (in complex cases).

The third category of ECC activities relates to involvement in EU consumer policy making. The ECCs are an invaluable—yet still not fully utilised[80]—source of data and feedback from consumers. With this in mind, they could be of help to policymakers, identifying the most relevant consumer concerns in the context of B2C transactions.[81]

Past surveys and reports have repeatedly shown the great potential of ECCs for facilitating cross-border B2C transactions, and have provided workload and resources data.[82] More recent data show that ECCs handled a total of more than 650,000 contacts (information requests and complaints) in the first 10 years, ie from 2005 to 2014.[83] The annual numbers have (in principle[84]) steadily risen over the years, peaking at slightly more than 93,000 annual contacts in 2014.[85] In 2011, the external CPEC took a closer look at the significance of ECC-Net and arrived at the following conclusions, drawn from a comprehensive survey.[86] Roughly one-third of respondents (29 per cent) stated that their confidence in cross-border shopping had risen due to ECC assistance. At the same time, however, 19 per cent had experienced the opposite effect, ie their confidence had fallen. Nevertheless, three in four consumers stated that they were principally satisfied with the ECCs' work. Overall, the CPEC calculated that ECC-Net 'delivered direct financial benefits to consumers of at least 1.77 times its cost to the taxpayer during 2010'.[87]

Empirical data have, however, spotlighted several deficiencies. The most striking involve a shortage of funding and personnel—for example, only one ECC (ECC Germany) had more than a total of 10 full-time equivalents (FTEs) in 2013 and the

---

[79] Elsewhere, one of the authors referred to this as 'facilitating intermediary consumer law enforcement'. For details on this and the following, see ibid, 304–05.

[80] See Consumer Policy Evaluation Consortium (CPEC), 'Evaluation of the European Consumer Centres Network' (2011) 87, where it is explained that there is the need 'to optimise the feedback of the ECCs for policy-making purposes', ec.europa.eu/consumers/ecc/docs/final_report_cpec_en.pdf.

[81] ibid, 46–51.

[82] Comprehensive data can be found in, eg, CPEC, ibid; European Commission, 'Help and Advice on Your Purchases Abroad—The European Consumer Centres Network 2012 Annual Report' (2013) ec.europa.eu/consumers/ecc/docs/report_ecc-net_2012_en.pdf.

[83] For details, see European Commission, 'The European Consumer Centres Network—10 Years Serving Europe's Consumers; Anniversary Report 2005–2015' (2015), www.consumer.ee/public/ECC_NET_-_Anniversary_Report_2015_corrected_FINAL_28052015.pdfwww.consumer.ee/public/ECC_NET_-_Anniversary_Report_2015_corrected_FINAL_28052015.pdf.

[84] See European Commission, n 82, 11 (showing that twice—in 2009 and 2011—there was a slight decrease).

[85] See the 2013 ECC-Net infographic at ec.europa.eu/consumers/ecc/infographic/02_14_infograph-eccnet_2013.pdf.

[86] For the following data, see CPEC, n 80, iii.

[87] ibid.

vast majority of ECCs had less than five each[88]—low consumer awareness with respect to the existence of ECCs (consumer ECC awareness),[89] quality inconsistencies among the ECC-Net members and limited competences when it comes to actively supporting consumers in getting their interests satisfied.[90]

What conclusions can be drawn from these findings? Overall, the work of ECCs should be considered as positive from the viewpoints of consumer satisfaction and improving consumer confidence. However, in order to take the facilitating intermediary consumer support offered by ECCs to the next level, one needs to address the listed key concerns. Two key measures seem to be the most urgent ones in this respect. First, and taking into consideration that approximately only one consumer in four has ever heard of ECCs,[91] consumer ECC awareness needs to be increased. Second, human and financial resources need to be increased. The measures go hand in hand. Increased awareness would (at least in the short and mid-term)[92] lead to more work for the ECCs (and hence to the need for more human and financial resources). Without additional resources it would, however, be difficult to rapidly raise awareness. Recommended steps to be taken to achieve an improvement in both areas include (as explained in more detail elsewhere[93]) a stronger Commission initiative to vest ECCs with more human and financial resources (eg via rechannelling existing funds from less sustainable projects to the ECC-Net; enabling and motivating ECCs to expand self-promotion and self-financing activities), as well as intensifying current activities and engaging in new ones. With respect to current activities, ECCs could broaden their information initiatives, eg by being given a stronger media presence or organising additional public information events. As for assisting in consumer dispute resolution, another example of a generally already existing ECC task, both the ADR Directive and the ODR Regulation show that ECCs can be granted important roles in this respect.[94]

The ECCs might also engage in additional projects to tackle some more of the B2C transaction obstacles identified earlier. Two language-related examples exemplify this. One idea would be to establish cooperation between ECCs and certified translation services that specialise in legal matters. Ideally, ECCs would employ specially trained translation staff to support consumers and businesses in cross-border issues, both at the stage of contractual negotiations and when it comes to dispute resolution.

---

[88] For concrete data (that also show that there has not yet been much positive change in terms of an increase in FTEs per ECC) see Wrbka, n 18, Table 6.

[89] Pertinent reports have repeatedly pointed out the low consumer ECC awareness (although there has been a slight improvement)—see CPEC, 'Evaluation of the European Consumer Centres Network' 6 (Table 1:2) and TNS Political & Social, 'Consumer Attitudes towards Cross-border Trade and Consumer Protection', Flash Eurobarometer 358 (2013) 42, which show that the consumer ECC awareness was 15 per cent in 2011 and 22 per cent in 2013 (ec.europa.eu/public_opinion/flash/fl_358_en.pdf).

[90] For all these issues in more detail, see CPEC, 'Evaluation of the European Consumer Centres Network' 84, and a commentary in Wrbka, *European Consumer Access to Justice Revisited* 306–12.

[91] See already above n 90.

[92] It must be hoped that eventually the number of annual contact would level off at a certain level (or might even decrease). In this way, one can understand the ultimate goal of ECC-Net expressed in 2011 as follows: 'to reduce the number of 'interested users' [ie of consumers who ask ECCs for legal information] because consumers … are getting *satisfactory* service from traders selling cross border' (see CPEC, 'Evaluation of the European Consumer Centres Network' 88; emphasis added).

[93] For details, see Wrbka, n 18, 312–17.

[94] Art 14(2) ADR Directive; Art 7(1) ODR Regulation.

Second, one could think of even more strongly law-focused language support. This could eventually have a positive impact on consumer confidence, because it addresses what is arguably the strongest (primarily) non-law related cross-border B2C transaction impediment: ECCs could be given the competence to check and (if in line with legal requirements) approve businesses standard terms used in cross-border B2C transactions. Businesses could be offered the chance to get their standard terms (once approved) translated into foreign languages by the ECCs or their translators. Approval (and translation) by ECCs could—especially in combination with visible 'ECC approval seals'—assure consumers that they can trust in the legal compliance of standard terms, thus increasing overall consumer confidence in the B2C market.[95]

So ECCs might be the key consumer contact when it comes to cross-border B2C issues. However, similar underlying thoughts, in particular the wish for increased stakeholder support, can be used to justify the stronger involvement of comparable bodies at a sectoral level, eg with respect to e-commerce, as well as in the cases of domestic issues and business support. With respect to domestic issues, Member States have been taking different approaches, choosing (in principle) between public authorities[96] and private bodies.[97] (We shall briefly return to them in Chapter 4 on compensatory collective redress and alternative dispute resolution.) Direct business support should not be left unmentioned either, since pertinent studies indicate the need for an improvement in this respect too. Not only the aforementioned 2011 B2C Contract Survey, but also newer studies explain that a considerable number of businesses are not yet well enough informed about consumer law standards—sometimes even if the mandatory standards are part of their own jurisdiction's legislation. The 9th Consumer Conditions Scoreboard[98] as well as the 2013 Eurobarometer report on retailers' attitudes towards cross-border trade and consumer protection (2013 Cross-border Retailer Eurobarometer report)[99] imply that in various instances, far less than half of the traders were able to answer consumer law-related questions correctly.[100]

To remedy the lack of legal knowledge on the business side, one could think of the stronger involvement of institutions comparable to the ECCs. Actually, a possible addressee already exists. In 2008 the Commission launched the Enterprise Europe Network (EEN). Crafted as a 'one-stop shop for all ... business needs',[101] the EEN aims to support businesses in various business-related matters with the help of a network of several hundred local contact points within and even outside of the EU.[102]

---

[95] It should not go unmentioned that standard terms compliance checks in cooperation with ECCs already occur in some instances, eg by business support member bodies of the Enterprise Europe Network. However, an enhanced institutionalised approach in combination with a comprehensive language support element and ECC quality seals would be a more effective method to raise consumer confidence.

[96] See, eg, the UK with its former Office of Fair Trading (OFT; dissolved in 2014) and its successors, the Competition and Markets Authority (CMA) and the Financial Conduct Authority (FCA).

[97] The private body approach had, eg, prevailed in Germany, the Netherlands and Austria.

[98] European Commission, 'The Consumer Conditions Scoreboard: Consumers at Home in the Single Market—9th edition' (2013), ec.europa.eu/consumers/consumer_evidence/consumer_scoreboards/9_edition/docs/cms_9_en.pdf.

[99] TNS Political & Social, 'Retailers' Attitudes towards Cross-border Trade and Consumer Protection', Flash Eurobarometer 359 (2013), ec.europa.eu/commfrontoffice/publicopinion/flash/fl_359_en.pdf.

[100] For details, see Wrbka, n 18, 317–19 with further references.

[101] www.een.ec.europa.eu/about/mission.

[102] For details, see een.ec.europa.eu/about/branches.

Providing businesses with legal information is one of the main EEN tasks. Although not (yet) declared as a key factor in this respect, consumer law-related information is clearly one area of law in which EEN could offer assistance.[103] Increased business awareness about the existence of EEN and a stronger initiative on the part of EEN could undeniably help to dispel businesses' concerns about different national sales laws.

Within the access to justice 2.0 concept, facilitating intermediaries undeniably play a crucial role, because they aim to provide consumers with invaluable legal information and support when it comes to cross-border B2C transactions. However, to guarantee a genuine level playing field for both businesses and consumers, one might have to complement this with a suitable legal framework. For the sake of simplicity, this additional layer can be called the 'legislative approach'.

The legislative approach can be subdivided into two groups: procedural law, on the one hand, and substantive law, on the other. The procedural law pillar comprises mechanisms of rights enforcement, regardless of whether they relate to direct enforcement by consumers themselves or indirect enforcement via consumer representation bodies. Existing specific EU tools that fall within this category include the Injunctions Directive,[104] the Legal Aid Directive,[105] the Consumer Protection Cooperation Regulation[106] and the Small Claims Regulation,[107] as well as the ADR Directive and ODR Regulation mentioned previously. Single provisions in substantive law instruments can be added.[108] The success and potential of rights enforcement devices can be assessed with the help of five specific criteria, which one of the authors has referred to elsewhere as awareness (of involved stakeholders), skills/experience (of involved stakeholders), availability (of mechanisms in a concrete case), usability (of the available mechanism) and effectiveness (of the mechanism/its outcome).[109]

Taking a closer look at the existing mechanisms, and in particular at available empirical assessments, one will see that none of them satisfies all five criteria. In most cases the mechanisms reveal deficiencies with respect to more than one, or even all five, criteria. To improve the overall success of these mechanisms, one would have to address the shortcomings in turn. The facilitating intermediaries approach discussed earlier could be used to remedy the deficiencies with respect to the awareness and skills/experience criteria. The more 'technical' issues (availability, usability and effectiveness), on the other hand, require legislative action, in the sense that one would have to adapt relevant provisions of the directives/regulations to cope with the problems identified. The 2015 amendment of the European Small Claims Procedure[110] can be understood as one example of how surveys can lead to attempts to set procedural tools aright.

---

[103] Confirmed by the Commission (DG ENTR—Unit D2) via email on 4 March 2014 (on file with the authors).
[104] Directive 2009/22/EC, [2009] OJ L110/30.
[105] Directive 2003/8/EC, [2003] OJ L26/41.
[106] Regulation (EC) 2006/2004, [2004] OJ L364/1.
[107] Regulation (EC) 861/2007, [2007] OJ L199/1 as amended by Regulation (EU) 2421/2015, [2015] OJ L341/1.
[108] See, eg, the examples in Wrbka, n 18, 34.
[109] For details and examples, see ibid, 269–74.
[110] See above n 107.

Substantive consumer laws constitute the second layer of the legislative approach and should be mentioned in the same breath as rights enforcement tools. Even the best crafted procedural devices would not be of much use if the protective level offered by substantive laws were insufficient. Hence, the question in this respect is how the EU legislator should approach the 'inner' side of consumer protection, ie what the content of substantive rights should be?[111]

One of the starting points in discussions on substantive consumer law is Article 114(3) of the Treaty on the Functioning of the European Union, which requires the EU legislator to apply a 'high level of protection'. Put into context with the idea of regulating broader consumer issues at the EU level and the recent (at least partial) trends to utilise full harmonisation, EU policymakers face a dilemma that could create detrimental effects for national policymakers. Article 114(3) does not require the highest possible level of protection to be adopted: EU consumer laws need to be structured alongside 'only' a relatively high level, but may not succeed in reaching the level of some 'leading' Member States. Examples from the past show that EU law making indeed requires compromises to be made. While in the case of minimum harmonisation, compromises would still allow national legislators to apply consumer-friendlier standards, this possibility does not exist in the case of full harmonisation. The greater the extent of full harmonisation and the broader the scope of the EU legislation covered, the higher is the risk for (at least) some national consumer regimes to suffer partial damage (in terms of the protective standard) and for us to face a 'race to the bottom' in terms of the average consumer protection standard.[112]

Several authors add further concerns regarding full harmonisation. These include the following:

(1)   The risk of falling under different protective levels depending on the type of transaction (depending on the good/service in question, a particular transaction might fall either under the EU legislation, or under national legislation which might—due to the fact that EU law would not apply to that good/service—follow a different protective standard).[113]

(2)   Proportionality concerns, ie the question whether full harmonisation is actually the least restrictive means to achieve a level playing field to enhance the internal market.[114]

---

[111] On the EU consumer policy dilemma, see, in particular, S Wrbka, 'The Dilemma of European Consumer Representation in Deliberative Networks—the Democratic Deficit in the Context of the Drafting of the Common European Sales Law' in M Fenwick, S Van Uytsel and S Wrbka (eds), *Networked Governance, Transnational Business & the Law* (Tokyo, Springer, 2014) 145.

[112] In a similar vein are, eg, Tamm, n 5, 241; M Stürner, 'Das Konzept der Vollharmonisierung' in M Stürner (ed), *Vollharmonisierung im Europäischen Verbraucherrecht?* (Munich, Sellier, 2010) 3; K Trietz, 'Verbesserung des Verbraucherschutzes durch die Vollharmonisierung?—Ein Praxisbericht im deutsch-polnischen Verhältnis' in M Stürner (ed), *Vollharmonisierung im Europäischen Verbraucherrecht?* (Munich, Sellier, 2010) 197; AC Mittwoch, *Vollharmonisierung und Europäisches Privatrecht. Methode, Implikationen und Durchführung* (Berlin, de Gruyter, 2013) 138–39; C Herresthal, 'Vertragsrecht' in K Langenbucher (ed), *Europäisches Privat- und Wirtschaftsrecht*, 3rd edn (Baden-Baden, Nomos, 2013) 69, 84–85.

[113] Stürner, 'Das Konzept der Vollharmonisierung', n 112, 7.

[114] Stürner argues in a similar vein (see ibid, 6–7).

(3)   The risk of legislative stagnation at the national and the EU levels, because the loss of national test sites would complicate further development with the help of practical feedback from the Member States. Götz Schulze refers to this situation as a state of 'fossilisation' (*Versteinerung*).[115]

Rather than relying on full harmonisation, one could reach a result that achieves satisfaction of the call for more certainty/simplicity without depriving Member States of the possibility to apply consumer-friendlier standards with a combination of two different mechanisms—the aforementioned facilitating intermediaries approach (to enhance legal information and support), paired with a concept that one might call 'high-level minimum harmonisation'.[116] High-level minimum harmonisation can be understood as applying minimum standardised protection at the EU level that sets a comparatively high standard. At the same time, it would (due to its minimum harmonisation character) allow national legislators to maintain or introduce higher standards (if exceptionally needed). To determine the appropriate level of protection to be introduced with the help of high-level minimum harmonisation, one could/would have to have recourse to comparative studies of known protective standards, eg from the Consumer Law Compendium or the DCFR project. To achieve the highest possible/best acceptable level of legal certainty, and to reduce the necessity to go beyond the pan-EU level, at the national level one should aim for a level of protection that would satisfy the consumer policies of the vast majority of Member States.

V. Concluding Remarks

This chapter has focused on consumer law (in the EU). It has explained that consumer law is a very relevant area of law that affects the daily lives of business and consumers. Consumer law is still developing, and both legal academics and policymakers are looking for the most suitable direction in which to satisfy as many interests as possible. In the EU, for example, the biggest issue to be addressed might be the question of how to reconcile business and consumer interests in a way that both strengthens the market and safeguards justified consumer interests.

---

[115] G Schulze, 'Ökonomik der Vollharmonisierung im Gemeinschaftsprivatrecht' in B Gsell and C Herresthal (eds), *Vollharmonisierung im Privatrecht* (Tübingen, Mohr Siebeck, 2009) 63, 81. For an argument along similar lines, see B Tilleman and B Du Laing, 'Directives on Consumer Protection as a Suitable Means of Obtaining a (More) Unified European Contract Law?' in S Grundmann and J Stuyck (eds), *An Academic Green Paper on European Private Law* (The Hague, Kluwer Law International, 2002) 81, 97.

[116] For details, see Wrbka, n 18, 328–32, where the author furthermore touches upon the potential of (additional) general, binding principles for national legislators to ensure a certain overall level of protection. In this context, it is in particular Hugh Collins' idea of a European Civil Code, made up of legal principles as a guiding tool for national legislators, that needs to be mentioned. For details, see H Collins, *The European Civil Code: The Way Forward* (Cambridge, Cambridge University Press, 2008) 144–45.

History has shown that (at the EU level) one can distinguish between different approaches. Originally the focus was put on sector-specific issues and aligning national consumer law regimes without depriving national lawmakers of their competences to enact or maintain stricter standards. In the early years of the new millennium the Commission has begun to gradually shift from minimum to full harmonisation, aiming to regulate broader legal issues in more comprehensive, merged legislation. These endeavours have suffered a setback, primarily because the Member States have not been willing to renounce their legislative freedom to go beyond a particular EU standard. More recent trends point to a mixed solution: the CRD, the new Package Travel Directive, and both the 2015 Proposal for a Directive on certain aspects concerning contracts for the supply of digital content and the 2015 Proposal for a Directive on certain aspects concerning contracts for the online and other distance sales of goods[117] are good examples of mechanisms based on targeted full harmonisation, that is, a combination of fully harmonised issues and minimum standards (where the policymakers do not believe it is necessary to achieve one single standard). Whether this is the most appropriate (and in terms of proportionality most suitable) approach is unclear. The high-level minimum approach introduced in this chapter might show similar results without depriving national parliaments of their legislative freedom to protect consumers in a better way.

Another issue that needs to be addressed in the future is how to strengthen consumer confidence in the B2C market by means other than 'just' enacting laws. The facilitating intermediaries approach discussed here can be understood as one mechanism to answer practical concerns—at both the consumer and the business level. Facilitating intermediaries can function as important platforms to provide stakeholders in B2C contracts with legal information and support, irrespective of whether this should happen in the EU or anywhere else in the world.

Consumer law has not reached its peak yet. Contemporary discussions of how to improve the legal framework for e-commerce and how to enable consumers to get their rights enforced more easily are the best proof for this. We shall return to these issues later in this book.[118]

Selected Further Reading

Benöhr, I, *EU Consumer Law and Human Rights* (Oxford, Oxford University Press, 2013)

Boele-Woelki, K and Grosheide, W (eds), *The Future of European Contract Law* (Alphen aan den Rijn, Kluwer Law International, 2007)

---

[117] See above n 61.

[118] See ch 7, 'E-Commerce Law' and ch 4, 'Compensatory Collective Redress and Alternative Dispute Resolution'.

Howells, G, Ramsay, I, Wilhelmsson, T and Kraft, D (eds), *Handbook of Research on International Consumer Law* (Cheltenham, Edward Elgar, 2010)

Howells, G and Weatherill, S, *Consumer Protection Law*, 2nd edn (Aldershot, Ashgate, 2005)

Karanikic, M, Micklitz, H-W and Reich, N (eds), *Modernising Consumer Law: The Experience of the Western Balkan* (Baden-Baden, Nomos, 2012)

Micklitz, H-W, Stuyck, J and Terryn, E (eds), *Cases, Materials and Text on Consumer Law*, 2nd edn (Oxford, Hart Publishing, forthcoming)

Nebbia, P and Ashkam, T, *EU Consumer Law* (Oxford, Oxford University Press, 2004)

Ramsay, I, *Consumer Law and Policy*, 3rd edn (Oxford, Hart Publishing, 2012)

Reich, N and Micklitz, H-W, *Europäisches Verbraucherrecht*, 4th edn (Baden-Baden, Nomos, 2003)

Reich, N, Micklitz, H-W, Rott, P and Tonner, K, *European Consumer Law*, 2nd edn (Cambridge, Intersentia, 2014)

Reich, N and Woodroffe, G (eds), *European Consumer Policy after Maastricht* (Dordrecht, Kluwer Academic, 2010)

Schulte–Nölke, H, Twigg–Flesner, C and Ebers, M (eds), *EC Consumer Law Compendium: The Consumer Acquis and Its Transposition in the Member States* (Munich, Sellier, 2008)

Twigg-Flesner, C, *A Cross–border–only Regulation for Consumer Transactions in the EU: A Fresh Approach to EU Consumer Law* (New York, Springer, 2012)

Weatherill, S, 'Consumer Policy' in P Craig and G de Búrca (eds), *The Evolution of EU Law*, 2nd edn (Oxford, Oxford University Press, 2011) 837–76

Weatherill, S, *EU Consumer Law and Policy*, 2nd edn (Cheltenham, Edward Elgar, 2013)

Wrbka, S, *European Consumer Access to Justice Revisited* (Cambridge, Cambridge University Press, 2015)

2

Product Liability Law

I. Outline

Product liability law constitutes an important field of law, in practice especially when one considers the number of cases. In 2014, David G Owen estimated that in the US alone people 'may suffer upwards of 200 million product injuries, illnesses, and deaths each year, at a national cost approaching $10 trillion'.[1] Many of these incidents reach the courts. In the US in particular, the last few decades have seen an increasing amount of specialisation in product liability law, with respect both to law firms and to legal departments in major corporations. This has led Owen to argue that 'products liability now ranks as one of the most important fields of law'.[2] Again from a business point of view, managing the legal risk that product liability law has created constitutes a substantial challenge for all companies, irrespective of size or type of business.

Lawmakers in the EU replied to comparable developments at a national level with one of the first directives—the Product Liability Directive (PLD) in 1985—to standardise product liability rules throughout the EU.[3] Many other jurisdictions around the globe have followed this example and introduced special product liability regimes.

Product liability law—in this chapter understood as the set of legal rules that governs the consequences of damage caused by defective products—is a complex area of law that can be approached in a number of different ways.

Let us take a look at one example: Buyer C purchases a fire extinguisher from seller B that was manufactured by producer A. When C puts the extinguisher to use, the discharge lever breaks and the extinguisher depressurises instantly. Parts of the

---

[1] DG Owen, *Products Liability Law*, 3rd edn (St Paul, MN, West Academic, 2015) 1.
[2] DG Owen, *Product Liability in a Nutshell*, 9th edn (St Paul, MN, West Academic, 2015) 12.
[3] Directive 85/374/EEC, [1985] OJ L210/29.

lever are sent flying in various directions. One part hits C's eye; another one a mirror behind C, breaking it into pieces; a third piece slices through the arm of C's brother, D.

Product liability law aims to enhance law enforcement by providing possible claimants with simplified rules on compensation. But several questions arise. First, who can be held liable? Second, to what extent is culpability relevant? Third, who may sue and what types of damage are covered? The simple, but likely unsatisfying answer is that the solutions differ from jurisdiction to jurisdiction, further complicating the situation for all. In this chapter, we shall encounter some of these complications.

In times of increasing market globalisation one further question should be emphasised. Producers, sellers and buyers/users of defective products often operate from and reside in different countries. The extended and often global character of contemporary supply chains add to the complexity of this field of law. Against this background, it is obvious that product liability is increasingly becoming an area of international and cross-border interest. Bearing in mind the conceptual differences between existing product liability regimes, calls for increased unification of product liability law become understandable.

For the sake of clarity, it should further be noted that readers might get confused by similar-looking terminology that is used in the literature. While the terms 'product liability law' and 'products liability law' can be used interchangeably (*note*: in this chapter, we use the former), one should be aware that 'product liability law' is conceptually different from (but to some extent interlinked with) 'product safety law'. The private law concept of product liability concerns itself with the legal consequences of damage caused by defective products. In this respect, it can be considered as a set of rules that apply *ex post*, ie as provisions that are used to resolve disputes arising from damage caused by defects. Product safety law, on the other hand, in principle comprises *ex ante* rules (and is usually exclusively located in public law.) It is concerned with (regulatory) rules that define product safety standards to be met by producers/manufacturers of products to prevent possible defects and damage.[4] Although violations of product safety law standards might lead to the application of product liability law (in cases where product safety law infringements cause product law-relevant, defect-caused damage), product liability law covers defect-caused damage more comprehensively, which does not necessarily involve breaches of safety standards. We shall briefly return to this issue in the context of the definition of product liability-relevant defects.

---

[4] In a similar vein see, eg, David Owen, who refers to the difference between these two concepts as follows: 'What products liability law is *not* is "product safety" law. "Products liability" and "product safety" are terms conventionally used in America to describe the law that broadly covers product-related dangers, accidents, and illnesses. A central issue in both products liability law and product safety law is establishing how products should be classified as "excessively" or "unduly" hazardous, "unreasonably" dangerous, or "defective." Both areas of law seek to reduce the toll of accidents from such hazards to improve product safety. But there they begin to diverge. ... The law of product safety is *regulatory* law ... Product safety law operates *ex ante*, seeking to prevent product-caused accidents and diseases before they occur. ... In contrast to product safety law, products liability law governs the private *litigation* of product accidents (see Owen, n 1, 1–3).' For further comments on product safety law from an EU perspective, see, eg, C Hodges, *European Regulation of Consumer Product Safety* (Oxford, Oxford University Press, 2005). See further G Howells, *Consumer Product Safety* (Aldershot, Ashgate, 1998).

II. General Remarks and Early History of Product Liability Law

Product liability law can, broadly speaking, be understood as the legal regime that governs the legal consequences with respect to damage caused by defective products. This definition poses several questions, five of which are addressed here. First, what does 'defective' mean? Second, what liability standard is applied: does product liability rest on negligence, or is it 'strict' in the sense that no culpable behaviour is needed? Third, which types of damage fall under the product liability regime: damage to persons themselves, as well as to their property? Fourth, who can be held liable: the producer of a defective good, its seller, the importer (of defective products manufactured abroad)? Fifth, who is protected by product liability laws: only the buyer, or any injured party? Lawmakers have to make difficult policy decisions. The examples discussed in this chapter show that different jurisdictions balance the interests of the stakeholders involved in different ways.

Notwithstanding the fact that product liability law is an often-litigated area in today's world, it is not a recent concept. One can actually trace it back to Roman times, when the foundations for both contractual and delictual/tort product liability were laid.

In early times the phrase *caveat emptor* ('buyer beware') significantly characterised the legal situation with respect to damage caused by defects (understood in a wide sense). Although the buyers' remedies for defective products were limited, people suffering damage were not absolutely powerless. Even under Roman law, certain remedial actions existed. Traders could, for example, be held liable if they delivered less than the explicitly agreed quantity.[5] With respect to the quality of 'goods' possible actions were sparser and initially limited to certain latent defects of slaves. Justinian later broadened the scope to cover quality related issues at a more general level. The Justinian model was complex, and distinguished between situations in which the seller knew about the defect and those where he or she did not. In the latter situation, the seller had the opportunity to generally exclude liability for latent defects. If he or she failed to do so, the buyer could exercise two actions: the *actio redhibitoria* to claim the payment back, or the *actio quanti minoris* to get a price reduction. If the seller was aware of the defect, the situation was different in two ways. First, he or she could not exclude liability. Second, the buyer had the opportunity to claim for damages that went beyond mere price reduction.

With respect to tort law it was the *Lex Aquilia* that—in the third century BCE— first introduced a potentially suitable mechanism. However, just as was the case with

---

[5] R Zimmermann, *The Law of Obligations, Roman Foundations of the Civilian Tradition* (Cape Town, Juta & Co Ltd, 1990) 30.

contractual liability, the injuring party could only be held liable if his or her behaviour was (at least) negligent. To summarise, neither tort nor contractual liability law knew a special product liability regime that could have been applied regardless of culpable behaviour.

In the following section we highlight more recent advancements in product liability law in selected regions. We shall see, in particular, how different jurisdictions have addressed the issues outlined in the previous paragraphs.

III. Product Liability in Selected Jurisdictions

A. Product Liability Law in the US

Product liability in the US is a complex regime and—despite some special features—a good example of how product liability law has evolved over the years. Modern product liability law in the US is dominated mainly by warranty law and (more recently) strict (tort) liability, with—to a lesser extent—additional input by traditional (negligence-based) tort law and tortious misrepresentation.

Early US product liability law took a relatively narrow approach. One of the default bases for suing for compensation was negligent behaviour. People who suffered harm as a result of defective products could have recourse to conventional tort law if manufacturers or sellers negligently caused the defect (or negligently did not prevent harm). With respect to sellers who were not at the same time manufacturers, negligence-based tort actions were not very promising though. In the vast majority of cases sellers did not know (and were not able to know) that products they sold were defective. Hence, the ordinary range of possible defendants was in practice limited to manufacturers. However, initially two factors in particular complicated the situation with respect to manufacturers too. First, US product liability negligence law initially adopted a contract law defence: the privity principle allowed manufacturers to fend off product liability claims with the argument that injured parties were too remote, in the sense that manufacturers' duty of care did not extend to include parties with whom those manufacturers were not in direct contact. In the first half of the twentieth century the privity principle had gradually lost most of its importance with respect to manufacturers' negligence cases. Starting with foodstuffs and products that were imminently dangerous, privity was subsequently less often considered as a possible defence in manufacturers' negligence cases.[6]

---

[6] See, eg *MacPherson v Buick Motor Co* (1916) 217 NY 382, 111 NE 1050, 1053, where the court argued that if products 'will be used by persons other than the purchaser, and used without new tests, then, irrespective of contract, the manufacturer of the thing of danger is under a duty to make it carefully'.

Second, from a more practical perspective, the plaintiff's obligation to prove the defendant's negligence caused difficulties. Neither was it entirely clear how high the expected level of care should be, nor was the plaintiff usually in a situation where he or she had easy access to evidence that the manufacturer actually acted culpably. Courts had gradually started to lower the evidential threshold by allowing circumstantial, ie non-direct, prima facie evidence to indicate negligent behaviour. If the circumstances were obvious enough to convince the court that the manufacturer acted negligently, no direct evidence was needed. This idea, the *res ipsa loquitur* ('*res ipsa*') doctrine, simplified the situation significantly, but—over the years—it came under fire, as some commentators began to consider product liability litigation as becoming too excessive. On top of that, applying the *res ipsa* mechanism too generously posed challenges for legal predictability and clarity. Hence, from a doctrinal point of view, many observers asked for a different solution.

Tortious misrepresentation forms a second traditional category of possible product liability claim bases. Understood as negligently or knowingly communicating wrong or misleading information about product facts that causes harm to a person relying on the truth of the communication, it does not necessarily describe a typical form of product liability.[7] In the case of tortious misrepresentation, a defect is constituted if the communicated 'fact' turns out as either wrong or not in the way the communication was to be commonly understood by a third party. A classic example would be the (negligent) promise that the rungs of a ladder can carry up to 150 kg, but they in fact break under a weight of 100 kg, injuring the buyer who has climbed up the ladder. In practice, tortious misrepresentation has turned out more or less as unsuccessful as negligence-based claims, because both the question of what was communicated and whether there is any culpability on the defendant's side might create practical evidence issues for the plaintiff.

Very likely in light of the disadvantages of these two mechanisms, US product liability law has increasingly sought to apply alternative instruments. For a long time, US-style warranty law was the sole means to compensate for the difficulties with respect to demonstrating negligence on the defendant's side.

The basic idea behind product liability-relevant warranty law is that the underlying contract provides the basis for guaranteeing the absence of product defects. The product liability warranty regime distinguishes, in principle, between three different warranty types in this respect. The simplest form is the group of express warranties. In this case the seller would explicitly warrant the 'defectlessness' of a product. From a practical perspective, more relevant are arguably two implied warranty forms: the implied warranty of merchantability ('implied merchantability warranty') and the implied warranty of fitness for particular purpose ('implied fitness warranty'). The implied merchantability warranty relates to the specific quality of a product as generally to be expected. It refers to the seller's obligation to warrant that the product can be used for the purpose for which it is usually used. If a buyer purchases a chainsaw, he or she can reasonably expect that the blades are fixed properly. To complement the implied merchantability warranty concept, the seller of a product can be held

---

[7] See, eg Owen, n 2, 195, where Owen explains that '[m]isrepresentation … is not generally classified as a product "defect"'.

liable under the implied fitness warranty if the product cannot be used for a particular purpose communicated by the buyer.

The warranty regime simplified the overall situation for the plaintiff, because—in contrast to claims based on general tort law and tortious representation—it did not require the existence of culpable behaviour. At the same time, however, several factors still complicated litigation. Aside from possible disclaimers and limitations of remedies expressed by the seller (*note*: these defences are of less relevance in consumer cases)[8] and the harmed party's duty of timely notice of breach, for a long time the aforementioned privity element (with respect to manufacturers' liability) significantly limited the potential of warranty claims. To escape non negligence-based product liability, manufacturers chose to 'outsource' the distribution of their products to sellers who would contract with the purchasers independently. When sued by injured parties, manufacturers could—in early times—succeed with lack of privity arguments. Their contractual relationship with the sellers did not entail liability consequences if purchasers (who only contracted with the sellers and not the manufacturers) suffered harm. In the early twentieth century, courts decided to partially limit the potential of the privity defence, by not accepting it in foodstuff product liability cases.[9]

It took a couple of decades until courts and commentators came up with calls and ideas for expanding non-negligence liability to include manufacturers.[10] In the 1944 decision in *Escola v Coca-Cola Bottling*, one of the judges, Justice Traynor, asked for traditionally negligence-based manufacturers' liability to be rethought, as follows:

> Even if there is no negligence, however, public policy demands that responsibility be fixed wherever it will most effectively reduce the hazards to life and health inherent in defective products that reach the market. It is evident that the manufacturer can anticipate some hazards and guard against the recurrence of others, as the public cannot. Those who suffer injury from defective products are unprepared to meet its consequences. The cost of an injury and the loss of time or health may be an overwhelming misfortune to the person injured, and a needless one, for the risk of injury can be insured by the manufacturer and distributed among the public as a cost of doing business. It is to the public interest to discourage the marketing of products having defects that are a menace to the public. If such products nevertheless find their way into the market it is to the public interest to place the responsibility for whatever injury they may cause upon the manufacturer, who, even if he is not negligent in the manufacture of the product, is responsible for its reaching the market. However intermittently such injuries may occur and however haphazardly they may strike, the risk of their occurrence is a constant risk and a general one. Against such a risk there should be general and constant protection and the manufacturer is best situated to afford such protection.[11]

Justice Traynor argued that broadening the manufacturer's liability would not cause major issues, since it would only mean a simplification of the compensation chain. Applying the traditional warranty regime, harmed purchasers could sue sellers for

---

[8] For details, see ibid, 114 et seq.

[9] See, in particular, *Mazetti v Armour & Co* (1913) 75 Wash 622, 135 Pac 633.

[10] One of the most influential works in this respect was authored by William Prosser, to whom courts subsequently referred when asking for a broader application of non-negligence manufacturers' liability. For details see WL Prosser, *Handbook of the Law of Torts* (St Paul, MN, West Publishing, 1941).

[11] *Escola v Coca-Cola Bottling Co* (1944) 24 Cal.2d 453, 150 P.2d 436.

warranty liability. Sellers in return could hold themselves harmless by having recourse to the manufacturer. Still, privity considerations, in particular, might have been one reason why holding manufacturers liable under contract law proved difficult.

The early 1960s marked the birth of the rise of strict tort liability. In *Henningsen v Bloomfield Motors*, the New Jersey High Court ruled in favour of the plaintiff, holding the manufacturer of a defective product liable.[12] The judgment can be understood as a first step towards manufacturers' strict tort liability. Although the case was decided under considerations of breach of implied warranty of merchantability, it pointed to the manufacturer's strict liability, declaring privity considerations not to be applicable in the particular case.

Express reference to manufacturers' strict *tort* liability was made three years later in the ground-breaking *Greenman v Yuba Power Products* decision.[13] The plaintiff, William B Greenman, sued Yuba Power Products, Inc, the manufacturer of a 'Shopsmith' (ie a machine that combines a saw, drill and wood lathe) for compensation with respect to an injury allegedly caused by a product defect. Unlike in the earlier *Escola* case, the California Supreme Court held the manufacturer strictly liable. Justice Traynor, again co-deciding judge, explained the court's (new) approach as follows:

> Moreover, to impose strict liability on the manufacturer under the circumstances of this case, it was not necessary for plaintiff to establish an express warranty ... A manufacturer is strictly liable *in tort* when an article he or she places on the market, knowing that it is to be used without inspection for defects, proves to have a defect that causes injury to a human being.[14]

The court added fairness considerations, arguing that strict liability serves to guarantee 'that the costs of injuries resulting from defective products are borne by the manufacturers that put such products on the market rather than by the injured persons who are powerless to protect themselves'.[15]

Just one year after *Greenman*, strict tort liability saw a further development. In *Vandermark v Ford Motor et al*, the plaintiff sued, inter alia, a car dealer who had sold him a defective car.[16] The Californian court explained that strict tort liability can be used even to explain the seller's strict liability:

> Retailers like manufacturers are engaged in the business of distributing goods to the public. They are an integral part of the overall producing and marketing enterprise that should bear the cost of injuries resulting from defective products. ... In some cases the retailer may be the only member of that enterprise reasonably available to the injured plaintiff. In other cases the retailer himself may play a substantial part in insuring that the product is safe or may be in a position to exert pressure on the manufacturer to that end; the retailer's strict liability thus serves as an added incentive to safety. Strict liability on the manufacturer and retailer alike affords maximum protection to the injured plaintiff and works no injustice to the defendants, for they can adjust the costs of such protection between them in the course of their continuing business relationship.[17]

---

[12] *Henningsen v Bloomfield Motors, Inc* (1960) 32 NJ 358, 161 A.2d 69.
[13] *Greenman v Yuba Power Products, Inc* (1963) 59 Cal.2d 57.
[14] ibid, recital 5 and 6 (emphasis added).
[15] ibid, recital 9.
[16] *Vandermark v Ford Motor Co* (1964) 61 Cal.2d 256.
[17] ibid, recital 7.

In the same year as *Vandermark*, the American Law Institute (ALI) confirmed the expanded strict (tort) liability regime in Section 402A of the Restatement of Torts, Second ('Section 402A').[18] As a basic principle, strict (tort) liability, ie non negligence-based (tort) liability, shall build the basis for product liability claims if the product was sold 'in a defective condition unreasonably dangerous'.[19]

By the end of the 1960s strict (tort) liability was further broadened to include third party beneficiaries. *Elmore v American Motors*,[20] decided in 1969, clarified that not only the purchaser of a defective good, but also third parties who are injured by the defective good should enjoy protection under the strict (tort) liability regime.

In the following decades, the significance of strict (tort) liability had grown further, establishing it as a popular alternative to liability out of warranty breaches. With respect to manufacturers it can even be considered the primary instrument (due to privity considerations).

The rise of strict liability was appreciated by consumers and consumer representatives all over the country. But critical voices noted that product liability, with its basically limitless manufacturers' and sellers' strict liability rules, would impair manufacturers' and sellers' interests too much. By the end of the twentieth century several State courts had thus aimed to apply a more nuanced approach that would differentiate between strict liability and negligence, based on the circumstances of the respective case. This revised regime had not gone unnoticed. In 1998, the ALI issued its Restatement of the Law Third (Torts/Product Liability),[21] § 2 of which partially returns to negligence as the basis for product liability claims. It differentiates between three types of defects: manufacturing defects; design defects; and defects as a result of inadequate instructions (warning defects). It reads as follows:

> A product is defective when ... it contains a manufacturing defect, is defective in design, or is defective because of inadequate instructions or warnings. A product:
>
> (a)   Contains a manufacturing defect when the product departs from its intended design even though all possible care was exercised in the preparation and marketing of the product;
>
> (b)   Is defective in design when the foreseeable risks of harm posed by the product could have been reduced or avoided by the adoption of a reasonable alternative design by the seller or other distributor, or a predecessor in the commercial chain of distribution, and the omission of the alternative design renders the product not reasonably safe;
>
> (c)   Is defective because of inadequate instructions or warnings when the foreseeable risks of harm posed by the product could have been reduced or avoided by the provision of

---

[18] American Law Institute, *Restatement of the Law, Second*, vol 2: *§§ 281–503* (St Paul, American Law Institute Publishers, 1963) § 402 A. Although § 402 A is entitled 'Special Liability of Seller of Product for Physical Harm to User or Consumer', the provision relates to the liability of not only (intermediary and final) sellers, but also manufacturers—see ibid, 355.

[19] Pursuant to the view of the ALI, the 'unreasonably dangerous' limitation shall function to distinguish product liability-relevant cases from 'ordinary' incidents (that relate to 'acceptable' or 'necessary' product risks). A product danger is relevant only in cases where the defect is 'dangerous to an extent beyond that which would be contemplated by the ordinary consumer who purchases it, with the ordinary knowledge common to the community as to its characteristics' (ibid, 352).

[20] *Elmore v American Motors* (1969) 70 Cal.2d 578.

[21] American Law Institute, *Restatement of the Law Third (Torts/Product Liability)* (St Paul, MN, American Law Institute Publishers, 1998) § 2.

reasonable instructions or warnings by the seller or other distributor, or a predecessor in the commercial chain of distribution, and the omission of the instructions or warnings renders the product not safe.

This provision draws a basic distinction between manufacturing defects on the one hand and design and warning defects on the other. While the first category follows the strict liability doctrine, design and warning defects by definition include a negligence component.

Although § 2 Restatement of the Law Third reflects the situation of a large number of US states, a significant number of courts still follow the older, broad strict liability approach (that does not apply standards of care to some of the defect categories).[22] Overall, the situation in the US with respect to product liability remains in a flux. It will be interesting to see which approach will dominate in the future.

B. Product Liability Law in the EU

i. General Remarks

Product liability law in the EU shows some parallels to its US counterpart, although practically important differences can be identified. In terms of litigation relevance, for example, observers stress that product liability cases contribute to the US courts' agenda to a higher degree than in the EU. Christopher Hodges, for instance, notes that '[t]he level of product liability claims in Europe has consistently remained far lower than that which has been produced in the USA'.[23]

The difference in the litigation relevance of product liability (understood as the number of product liability cases decided by courts) might primarily be explained by procedural law distinctions rather than by substantive law divergences (to which we shall return briefly). It is fair to say that some features of US procedural law provide for comparatively higher incentives to sue and a lower inhibition threshold. Unlike in the EU, the US product liability regime rests, for example, on the extensively used concept of punitive damages, which allows plaintiffs to sue for additional amounts of money that go beyond the actual damage caused, sometimes reaching exorbitantly high levels. Pre-trial discovery can be listed as an additional facilitator of US litigation, as it easily allows the parties to collect evidence before a lawsuit is actually launched. A third, litigation-stimulating factor is contingency fees. This cost allocation system allows possible plaintiffs to launch proceedings without having to face financial risks. If a lawsuit is unsuccessful, the losing plaintiff would not have to bear lawyers' fees. In the event of a win, however, a significant portion of the amount won goes to the plaintiff's lawyer—usually between 25 and 30 per cent. In contrast to this, the loser-pays-principle, which is the dominant cost allocation system in most EU Member States, aims to single out more promising cases and keep less promising ones from

---

[22] Owen, n 2, 19–20.
[23] C Hodges, 'Approaches to Product Liability in the EU and Member States' in D Fairgrieve (ed), *Product Liability in Comparative Perspective* (Cambridge, Cambridge University Press, 2005) 192, 201.

being litigated. This is largely achieved by the fact that losing the case leads to the plaintiff's having to bear not only the court costs and his own lawyer's fees, but also the defendant's lawyer's fees. This, it is generally hoped, will help to prevent malicious and hopeless cases from being brought before the courts.

Returning to substantive product liability law, one can note that EU product liability law is, in principle, structured upon a framework of different mechanisms comparable to those in the US. At least theoretically, negligence, tortious misrepresentation, breaches of warranty, as well as strict tort liability can all be used to pursue a legal interest in being compensated for damage—at least to some extent. It has to be noted, though, that the last of the four categories, ie strict tort liability, dominates in practice due to the insufficiencies and practical issues surrounding the other options. The legal remedies available under warranty law, for example, are very limited and (in absence of culpability) do not go beyond compensating for defects in the product itself. Depending on the particular circumstances, the injured party could merely claim for repair, replacement, a price reduction or rescission of the contract, but not ask for any further compensation. Negligence-based remedies are not of much help either, most notably because plaintiffs usually find it difficult to produce evidence of culpable behaviour.

Because of the limited potential of other options, some Member States had—already prior to the (shortly to be discussed) 1985 PLD—developed specific strict tort liability solutions.[24] However, looking at the pan-European level, it is fair to say that modern product liability law developed later than in the US. Discussions first arose in the late 1950s and early 1960s, when Europe was also struck by a thalidomide scandal that caused severe physical harm. Producing evidence for culpable behaviour proved to be difficult. Against this background it was no surprise that policymakers intensified discussions to strengthen product liability law at a more general, ie pan-EU, level. It was not before 1977, however, that some concrete steps were taken, when the Council of Europe issued the European Convention on product liability in regard to personal injury and death (1977 Strasbourg Convention). One of the key features of the Convention was the introduction of strict tort liability in cases of physical damage (including death). For many Member States this would have meant a significant change in their product liability regimes. But the 1977 Strasbourg Convention proved to be an unpopular instrument. With only four signatories and not a single ratification (as of July 2016), it has not yet entered into force.[25]

Motivated by the 1977 Strasbourg Convention, EU policymakers intensified their deliberations on a pan-EU product liability regime. One of the core issues was the question of how to balance the interests of manufacturers and distributors, on the one hand and buyers, and users of defective products, on the other. While the first two groups feared that overly harsh rules could impair competitiveness in the global market, the last two believed that not raising the bar significantly would open the doors to an increasing number of potentially harmful products.

---

[24] For a more detailed overview of early developments of product liability law in Europe, see, eg, the contributions in S Whittaker (ed), *The Development of Product Liability* (Cambridge, Cambridge University Press, 2010); and Fairgrieve (ed), n 23.

[25] For a chart of signatures and ratifications see, eg, www.coe.int/en/web/conventions/full-list/-/conventions/treaty/091/signatures?p_auth=ndfT4Phj.

In 1985 the EU legislator finally reached a compromise and adopted the PLD.[26] In a fully harmonised way, the Directive enshrined provisions that widely standardised national product liability regimes.[27] It can be considered as a breaking point in EU product liability law, because it introduced an EU-wide obligation for the Member States to adopt a strict product liability standard. The aforementioned alternatives—warranty law, negligence, and tortious misrepresentation—though not entirely disappearing, have lost their significance to answer product liability ever since.

The PLD can be considered as one of the first, if not the first substantive EU consumer laws. Although the Directive is mostly discussed in the context of consumer law, it should nevertheless be noted that—with the exception of damage to property—it goes beyond B2C situations and can be applied regardless of whether the injured party is a consumer or a professional.[28] If, for example, a carpenter loses his finger as a result of a defective chainsaw, he or she can have recourse to the respective national implementation of the PLD.

ii. Selected Issues

Since its introduction in 1985, the PLD has, in principle, remained unchanged.[29] This does not mean, however, that the implementation and application of the PLD has always been unproblematic. Several issues have made it necessary for the CJEU to clarify the PLD regime, or at least have been brought into question. Some of these are discussed in the following paragraphs.

Article 6 PLD, for example, defines the underlying defect concept, ie the central parameters that must exist to apply the regime. Its first paragraph reads as follows:

> A product is defective when it does not provide the safety which a person is entitled to expect, taking all circumstances into account, including:
>
> (a)   The presentation of the product;
> (b)   The use to which it could reasonably be expected that the product would be put;
> (c)   The time when the product was put into circulation.

Pursuant to this definition, the central starting point for assessing the possible defectiveness of a product is the level of protection people may expect. The sub-provisions of Article 6(1) offer some guidance regarding this 'consumer expectations test'. The case law of the CJEU applies a relatively flexible scheme. Depending on the product and the precise range of possible users, differently high levels should be taken into

---

[26]   See above n 3.

[27]   The fully harmonised character of the PLD was first confirmed by the CJEU in Case C-52/00 *Commission v France* [2002] ECLI:EU:C:2002:252 and Case C-154/00 *Commission v Greece* [2002] ECLI:EU:C:2002:254. It should be noted, though, that the PLD failed to introduce a conclusive set of rules, because some issues were left outside its scope. Most notably, it does not touch upon the question of possible non-material damage caused by defective products. Its possible regulation was left to the discretion of the Member States.

[28]   For details, see Art 9 PLD.

[29]   The only exception was an amendment in 1999 that—in response to concerns in the context of an occurrence of bovine spongiform encephalopathy (BSE) in Europe—extended the scope of the Directive to agricultural and fishery products. For details, see Directive 1999/34/EC, [1999] OJ L141/20.

consideration. In the vast majority of cases the court applies an objective standard, in the sense that it refers to the needs, expectations and experience of a typical user group and not the injured plaintiff as an individual. In this context, it should also be noted that pursuant to its Article 4, the PLD follows the general burden of proof in tort cases, which means that it is still the injured party who needs to prove that a product is defective.

In a more recent case the CJEU took the chance to refine the consumer expectations test with respect to mass-produced articles, and to a certain extent simplified the plaintiffs' argumentation. In *Boston Scientific Medizintechnik GmbH v AOK Sachsen-Anhalt and Others* ('*Boston Scientific*'),[30] the CJEU had to answer the question whether a particular product can be called defective if products in the same product series are potentially or actually defective, without the need to show that the good in dispute itself displays a defect. The CJEU answered this question in the affirmative, and argued that in particular in cases of vital and potentially harmful products— the case in issue involved pacemakers and defibrillators—a considerably high level of safety has to be met. Potential and actual defects of goods in the same product series could lead to the conclusion that all products in that product series/product group are defective—without the need to prove the particular good itself to be defective. The judgment might be of significant practical relevance, because it can be seen as compensating for the (later to be discussed) development risk defence, which allows producers to parry product liability claims.

One of the most relevant differences between the PLD and the US approaches in practice is undeniably the fact that Article 1 PLD—in line with the 1977 Strasbourg Convention—limits the range of principally liable stakeholders to producers of defective products.[31] Although the Directive primarily focuses on manufacturers, one should note two things. First, the term 'producer' is defined in a broad sense. It does not refer only to the (main) manufacturer of the product, but additionally to 'the producer of any raw material or the manufacturer of a component part and any person who, by putting his name, trade mark or other distinguishing feature on the product presents himself as its producer'.[32] Second, Article 3(2) and (3) PLD broaden the scope beyond manufacturers in two cases. Article 3(2) introduces the liability of importers of defective products into the EU.[33] Article 3(3) includes the only situation in which a seller (even if he or she is not identical with the producer or the importer) might be liable under the PLD. Sellers can be held liable if they fail to inform the injured party about the producer (or, where he or she purchased the product from another seller, about that seller) 'within a reasonable time'.[34]

---

[30] Joined Cases C-503/13 and C-504/13 *Boston Scientific Medizintechnik GmbH v AOK Sachsen-Anhalt— Die Gesundheitskasse und Betriebskrankenkasse RWE* [2015] ECLI:EU:C:2015:148.

[31] This means that any seller in the distribution chain of a defective product is exempted from the strict liability regime of the PLD. Sellers would, of course, still be liable under 'ordinary' rules, ie negligence-based tort law or breach of warranties (if national regimes include this option).

[32] Art 3(1) PLD.

[33] The practical relevance of this provision can be explained by two arguments. First, due to language issues, questions of court competence and financial considerations, in practice it might be difficult to sue a producer from a non-EU country. Second, even if one succeeded in suing and won the case, the question of enforceability of a judgment would arise. Depending on where one sues, complex rules might complicate enforcement—or even make it impossible.

[34] Neither the PLD nor its Explanatory Memorandum defines what is meant by 'within a reasonable time'. The latter merely explains that the aim of this clause is to introduce 'a substitute liability of

In light of the basic limitation of the personal scope of strict tort liability to producers and the full harmonisation character of the Directive, Article 13 PLD contains a
potentially important exception. It allows Member States to maintain certain liability
rules that already existed at the national level prior to the notification of the PLD
to the Member States. Article 13 differentiates between three categories: contractual
liability rules; non-contractual liability rules; and rules that are based on a special
liability system. Some Member States tried to have recourse to the—at first sight—
all-encompassing wording of Article 13 PLD and aimed to apply a broader approach
(to include sellers within the implemented strict liability rules).[35]

In 2006 the CJEU had to concern itself with this strategy in a Danish case. In *Skov
v Bilka*,[36] the Court had to deal with a salmonella poisoning case that involved both
the 'producer' of the eggs, Skov, and the owner of the distributing supermarket, Bilka.
Under traditional Danish law, sellers were widely treated equally with producers in
terms of liability. Danish case law developed general liability rules that could hold
sellers liable in lieu of manufacturers, even in cases of strict liability. The CJEU had
to decide whether this approach was permissible, in particular considering the leeway
that Article 13 PLD granted the Member States. The Court ruled against the Danish
solution and explained 'that Article 13 could not be interpreted as leaving it open to
the Member States to maintain a *general* system of product liability different from
that provided for in the Directive'.[37] This decision basically meant that the exceptions
provided by Article 13 have to be understood in a narrow sense. Equal strict liability
treatment of producers and sellers would only be permissible in cases of national pre-
PLD legislation if that legislation were sectoral, in the sense that it applied to a distinct
group of possible product liability cases, eg pharmaceutical products.

Another, practically important feature of the PLD is the optional[38] 'development
risk clause/defence' found in Article 7(e). The development risk defence ('DRD') is
part of a catalogue of liability limitations with the purpose of serving the interests
of the innovation market in staying competitive. Pursuant to this rule, a producer
(likewise any other potentially liable person/entity) is—as will be shown shortly—not
liable under the PLD regime if he or she can prove that in light of 'the state of scientific

---

each supplier in order to compel him to reveal the actual circumstances, in particular the identity of the
producer'—see Explanatory Memorandum accompanying the Directive Proposal, 23 July 1976, COM(76)
372 final, recital 9. Some Member States decided to define the term by introducing time frames. Examples
include Germany (1 month; §4(3) Product Liability Act), France (3 months; Art 1386(7) French Civil Code),
Italy (3 months; Art 4 Presidential Decree No 224 of 24 May 1988) and Spain (3 months; Art 4(3) Law on
Product Liability). The CJEU has—to date—not commented on these domestic solutions.

[35] For some Member States, implementing the strict liability concept of the PLD only with respect
to producers meant that they had to introduce different product liability standards for producers (strict
liability) and sellers (negligence-based liability).

[36] Case C-402/03 *Skov Æg v Bilka Lavprisvarehus A/S* [2006] ECLI:EU:C:2006:6. For further comments
on this case, see, eg G Howells and JS Borghetti, 'Product Liability' in HW Micklitz et al (eds), *Cases,
Materials and Text on Consumer Law* (Oxford, Hart Publishing, 2010) 439, 450–51.

[37] *Skov v Bilka*, n 36, recital 39 (emphasis added).

[38] To strike a balance between the interests to strengthen competitiveness (by introducing the DRD) and
to safeguard consumers' interests to be protected against unnecessary developmental risks, the defence was
crafted as a Member State option. Art 15(1)(b) allows Member States to apply a stricter regime and declare
producers liable, even in cases where they can prove 'that the state of scientific and technical knowledge at
the time when [they] put the product into circulation was not such as to enable the existence of a defect to
be discovered'.

and technical knowledge', one cannot refer to a 'defect'. (Liability under conventional negligence rules is not affected by Article 7(e). However, it is hard to imagine that a producer can be acting culpably if the state of scientific and technical knowledge at the relevant time does not indicate a defect.)

In terms of protection, the insertion of the DRD into the PLD meant a step backwards compared with the 1977 Strasbourg Convention (as the latter instrument did not know a comparable liability exclusion). But its incorporation was a necessary move to win approval from the business side, largely because producers felt that in absence of the defence, they would be at a competitive disadvantage compared to producers abroad who would not—at least not directly—fall under the applicability of the new European regime.[39]

Ever since the adoption of the PLD, the DRD has remained a frequently discussed feature. In 2002 the Fondazione Rosselli, mandated by the European Commission ('Commission'), published a report on the analysis of the economic impact of the DRD.[40] Looking at the DRD from an implementation point of view, the Fondazione Rosselli PLD Report showed that Member States have reacted to the DRD option in different ways. Although the majority of the 15 jurisdictions examined implemented the defence in full, three Member States have done so only with respect to certain products/circumstances, while two—Finland and Luxemburg—decided not to make use of the Article 7(e) option.

In terms of the overall desirability of maintaining the DRD, the Report—in line with the aforementioned business considerations—pointed out the alleged importance of the defence for stimulating innovation and keeping product liability insurance costs at an acceptable level. However, it also expressed concern over a possible decrease in safety standards. Using the respective state of scientific and technical knowledge as the decisive threshold, developers could easily carry out research that would have a potentially harmful effect on the environment and people in general. If the expected benefits for society are not of a significant scale, the justifiability of the DRD would be questionable.[41] To compensate for this concern, the Report suggested the introduction of special 'prevention and protection schemes'.[42] These measures could include, in particular, extended social insurance services and state funds to safeguard the financial interests of potentially affected consumers, as well as a possible stronger alignment of product liability law with product safety standards. The suggestions are still widely unimplemented. The possible implementation of compensation funds, in particular, has been criticised for not being sufficiently well-conceived.[43]

---

[39] See, eg M Clarke, 'Product Liability Briefing: The Future of the Development Risk Defence in Europe' (2004) 1–2 (copy with the authors), where the author explains that the DRD should be considered as conserving 'the balance between commercial innovation and consumer protection'.

[40] Fondazione Rosselli, 'Analysis of the Economic Impact of the Development Risk Clause as provided by Directive 85/374/EEC on Liability for Defective Products' (2002) ('Fondazione Rosselli PLD Report').

[41] ibid, 4, where the Report arrives at the conclusion 'that there are specific and crucial instances in which the DRC [ie the Development Risk Clause] could fail to provide producers with the right incentives to advance the technological state of the art, to the point that would be socially desirable in product safety matters'.

[42] ibid, 5.

[43] Arguments against the introduction of a compensation fund include primarily the questions of how to determine pro rata contributions to the fund and the allocation of rights of use per industry sector. For details, see, eg, Clarke, n 39, 2.

Despite some controversial issues—some of which have been pinpointed in previous paragraphs—the PLD has, in terms of substance, remained unchanged to date.[44] Possible product liability related developments can rather be expected in the area of product safety law. Safety standards have principally been regulated by the 2001 General Product Safety Directive[45] and (more narrowly) the 1987 Food Imitation Products Directive.[46] Based on the view that directives (due to their basic lack of direct applicability) usually do not achieve the same degree of harmonisation as regulations, the Commission decided to present a refined framework on product safety.[47] In 2013 it published CPS Regulation Proposal that—if and once adopted—would repeal the 1987 and 2001 Product Safety Directives.

By opting for a regulation, the Commission sought to kill two birds with one stone. Most notably, the CPS Regulation Proposal tries to react to the different definitions and evaluations of 'safety' found at the Member States level by introducing a set of standardised safety criteria that mainly builds upon EU safety standards. A special, centralised market surveillance mechanism would contribute to the idea of EU product safety.[48] To complement the proposed CPS Regulation from a technical perspective, the Commission proposed a special market surveillance regulation—the Regulation on market surveillance of products (PMS Regulation)—that (once and if adopted) would repeal and harmonise more than 10 sectoral EU surveillance instruments.[49] By doing so, the PMS Regulation would further contribute to the standardisation of safety surveillance with respect both to the affected industries and the Member States' legislation.

Overall, the two proposed instruments—the CPS Regulation and the PMS Regulation—would obviously have the potential to (at least) enhance the information flow and disclosure with respect to unsafe products. As far as the possible impact on the PLD is concerned, it could be expected that courts might more frequently have recourse to the safety evaluation criteria of the CPS Regulation (and by doing so could answer the aforementioned call of the Fondazione Rosselli PLD Report for improved prevention and protection schemes). It should be added, however, that any possible clarifying effect of the CPS Regulation with respect to the determination of defects would—if the proposal were to be adopted in the suggested form—be of a direct nature only in relation to consumers. Article 2(1) of the CPS Regulation Proposal limits the scope of the Regulation to products used by consumers. The PLD—although usually associated with incidents involving consumers, and although damage to and

[44] See above, n 27.
[45] Directive 2001/95/EC, [2001] OJ L11/4.
[46] Directive 87/357/EEC, [1987] OJ L192/49.
[47] The European Commission put this argument as follows: 'A Regulation is the appropriate legal instrument as it imposes clear and detailed rules which do not give room for divergent transposition by Member States. A Regulation ensures that legal requirements are applicable at the same time throughout the Union' (see recital 2, Regulation Proposal, 13 February 2013, COM(2013) 78 final (CPS Regulation Proposal).
[48] The Regulation would impose harmonised safety documentation obligations on selected stakeholders—most notably on manufacturers. See, in particular, c II, CPS Regulation Proposal ('Obligations of economic operators').
[49] Regulation Proposal, 13 February 2013, COM(2013) 75 final. Pursuant to its accompanying Explanatory Memorandum, the Regulation on market surveillance of products would present a 'one-tier system in which all market surveillance rules are brought together in a single instrument and in which RAPEX [ie the Rapid Exchange of Information System, an EU product safety alert system] will be the single alert system regarding products presenting a risk'.

destruction of property necessitates that the affected property is for private consumption/use (Article 9(b) PLD)—is to some extent wider in its scope. Death and personal injuries are covered by the PLD, regardless of the capacity in which the injured person functioned (Article 9(a) PLD).

C. Product Liability Law Elsewhere

i. General Remarks

Inspired by developments in the US and the EU, numerous jurisdictions throughout the world have decided to introduce or, where already existing, revise their product liability laws.[50] This trend towards special product liability regimes based on strict (tort) liability started in the late 1980s and early 1990s, when several South American (eg Brazil, Peru and Argentina),[51] Asian (eg Japan and Taiwan)[52] and European non-EU countries[53] (Norway, Iceland and Switzerland), as well as Russia,[54] introduced initiatives. The introduction of strict liability was not limited to civil law jurisdictions, though. Australia is a prominent example, with its reform of the Trade Practices Act 1974 in 1992.[55] In some cases, product liability reforms took longer. Malaysia[56] and South Korea,[57] for example, followed in 1999 and 2000 respectively, and Thailand[58] even more recently.

ii. The People's Republic of China as One of the More Recent Strict Liability Examples

One of the latest countries to introduce a special strict liability based product liability regime is the People's Republic of China. With the adoption of its Tort Law in 2009

---

[50] Several practitioners' guides offer (in some cases difficult to access) information on national product liability regimes. Some of the more recent materials include: I Dodds-Smith and M Spencer (eds), *The International Comparative Legal Guide to Product Liability 2016*, 14th edn (London, Global Legal Group, 2016); CD Varner and BW Pratt (eds), *The Product Regulation and Liability Review* (London, Law Business Research, 2014); Rödl & Partner (eds), *Handbuch international Produkthaftung*, 2nd edn (Cologne, Bundesanzeiger Verlag, 2014).

[51] On Brazil, see, eg, G Brüggemeier, *Modernising Civil Liability Law in Europe, China, Brazil and Russia* (Cambridge, Cambridge University Press, 2011) 235. On South America in general, see, eg, JM Iturraspe, 'General Trends in South American Product Liability Law: An Overview' (2003) 20 *Arizona Journal of International and Comparative Law* 115.

[52] On Japan, see, eg, L Nottage, *Product Safety and Liability Law in Japan: From Minamata to Mad Cows* (London, Routledge, 2004). On Taiwan, see, eg, Lee and Li Attorneys-at-Law, 'Taiwan', iclg.com/practice-areas/product-liability/product-liability-2017/Taiwan.

[53] HC Taschner, 'Harmonization of Products Liability Law in the European Community' (1999) 34 *Texas International Law Journal* 21.

[54] Brüggemeier, n 52, 235.

[55] J Kellam and B Arste, 'Current Trends and Future Directions in Product Liability in Australia' (2000) 27 *William Mitchell Law Review* 141.

[56] N Amin, *Product Liability in Malaysia* (Selangor, Sweet & Maxwell, 2007).

[57] SH Han et al, 'Korea' in Varner and Pratt (eds), n 51, 103.

[58] S Thanitcul, 'Law and Legal Process of the Product Liability Act in Thailand' (2013) 20 *Journal of International Cooperation Studies* 27.

the top five GDP countries had turned to strict tort liability as their central product liability standard.[59] Like most of the jurisdictions mentioned in the preceding subsections, China based its new regime largely (but as will be seen, not exclusively) on the EU model.

Article 41 of the Tort Law, for example, exempts sellers (and anybody else in the distribution chain other than the producer) from strict product liability. Stated differently, as a basic principle only manufacturers (including sub-manufacturers, ie producers of parts of the final product) are covered by the strict liability regime, whereas all other stakeholders can only be held liable if they act culpably. Article 42(2) introduces an exception that we have already met in the context of EU product liability. If the manufacturer of the damage-causing, defective product cannot be identified and the seller is unable to provide relevant information, the seller may be held strictly liable.

One complicating factor with respect to Chinese product liability law is the fact that the Tort Law regime is not as comprehensive as, for example, the PLD. When confronted with product liability claims, one needs to additionally consult supporting laws, some of which are more general, others more specific in a sense that their scope is limited to certain product categories. The most important complementary instrument, the Product Quality Law of the People's Republic of China (PQL) dates back to the early 2000s. Unlike the Tort Law (and the PLD), it contains a defect definition. Pursuant to Article 46 PQL, a defect is generally constituted if a product causes 'an unreasonable threat to personal safety or to safety of another person's property'. Alternative parameters include, in particular, non-compliance with 'national or sectoral standards for ensuring human health, personal safety and safety of property' (where existing).[60]

The practically important 'unreasonable threat' parameter is statutorily not conclusively defined. Article 26 PQL provides some indications, though. It reads as follows:

Producers shall be liable for the quality of the products they produce. The products shall meet the following quality requirements:

(1)   Constituting no unreasonable threats to personal safety or safety of property, and conforming to the national standards or the sectoral standards for ensuring human health, personal safety and safety of property, where there are such standards;

(2)   Possessing the properties as required, except for those with directions stating their functional defects; and

(3)   Conforming to the product standards marked on the products or on the packages thereof, and to the quality conditions indicated by way of product directions, samples, etc.[61]

When deciding whether a relevant defect exists, authorities additionally have recourse to guidelines issued by the Chinese General Administration of Quality Supervision, Inspection and Quarantine (AQSIQ). In its Regulatory Interpretations about Product Liability Law, the AQSIQ adds a further criterion that (at least on paper) somewhat resembles the objectiveness element known from the consumer expectations test

---

[59] J Binding and C Eisenberg, 'Product Liability in the People's Republic of China' (2014) 15 *Business Law International* 19.

[60] Art 46 PQL. For an English translation of the PQL, see, eg, Ministry of Commerce, People's Republic of China, 'Product Quality law of the People's Republic of China', english.mofcom.gov.cn/article/policyrelease/Businessregulations/201303/20130300046024.shtml.

[61] Ministry of Commerce translation, above n 61.

discussed earlier in the context of the PLD. A product could be called defective if it does not 'meet the general accepted expectations of society'.[62]

A further example of a question about which the Tort Law remains silent is possible limitations. The answer could again be found in the PQL. Its Article 41 lists possible defences that include, in particular, the developmental state of the art argument, which seems to show parallels with the PLD's consumer expectations test. However, to what extent Article 41 can be successfully applied in practice is—at the time of writing—not yet clear.

Although the revised Chinese product liability regime largely builds upon the PLD, there are exceptions. One of the arguably most relevant ones in practice can be found in Article 47 of the Tort Law. As is the case in the US, Article 47 allows for punitive damages (if the manufacturer or seller, knowing of the defect, continues producing/selling the defective product).[63]

iii. Canada—An Exception to the Rule

Although strict liability characterises the product liability regimes of most major countries, there are some exceptions to the rule. Most include some common law jurisdictions, eg India or Hong Kong, that have not yet followed the US approach. Arguably one of the most relevant and interesting examples in this respect is—due to its mixed legal background (common law in general, civil law in Québec)—given by Canada.

To date, Canada has largely not yet switched to strict liability. Instead, most Canadian provinces and territories still apply a culpability-based product liability regime, even with respect to manufacturers' liability.[64] Although this circumstance seems remarkable, some authors point out that the difference between Canadian product liability law and strict liability based product liability is rather doctrinal than practically relevant. According to this view, Canadian courts arrive at results that come close to strict liability as a consequence of applying detailed requirements that need to be fulfilled to prove non-culpability.[65]

Nevertheless, some provinces have introduced statutory legislation that explicitly bases the manufacturer's liability on a non-culpability standard. Respective rules can be found in New Brunswick's Consumer Products Warranty and Liability Act (Article 27),[66] Sasketchewan's Consumer Products Warranties Act (Article 27)[67]

---

[62] Binding and Eisenberg, n 60, 27.

[63] Some commentators point out, however, that Art 47 (thus far) is of little practical relevance. See, eg, Jones Day, 'Product Law Worldview' (2012) 92.

[64] D Harrison, *The Law of Product Warnings and Recalls in Canada* (Markham/Ontario, LexisNexis, 2013) 6.

[65] See, eg, J Cassels and C Jones, *The Law of Large-Scale Claims: Product Liability, Mass Torts, and Complex Litigation in Canada* (Toronto, Irwin Law, 2005) 96, where the authors conclude as follows: 'Canadian courts hold manufacturers to very high levels of accountability that arguably come close to strict liability'. In a similar vein, eg, DS Morritt and SL Bjorkquist, 'Product Liability in Canada: Principles and Practice North of the Border' (2000) 27 *William Mitchell Law Review* 177, 192.

[66] Art 27(4) Products Warranty and Liability Act: 'The liability of a person under this section does not depend on any contract or negligence.'

[67] Art 27 Consumer Products Warranties Act: 'A person mentioned in section 5 shall, as against the retail seller or manufacturer, be entitled to recover damages arising from personal injuries that he has suffered and that were reasonably foreseeable as liable to result from the breach.'

and Québec's Consumer Protection Act (Article 53 with regard to contractual product liability).[68] What is noteworthy in this context is the fact that—unlike the PLD but in line with US product liability law—all three statutes extend strict liability beyond manufacturers to include sellers.[69]

IV. Some Pending Issues

This brief excursion into national and regional product liability law has shown that product liability—in most parts of the world—has undergone far-reaching reforms to increase injured parties' chances of receiving compensation. Most notably in this respect, it is the concept of non-culpability based, ie strict (tort), liability that has enhanced the enforcement of legal interests and expanded the scope of legal risk.

Despite this trend, however, one must not forget two facts that limit the significance of strict product liability: first, as the explanations in the preceding section show, strict product liability has not yet been seamlessly implemented. Culpable behaviour still remains a requirement in some jurisdictions. Second, when comparing, for example, the US and EU product liability approaches, it must be noted that additional issues have been regulated in conceptually different ways. The range of principally strictly liable stakeholders should be pointed out. With respect to both issues, the decisive question remains how to weigh the interests of the affected stakeholders. While some jurisdictions aim to lower the threshold to pursue compensatory interests to the greatest possible extent, others seem to keep the manufacturers' and (especially) sellers' liability within narrower limits.

The importance of understanding the different approaches encountered in this chapter becomes very obvious when one takes a look at cross-border scenarios. The ever-increasing market globalisation shows that product liability discussions must not be kept within national borders. More and more products are exported/imported, which might complicate dispute resolution. Conflict of laws regimes can—to a certain extent—be of help in this regard. They are, however, not an all-clarifying solution. The geographically limited scope of their application—none of the existing conflict-of-law tools is universally applicable—springs to mind. Aside from that, a more fundamental question needs to be addressed. E-commerce aims to enhance cross-border shopping

---

[68] Art 53(3) Consumer Protection Act: 'The merchant or the manufacturer shall not plead that he was unaware of the defect or lack of instructions.'

[69] Canadian German Chamber of Industry and Commerce Inc, 'Produkthaftung in Kanada' 2–3 (file with the authors). On Québec see further, D Gibbens, 'Overview Of Quebec Product Liability Law Basic Principles Under The Quebec Civil Code and Consumer Protection Act' (2015) 37, where the author concludes that according to Art 53 Consumer Protection Act, 'the seller or manufacturer is clearly precluded from raising his ignorance of the defect or lack of instructions as a defence to avoid liability', (file with the authors).

by creating a market that is accessible by (basically) everyone, regardless of where he or she lives. To what extent are the conceptually different 'liability bases' and 'liability scopes' justifiable, desirable and detrimental in cross-border situations? Put differently, from a domestic market perspective, it might be reasonable to apply (more or less) unique standards. Yet should we not aim for a greater amount of product liability harmonisation in times of an increased 'blurring' of borders? Rules to treat importers similarly to manufacturers might be one answer (where existing). But this cannot be the end of the story.

Despite the increasing importance of cross-border sales, international product liability legislation is—at best—insignificant. For the vast majority of cases, the United Nations Convention on Contracts for the International Sale of Goods (CISG), for example, must be ruled out as a possibly applicable basis. There are several reasons for this. First, the CISG focuses on contractual issues. The principally liable party under national product liability law, the manufacturer, is, however, not a contractual party—unless he or she also sells the product. Contract law product liability extensions towards manufacturers—as known from older US law—is the exception rather than the rule. Second, Article 5 of the Convention explains that the CISG does not cover liability for personal damage. Even in those rare cases in which one could hold a party liable for product liability damage based on contract law, the most important product liability damage in practice, physical personal damage, would thus fall outside the scope of the CISG. Third and likely most importantly, the CISG does not apply to B2C situations. Many jurisdictions, however, consider their product liability regimes as primarily significant in B2C cases—and in some instances, eg the PLD with respect to property damages, limit the material scope to non-professional use of products. Hence, in the vast majority of cases in which one would consider product liability law relevant, the CISG would not be able to provide an answer.

In this light it must be regretted that none of the major institutions dealing with international private law issues—with the International Institute for the Unification of Private Law (UNIDROIT), the United Nations Commission on International Trade Law (UNCITRAL) and the Hague Academy of International Law leading the way—have shown concrete interest in intensifying debates on the possible internationalisation of product liability law.[70] Hence, in the absence of better aligned national legislation, conflict-of-law and comparative law expertise will—for the time being—remain of prime importance in the field of product liability law.

V. Concluding Remarks

This chapter has shown that product liability law—here understood as a set of rules that governs the financial consequences of damage caused by defective products—has

---

[70] For critical comment see, eg, FJ Bernardi, 'Einführung' in Rödl & Partner (eds), n 51, 4–5.

evolved over the centuries to facilitate rights enforcement of harmed stakeholders. None of the more traditional instruments, negligence-based tort law, tortious misrepresentation and warranty law, were capable of facilitating the position of injured parties satisfactorily when it came to damage in the form of financially existence-threatening consequences, or severe physical damage and death.

Major jurisdictions, with the US and the EU leading the way, have thus sought to simplify rights enforcement by introducing strict tort liability. Ideally, strict product liability would eventually prompt manufacturers, in particular, to exercise a higher level of diligence to avoid liability. Some few jurisdictions—the US can be listed as the prime example—extend strict liability rules to include sellers in general under this refined regime. The basic idea behind this move is to be seen in the likely pressure sellers could put on manufacturers to apply the highest possible safety standards. Regardless of which of the two approaches strict liability regimes follow, the situation for harmed stakeholders is undeniably significantly improved compared with older concepts.

Some examples in this chapter have proved, however, that strict liability has not yet been established as a general, gapless product liability standard. It remains to be seen whether the trend towards strict liability will continue. From an international or transnational perspective, it is to be hoped that there will be at least some further standardisation of product liability law. From a substantive law point of view, the two most pressing issues in this respect seem to be the question whether to introduce strict (tort) liability (where not yet done) and—with respect to those jurisdictions that base their product liability regimes on strict liability—who to hold liable under strict liability law. It remains to be seen whether academic debate will be able to stimulate policy discussions that might have further and increased effects on businesses around the globe.

Selected Further Reading

Dodds-Smith, I and Spencer, M (eds), *The International Comparative Legal Guide to: Product Liability 2016*, 14th edn (London, Global Legal Group, 2016)

Fairgrieve, D (ed), *Product Liability in Comparative Perspective* (Cambridge, Cambridge University Press, 2005)

Fairgrieve, D and Goldberg, RS, *Product Liability*, 3rd edn (Oxford, Oxford University Press, 2016)

Harrison, D, *The Law of Product Warnings and Recalls in Canada* (Markham, LexisNexis, 2013)

Hodges, C, *European Regulation of Consumer Product Safety* (Oxford, Oxford University Press, 2005)

Howells, G, *Consumer Product Safety* (Aldershot, Ashgate, 1998)

Howells, G and Borghetti, JS, 'Product Liability' in HW Micklitz, J Stuyck and E Terryn (eds), *Cases, Materials and Text on Consumer Law* (Oxford, Hart Publishing, 2010), 439–98

Lenz, T, *Produkthaftung* (Munich, CH Beck, 2014)

Nottage, L, *Product Safety and Liability Law in Japan: From Minamata to Mad Cows* (London, Routledge, 2004)

Owen, DG, *Product Liability in a Nutshell*, 9th edn (St Paul, MN, West Academic, 2015)

Owen, DG, *Products Liability Law*, 3rd edn (St Paul, MN, West Academic, 2015)

Rödl & Partner (eds), *Handbuch international Produkthaftung*, 2nd edn (Cologne, Bundesanzeiger Verlag, 2014)

Stapleton, J, *Product Liability* (Cambridge, Cambridge University Press, 1994)

Tulibacka, M, *EU Product Liability Law in Transition* (Farnham, Ashgate, 2009)

Van Dam, C, *European Tort Law*, 2nd edn (Oxford, Oxford University Press, 2014)

Varner, CD and Pratt, BW (eds), *The Product Regulation and Liability Review* (London, Law Business Research, 2014)

Whittaker, S (ed), *The Development of Product Liability* (Cambridge, Cambridge University Press, 2010)

3

Warranty Law

I. Outline

A common understanding in commercial transactions is that buyers have an interest in 'getting what they pay for'. This legitimate expectation would be undermined if sellers were not to perform in accordance with the contract or—broadly speaking—if the (principally) subjective equivalence between performance and counter-performance were to be impaired. One party could, for example, perform late, or even fail to perform. Another example can be seen in delivered goods or services that do not conform with the performance owed in terms of quality (material defects) or the legal consequences of the transaction (rights-related defects). In the preceding chapter, we discussed the sectoral issue of deficiencies in product safety. In this chapter, we would like to take a closer look at qualitative issues of performance, thus limiting our observations to material defects.

Defects in quality can occur in different situations, be it with respect to goods or services, sales transactions or other contractual frameworks, eg leases, tenancies or contracts for work and labour. In the present context, we shall primarily focus on the arguably most common scenario, the sale of goods.

The obligation to perform in conformity with the contract is the seller's main contractual obligation. This consideration might sound obvious and simple, but how to regulate issues of contractual non-conformity has been heavily debated ever since the emergence of sales transactions. Among the key challenges are the questions of how to balance the sellers' and buyers' interests, where to draw the line between party autonomy and objective equivalence, whether one should differentiate between professional and non-professional buyers, and how best to address the call for adequacy, proportionality and suitability of possible remedies. The brief overview in this chapter will highlight different approaches taken at different points in time and in different parts of the world. We do not intend to provide a conclusive overview of warranty law; the emphasis is rather on outlining underlying strategies and approaches, while pointing out some key challenges from a transnational perspective.

At least in modern times—we touch upon the pre-modern evolution of warranty law shortly—it has been the general belief that the seller's obligation to take responsibility for defects is generally beneficial to all stakeholders concerned. Colin Scott, for example, broadly claims that 'legal guarantees of quality are good for all'.[1] This claim results from two complementary considerations. First, buyers would be more highly motivated to purchase goods if they could rely on certain qualitative standards. Second, striving for higher quality could eventually and sustainably stimulate the market, both in terms of consumer satisfaction and with respect to technological development.[2]

At the same time, however, one can find voices which claim that producers could have an interest in applying strategies and techniques of premature product aging that would motivate, or even force, buyers to purchase new goods more frequently.[3] This phenomenon of shortening the lifecycle of goods—in the pertinent literature commonly referred to as 'planned obsolescence'—is increasingly and heavily debated at an interdisciplinary level. From a legal perspective, it can be noted that in more recent years, warranty law has been thought of as one potential solution. We would like to take the opportunity to briefly discuss this issue, in particular from a transnational perspective, in the second part of this analysis, to explain some of the biggest challenges for warranty law.

Following a brief look at the historical development of warranty law in early times, this chapter will examine different warranty regimes in selected jurisdictions. This will include national as well as regional and supra-regional concepts and legislative projects. The purpose of this is to showcase the development and current state of the art of warranty regulation. We shall then switch to a discussion of challenges for transnational trade from a warranty law perspective. This will particularly include the aforementioned planned obsolescence debate. For the sake of clarification, one should again notice that the analysis will, in principle, be limited to warranties with respect to material (and not rights-related) defects.

II. Warranty Law in Early Times

Warranty law constitutes a key sales law element in advanced jurisdictions. One central idea is to keep the transactional seller–buyer relationship well balanced, in the sense that sales law regimes offer mechanisms and tools to 'restore' the contractual balance if the seller's performance leads to an impairment. The equivalence of a contractual transaction could, for example, be compromised if the delivered good did not meet mutually agreed specifications. Not meeting generally expected quality standards can

---

[1] C Scott, 'Quality of Products' in P Cane and J Conaghan (eds), *The New Oxford Companion to Law* (Oxford, Oxford University Press, 2008) 973, 973.

[2] ibid.

[3] S Wrbka, 'Warranty Law in Cases of Planned Obsolescence—The Austrian Situation' (2017) 7 *Journal of European Consumer and Market Law* 67, 67.

be considered a further example of unsatisfactory performance. Warranty law aims to answer concerns regarding non-conformity with contractual standards by offering a minimum set of legal tools that can be applied if needed, and (basically) without any requirement of culpability on the seller's side.

Designing a framework of warranty rights and remedies requires a carefully considered act of risk allocation. In particular, three (to some extent interrelating) questions come to mind in this regard. First, to what extent should buyers be allowed to enjoy warranty rights even where the seller is not to blame for the non-conforming performance? Second, against what kind of defects should buyers be protected? Third, should corrective mechanisms not be based on the consensual agreement between the parties rather than on statute or case law? A look at the evolution and progress of warranty law shows us how jurisdictions have replied (at least) to (some of) these questions, and how warranty law has changed since its emergence.

The underlying idea behind warranty law is not entirely new. Warranty law actually dates back (at least) to ancient Roman times. Although we have already touched upon some related questions in the preceding chapter on product liability, it might make sense to add some observations for the sake of more easily understanding the present debates and different approaches taken in more recent times.

Historically speaking, buyers did not enjoy much protection against low-quality performance. In Roman times, for instance, sales transactions were, at least in the beginning, characterised by strong emphasis of the seller's position. The buyer had (for a long time) virtually no remedial right against the seller of a defective good. The buyer's only chance was to inspect the good beforehand and to reject it in the event of a defect. This construct, commonly referred to as the *caveat emptor* ('buyer beware') principle, helped the buyer only in a limited number of cases. Most notably, latent or hidden defects, ie defects that could not be detected at the time of performance, consequently fell into the sphere of the buyer's risk.

Over the decades, the *caveat emptor* principle was subject to a number of refinements that aimed to seek (limited) improvement of the buyer's situation. Selling defective goods with knowledge of the defect, for example, was soon considered as a case where the financial risk should pass to the seller. Allowing for express, contractual warranties is another example of an early advancement. However, showing that the seller had acted deceitfully proved difficult. And express warranties were not commonly found in transactions.

From a buyer's perspective, the most significant development was arguably the partial acceptance of implied warranties. Implied warranties concern aspects of quality that are neither specifically agreed by the parties nor explicitly guaranteed by the seller, but which can rather be generally expected from the good in question. The idea to apply implied warranties originated from the finding that some sales transactions—in particular the sale of slaves, cattle and beasts of burden—were excessively characterised by deceitful seller behaviour. Limiting the buyer's tools to thorough inspection did not necessarily work in these cases; none of the categories mentioned usually displayed patent defects. Furthermore, express warranties were not commonly found in these transactions either. Taking into consideration that the buyers of those 'goods' were often members of the upper class, it was just a matter of time before the risk allocation began to shift towards the seller. The development was slow. But ultimately deceitful seller behaviour and express guarantees did not necessarily constitute absolute conditions anymore. The buyer could (within a short period of time) ask either for rescission of the contract (*actio redhibitoria*), or for a price reduction (*actio quanti minoris*)—even if the seller was unaware of the defect.

Although these developments indicate a gradual improvement of the buyer's position, Roman warranty law was—in particular compared with some modern trends—conceptually limited. In his commentary on the evolution of warranty law, John Reitz, for example, emphasises four main differences.[4] First—and despite the extension of the implied warranty theory under Justinian to include specific goods (*Speziesschuld*) at a broader level—the regime was limited to *emptio venditio* sales transactions only. This basically meant that certain sales transactions, most notably 'generic goods from unidentified masses', fell outside the regulatory scope and were subject merely to the conventional warranty concepts of express warranty and deceit.[5] Second, the implied warranty theory was restricted to latent defects. The buyer was generally still under the obligation to inspect the good thoroughly beforehand. Third, compensation rights with respect to implied warranties were restricted to the loss in value of the good. Unlike the case in some (but not all) modern jurisdictions, consequential damages remained uncovered. Fourth, implied warranties were further treated in a different way from express warranties with respect to limitation periods, and consequently were subject to shorter limitation periods. Six-month (for cases of rescission) and one-year (for cases of price reduction) limitation periods meant significant reductions compared with the general limitation period of 30 years (applicable in certain cases of express warranties).[6]

III. Warranty Law in Modern Times

Over the centuries sales transactions have been subject to fundamental regulatory change, in terms both of scope and of the substance of regulation. What started with the sale of slaves, cattle and beasts of burden at Roman markets has turned into one of the most relevant branches of commercial regulation at national, regional and global levels.

The further development of the market asked for a reconsideration of the sales regime that, to a large extent, still rested on the *caveat emptor* principle. The Industrial Revolution, with its origins in eighteenth-century England, was arguably the most influential facilitator in this respect, at least in the Anglo-American world. Qi Zhou and Larry A DiMatteo, for example, suggest that courts began to shape buyer-friendlier rules in response to altered actual circumstances. These included in

---

[4] JC Reitz, 'History of Cutoff Rules as a Form of Caveat Emptor: Part II—From Roman Law to the Modern Civil and Common Law' (1989) 37 *American Journal of Comparative Law* 247, 252–55.

[5] ibid, 252–53.

[6] For details see, eg, ibid, 254–55 with further references.

particular 'enormous innovation and scientific development, significantly improved productive efficiency, the introduction of mass production, and the sale of commodities in large quantities'.[7] Simply put, as a result of these trends, examining goods prior to contracting and delivery proved difficult. Pre-delivery inspection by the buyer was, for example, intrinsically complicated in cases where the good was to be sent to the buyer. The technical complexity of goods constituted an additional issue, in particular when it came to non-professional buyers.[8] In this light, it does not come as a surprise that post-Industrial Revolution sales regimes began to apply modernised rules. The following subsections will discuss selected issues in selected jurisdictions. For the sake of comprehensibility, the focus will be put on certain noteworthy features. Details can be found in the cited literature and that listed in the 'Selected Further Reading' section.

A. Warranty Law in the United States

i. General Remarks

United States (US) warranty law is characterised by a complex system of different layers that rest on an interplay between the Uniform Commercial Code (UCC), the Magnuson-Moss Warranty Act (MMWA) and a number of more specific yet diverse State laws, commonly referred to as 'lemon laws'. Overall, one can note that different frameworks and rules might apply—mainly depending on whether the transaction at hand concerns a situation that involves only professional stakeholders on both sides (business-to-business or B2B transactions) or at least one non-professional actor. The most relevant example for the latter category comprises business-to-consumer transactions (B2C transactions). To understand the basic mechanisms of the relevant instruments more easily, it makes sense to briefly discuss some underlying ideas and concepts.

As already indicated, different non-conformity categories might be identified. The most relevant ones in terms of qualitative issues are the two broader categories of breaching express terms, on the one hand, and implied terms, on the other. Express terms refer to party statements that become part of the actual contract, regardless of whether this is done orally or in writing. Assessing whether party statements form part of the contract or not is of practical relevance, because non-compliance could lead to two different sets of legal consequences—depending on whether non-compliance involves contractual agreements or not. For the purpose of easier understanding, one should note that the present chapter focuses on the first group of party statements— contract-integrated statements.[9]

---

[7] Q Zhou and LA DiMatteo, 'Three Sales Laws and the Common Law of Contracts' in LA Di Matteo and M Hogg (eds), *Comparative Contract Law: British and American Perspectives* (Oxford, Oxford University Press, 2016) 347, 367.

[8] In a similar vein, see ibid.

[9] As far as the second category is concerned, ie the group of pre-contractual statements that do not form part of the contract, it should be noted that issues arising would not lead to warranty rights but be dealt with under the concept of (mis-)representation. The regimes differ conceptually. Most notably—and unlike in the case of warranties—the incorrect seller's statement must at least have been made negligently. Differences further exist with respect to the availability of remedies and the calculation of time limitations.

Implied terms form a second big group within the warranty scheme. Unlike express terms, the implied counterparts represent common or objective terms that would generally be expected as constituting an integral part of a comparable transaction—without the necessity of being specifically agreed upon by the parties. Implied terms can find their basis, for example, in relevant statutes (terms implied in law) or—where applicable—customary practice (terms implied by custom). In the present context of qualitative non-conformity, arguably of more practical relevance, however, would be the group of terms implied in fact. Here the decisive question is which quality criteria parties (including the parties at hand) would consider as so obvious that they do not need to be explicitly agreed.

ii. Warranty Law and the Uniform Commercial Code

Contract law in the US falls under the legislative competencies of the States. As a result of this, sales transactions have traditionally been subject to diverse standards. To secure the best possible alignment of the State regimes, the Uniform Law Commission has been drafting and proposing uniform acts since its establishment in the late nineteenth century. Arguably the most important output thus far is the UCC,[10] first published in 1952. The UCC gained momentum in the 1960s, when a couple of major US States began to introduce its regime. Over the decades, the Code has been adopted by all 50 US States, the District of Columbia and the US territories.[11] It is divided into 11 articles—Articles 1 to 9, plus Articles 2A and 4A—and covers commercial transactions very broadly. For the purpose of this section we focus on Article 2 UCC on sales transactions.

As a basic principle, the seller has the obligation to deliver goods in conformity with the contract ('perfect tender' rule).[12] Article 2 UCC contains a number of elements that help to determine the relevant contractual parameters in any given case. The concept is widely based on a mix of the earlier outlined groups of express and implied terms, dividing the latter into two sub-categories. Consequently, a breach of any of the following three categories could constitute a relevant non-conformity situation: express terms (§ 2-313), implied warranties of merchantability (§ 2-314), and the usage of trade and implied warranties of fitness for a particular purpose (§ 2-315).[13] While the first implied terms category would most notably refer to the usability of the respective good as usually to be expected, the 'fitness for a particular purpose' pillar covers cases that stand somewhere in between express terms and the merchantability criterion. Here the crucial question is whether the seller 'has reason to know any particular purpose for which the goods are required and that the buyer is relying on the

---

[10] References to statutory provisions made in this section refer—unless specified—to provisions of the Uniform Commercial Code.

[11] Louisiana was the last State to adopt the UCC, in 1990. For details, see www.sos.la.gov/BusinessServices/UniformCommercialCode/Pages/default.aspx.

[12] UCC § 2-601. K Chapman and MJ Meurer, 'Efficient Remedies for Breach of Warranty' (1989) 52 *Law and Contemporary Problems* 107, 110.

[13] Note, however, that the merchantability criterion—pursuant to the UCC—is only of relevance if the seller is 'a merchant with respect to goods of that kind'—see (UCC § 2-314).

seller's skill or judgement to select or furnish suitable goods'.[14] This category can be seen as a last resort for cases in which there is neither an express warranty nor a warranty of merchantability. If, for example, an ordinary motorcycle was sold to a buyer who expressed his or her intention to use it off-road and purchased the motorcycle after consultation with the seller and convinced by the seller's advice, that buyer could have recourse to the fitness-for-purpose category. This would be particularly helpful in cases where off-road usability did not form an express term of the contract.

To deal with non-conformity cases, buyers can basically rely on three remedies. They can either reject the good, revoke the acceptance of a good (if certain requirements are fulfilled) or claim damages.[15] While rejecting the good and revoking an acceptance are mutually exclusive—a rejection is only possible until a good is accepted—compensation can be paired with either one, or form the basis of a claim of its own. A rejection of the good—and likewise a revocation of an acceptance (*note*: it basically leads to similar practical consequences as an initial rejection if the 'non-conformity substantially impairs' the value of the good[16])—does not automatically lead to a refund of the price paid. The seller can (usually) avoid this by repairing the good or replacing it with one that is in conformity with the contract—both within a reasonable time.[17]

Accepting the good does not have to be done explicitly. As a basic rule, any act that points to an acceptance is sufficient.[18] The practical consequences can be significant. The burden of proof of (non-)conformity, for example, shifts to the buyer.[19] Revoking the acceptance—and thus having recourse to the warranty remedies of repair, replacement or refund of the price paid—is limited to a few scenarios only. These comprise, most notably, cases where the buyer makes 'the reasonable assumption that its [ie the good's] non-conformity would be cured and it has not been seasonally cured', or where the buyer accepts 'without discovery of such non-conformity if his or her acceptance was reasonably induced either by the difficulty of discovery before acceptance or by the seller's assurances'.[20]

The possibility to claim damages is relatively far-reaching. Buyers of non-conforming goods could ask for compensation for 'the loss resulting in the ordinary course of events from the seller's breach as determined in any manner which is reasonable'.[21] Possible claims might include compensation for 'any incidental and [foreseeable] consequential damages'.[22]

---

[14] UCC § 2-315.

[15] UCC §§ 2-601, 2-608 and 2-714.

[16] UCC § 2-608(3).

[17] UCC § 2-508.

[18] UCC § 2-606(1)(a). Sub-ss (b) and (c) introduce two alternative acceptance scenarios: 'fail[ing] to make an effective rejection' (*note*: this requires that 'the buyer has had a reasonable opportunity to inspect' the good); and 'do[ing] any act inconsistent with the seller's ownership'.

[19] UCC § 2-607(4).

[20] UCC § 2-608(1)(a) and (b). It should be noted that to secure the conforming rights the buyer would—as a general rule—have to notify the seller 'within a reasonable time' after discovery of the contractual breach—see UCC § 2-607(3)(a).

[21] UCC § 2-714(1).

[22] UCC § 2-714(3) in combination with § 2-715. On the foreseeability issue in the context of consequential damages, see, eg, B Stone, 'Recovery of Consequential Damages for Product Recall Expenditures' (1980) *Brigham Young University Law Review* 485 with further references.

Overall the UCC has had a great impact on US warranty law. Zhou and Di Matteo point out that it served as the basis for *Restatement* rules on contractual non-conformity.[23] This fact, so the authors claim, has significantly influenced the common law of contract, since courts have repeatedly made recourse to the *Restatement* regime as a pivotal source for their reasoning. Nevertheless, the UCC remains relatively 'seller-friendly', in particular in comparison with key legislation in other jurisdictions discussed later in this chapter. Most notably, the warranty regime introduced under the Code principally does not differentiate between B2B and B2C transactions. Furthermore, its rules are largely flexible, meaning, in particular, that (under the UCC regime) the use of warranties is generally not mandatory. Sellers can relatively easily limit warranties, or exclude them altogether.[24]

iii. The Magnuson-Moss Warranty Act

The US Federal Magnuson-Moss Warranty Act (MMWA) was enacted in 1975 primarily to answer consumer protection concerns.[25] The MMWA particularly addresses issues that the UCC left widely at the seller's discretion, or even unregulated. Dee Pridgen and Gene Marsh list three considerations as driving forces behind the adoption of the MMWA: (i) the overall complexity of and linguistic challenges posed by warranties in B2C sales transactions; (ii) the hidden limitations of warranties in contracts and contractual terms and conditions; (iii) the consumers' perceived subpar access to justice in warranty cases.[26]

Mirroring these concerns, the MMWA introduced mechanisms that (to a certain extent) have improved the situation for non-professional buyers. Three key features should be pointed out in the present context. First, as is the case with the UCC, the MMWA does not oblige sellers to offer warranties. However, if they issue warranties in writing, they have to make sure that they follow specific disclosure requirements published by the Federal Trade Commission (FTC) with the aim of establishing a standard of general intelligibility.[27] Second, if warranties are issued in writing, sellers further must not disclaim implied warranties.[28] Third, the MMWA introduced a (voluntary) informal alternative dispute resolution (ADR) mechanism. Sellers who offer these schemes have to make sure that the instruments comply with the specific FTC standards. Establishing minimum quality ADR criteria might be welcome. However, some authors point out that the actual relevance of ADR schemes as

---

[23] Zhou and DiMatteo, n 7, 376–77.

[24] On this issue see, eg, CD Rohwer et al, *Contracts in a Nutshell*, 8th edn (St Paul, MN, West Academic, 2017) 437–38; Zhou and DiMatteo, n 7, 374–75; and, in more detail, C Carter et al, *Consumer Warranty Law: Lemon Laws, Magnuson-Moss, UCC, Manufactured Home, and Other Warranty Statutes*, 5th edn (Boston, MA, National Consumer Law Center, 2015) ch 5.

[25] 15 USC §§ 2301–2312.

[26] D Pridgen and GA Marsh, *Consumer Protection Law in a Nutshell*, 4th edn (St Paul, MN, West Academic, 2016) 303–04.

[27] ibid, 305–06.

[28] 15 USC § 2308. One should note, however, that—under certain conditions—the possibility to limit the duration of warranties remains intact—see Pridgen and Marsh, n 26, 309.

recommended by the MMWA is not that significant. Professional sellers would rather commit to ADR schemes designed on commercial ADR models.[29]

iv. Lemon Laws

A few years after the enactment of the MMWA, the first US States began to introduce sectoral legislation to maximise the relevance of warranty law in B2C transactions. These State laws, commonly referred to as 'lemon laws', initially aimed to provide non-professional purchasers of new motor vehicles with comprehensive warranty remedies. Over the years some of the lemon laws were broadened in scope, most commonly to include used motor vehicles and, in some instances, also to apply to selected goods other than motor vehicles.[30] For the sake of simplicity the following observations will focus on the primary area of concern—the purchase of new cars. Where applicable, other goods covered by the respective lemon law are subject to generally comparable regulation.

With the lemon laws, State legislators sought to resolve a practical phenomenon. Motor vehicles in particular were, on occasion, found to suffer from significant problems regarding quality. However, neither the UCC nor the MMWA had introduced comprehensive, mandatory rules to address this. Hence, a stricter approach was felt necessary to avoid the nuisance of repeatedly having to send cars for repairs.

Although lemon laws differ with respect to scope and regulatory density, some ideas are generally shared to resolve warranty-relevant cases as quickly and in as unbureaucratic manner as possible. Three key features should be pointed out. First, lemon laws introduce a set of mandatory warranties that apply with respect to the goods covered by the respective law. This is a significant improvement for buyers compared with the UCC (which generally allows for disclaimers and limitations) and the MMWA (which slightly improves the buyer's position but fails to make warranties mandatory).

Second, lemon laws usually broaden the group of warranty addressees. Buyers are given the chance to resort to the vehicle's manufacturer directly to get the defective vehicle repaired or replaced. This cuts the liability chain and makes sense, in particular in those cases where the seller's resources are limited in terms of repair and replacement.[31]

Third, as is the case in the MMWA, ADR plays an important role in the lemon laws. In addition to emphasising quality standards (that principally follow the MMWA concept), most lemon laws further require buyers to resort to redress schemes offered under the respective lemon law (which would comply with the ADR standards) before

---

[29] See, eg, Pridgen and Marsh, n 26, 312–13.

[30] See, eg, 'What you need to know about warranty laws—You have more rights than you might think' (May 2013) *Consumer Reports*, www.consumerreports.org/cro/magazine/2013/05/the-word-on-warranty-protection/index.htm.

[31] Note that UCC case law already acknowledged certain cases of direct manufacturer liability in express warranty scenarios—for a discussion see, eg CR Reitz, 'Manufacturers' Warranties of Consumer Goods' (1997) 75 *Washington University Law Review* 357; JD Prince, 'Defective Products and Product Warranty Claims in Minnesota' (2005) 31 *William Mitchell Law Review* 1677; S Bonanno, 'Privity, Products Liability, and UCC Warranties: A Retrospect of and Prospects for Illinois Commercial Code 2-318' (1991) 25 *The John Marshall's Law Review* 177.

going to court. This strategy aims to support the use of dispute resolution mechanisms rather than the ordinary courts, which would—in normal circumstances—lead to faster results.

Although the lemon laws rest on some common basic considerations, divergences remain stark. In addition to the differences already outlined, for example relating to the scope or the mandatory nature of pre-litigation ADR, distinctions can be found with respect to the exercise and choice of possible remedies. Some States, for example, grant the buyer of a defective motor vehicle the right to choose between the available remedies, whereas others leave that choice to the seller. Others leave this question unanswered. Nevertheless, lemon laws considerably improve the situation of non-professional buyers when it comes to contractual non-conformity issues. They have further developed the initial idea of the MMWA to accommodate information deficits and differences in bargaining power, to provide harmed buyers with effective legal remedies.

Overall, the US development in the second half of the twentieth century can be understood as a more modern shift away from the *caveat emptor* principle. In particular, the direct link to the manufacturers (as commonly known under the lemon laws) and (to a certain degree) the possibility to claim incidental and consequential damages without needing to prove any culpability on the seller's part, have to be considered a major improvement for the buyers (compared in particular with the situation in some Continental European jurisdictions, for instance).[32]

B. Warranty Law in the EU

i. The pan-EU situation

The European Union (EU) legislator has thus largely failed in its attempts to conclusively standardise warranty law. Member States have been aiming to secure the highest possible degree of legislative leeway to autonomously regulate what can be considered as a pivotal area of contract law. Even in more recent years, warranty issues have remained difficult to comprehensively regulate at the EU level. Unlike its proposal (which included revised warranty rules), the finally adopted Consumer Rights Directive (CRD), for example, addresses warranty law only in passing.[33] As a consequence, the Consumer Sales Directive (CSD) remains as the first and thus far only broad instrument to (partially) regulate warranty issues at the pan-EU level.[34]

Adopted in 1999, the CSD resulted from the idea of harmonising the considerably fragmented warranty laws of the Member States, with a focus on B2C transactions. In particular, from the viewpoint of cross-border trade, fundamental inter-Member

---

[32] On the latter, see, eg, TK Graziano, *Comparative Contract Law: Cases, Materials and Exercises* (Basingstoke, Palgrave MacMillan, 2009) Case 6.

[33] Directive 2011/83/EU, [2011] OJ L304/64. The only reference to warranty law is to be found in Art 33 CRD, which inserted a reporting mechanism into the key directive on warranty law, the 1999 Consumer Sales Directive.

[34] Directive 1999/44/EC, [1999] OJ L171/12. References to statutory provisions made in this section refer—unless specified—to provisions of the CSD.

State differences were arguably counterproductive to securing a truly internal market. The situation might not have played such a significant role in B2B transactions. Here, warranty rules were—and still are—usually flexible and autonomously negotiated by the parties. With regard to B2C transactions, however, it was rare for legal terms to be discussed or negotiable. As a result of this, most jurisdictions traditionally decided to declare the relevant rules (at least to some extent) mandatory to protect non-professional buyers. This—paired with the fragmented approaches the regimes followed—led to a practically complex framework that in reality was difficult to understand, in particular for those not familiar with conflict-of-law rules.

The CSD was considered a milestone in supranational law making. Peter Shears, Francis Zoller and Sandra Hurd, for example, argued that it would be 'the biggest change to consumer rights for twenty years'.[35] Whether this was really the case will be left undecided here. It is safe to say, however, that the CSD touched upon a topic that the national legislators had autonomously—and in a remarkably fragmented way— regulated for decades; some even for centuries. Despite being based on minimum harmonisation,[36] the Directive prompted a number of Member States to significantly revise their regimes, at least with respect to B2C transactions. Some Member States even opted for broader transposition and redesigned their national warranty schemes as a whole. The Austrian legislator, for example, decided to comprehensively revise its then existing warranty rules accordingly—including non-B2C transactions.

The CSD forms part of the EU consumer acquis, a group of eight 'first generation', minimum harmonised consumer directives that (to a large extent) apply to B2C sales law.[37] The Directive is relatively narrow in scope—applying merely to B2C transactions—and (with 14 articles) short. Its key provisions include the introduction of a standardised conformity concept, a two-tiered remedy regime, a minimum time limit of two years, a (partially) reversed burden of proof and the entrenchment of the framework's mandatory nature.[38] Other key questions, such as possible damage claims and direct producer liability, are left to one side. Nevertheless, one of the biggest achievements of the CSD is arguably the fact that it introduced a minimum warranty standard in B2C transactions, which Member States had to implement in their respective regimes. All of the following examples prompted some Member States to broaden or enhance their respective warranty laws in the case of B2C sales.[39]

The warranty concept introduced by the CSD rests on the idea that the buyer should be given the chance to exercise certain remedies to restore the contractual conformity of the good if it is impaired. Article 2(2) CSD presents four basic criteria that merge express and implied terms. Goods are—on a rebuttable basis—presumed to be defect-free if they:

(a)   comply with the description given by the seller and possess the qualities of the goods which the seller has held out to the consumer as a sample or model;

---

[35] P Shears et al, 'It Will be the Biggest Change to Consumer Rights' (2000) 2 *Journal of Business Law* 262, 262.

[36] Art 8(2) CSD: 'Member States may adopt or maintain in force more stringent provisions, compatible with the Treaty in the field covered by this Directive, to ensure a higher level of consumer protection.'

[37] For details on the consumer acquis directives, see S Wrbka, *European Consumer Access to Justice Revisited* (Cambridge, Cambridge University Press, 2015) 169–72 with further references.

[38] Arts 2, 3, 5(1), 5(3) and 7 CSD.

[39] For details H Schulte-Nölke et al (eds), *EC Consumer Law Compendium* (Munich, Sellier, 2008) 409–50.

(b)   are fit for any particular purpose for which the consumer requires them and
      which he or she made known to the seller at the time of conclusion of the con-
      tract and which the seller has accepted;
(c)   are fit for the purposes for which goods of the same type are normally used;
(d)   show the quality and performance normal in goods of the same type and which
      the consumer can reasonably expect, given the nature of the goods and taking
      into account any public statements on the specific characteristics of the goods
      made about them by the seller, the producer or his representative, particularly in
      advertising or on labelling.

The list is relatively long and includes some elements—most notably the 'public
statement' criterion of Article 2(2)(d)—that prior to the CSD were not enshrined in a
number of Member States' laws.[40]

Article 3 CSD enshrines a comprehensive, two-tiered remedial system that encompasses four remedies: repair, replacement, price reduction and rescission. As a first step,
buyers can choose between repair and replacement. The seller is bound by the choice,
unless he or she can show that the chosen remedy is impossible or disproportionate.[41]
In the event that the seller fails to restore the contractual balance within a reasonable
time, or if both options prove impossible, the buyer has—as a second step—the right
to ask for a price reduction or (unless the non-conformity is merely of minor nature)
to have the contract rescinded.[42]

Article 5 enshrines a general liability for issues that become 'apparent within two
years as from delivery'.[43] Two caveats, in particular, have to be made. First, Article 7(1)
gives the Member States the option to shorten the limitation period to one year in the
case of second-hand goods. Second, Article 5(2) introduces the option of applying a
defect notification scheme. If exercised, buyers would have to notify the seller within
two months of detecting the non-conformity. We shall return to these two issues briefly.

A buyer-friendly innovation was introduced by Article 5(3) CSD. Non-conformity
issues that become apparent within the first six months from the time of delivery are—
on a rebuttable basis—deemed to have existed at the time of delivery. From a practical perspective, however, one should note that the actual benefit of this rule might be
limited. It only affects the question whether the non-conformity already existed at the
point of delivery. It does not apply to the question whether the good is in contractual
conformity or not. This still needs to be proved by the buyer.

In 2007 two studies were published that provided information on the transposition of the CSD into national law: the *EC Consumer Law Compendium* (*Consumer
Law Compendium*)[44] and the Communication on the implementation of Directive 1999/44/EC on certain aspects of the sale of consumer goods and associated
guarantees including analysis of the case for introducing direct producers' liability

---

[40]   ibid, 424. Note, however, that Art 2(4) introduces a subjective element by excluding the seller's liability
with respect to third party public statements, in particular in cases where 'he was not, and could not have
been, aware of the statement in question'. As a result of the minimum harmonisation character of the CSD,
not all Member States made use of this exclusion.
[41]   Art 3(3) CSD.
[42]   Art 3(5) and (6) CSD.
[43]   Art 5(1) CSD.
[44]   Schulte-Nölke et al (eds), n 39.

(CSD implementation communication).[45] The *Consumer Law Compendium* gave a broad overview of the implementation of all eight consumer acquis directives. With respect to the CSD, it arrived at the conclusion that the Directive—largely as a result of the mechanisms outlined above—achieved a significant level of harmonisation but failed to align the national warranty regimes in a way that would have truly led to a level playing at the inter-Member State level. This was obviously the result of a mix of four factors: the minimum harmonisation approach of the CSD; its narrow scope; the leeway granted to Member States with respect to the implementation techniques; and the broad catalogue of regulatory options that expressly gave Member States the choice between two alternatives in each case.[46] The just-mentioned options of shortening the limitation period in the case of second-hand goods and introducing a non-conformity notification scheme, for example, both met with a considerably divided response, lacking any red line in the sense that one could identify generally buyer-friendlier Member States.[47]

The CSD implementation communication arrived at generally similar results. In short, the communication concluded that further regulatory steps might be necessary to minimise the fragmentation of warranty law and to maximise its potential for the internal market.[48] It further added potentially important observations with respect to a possible extension of liable parties. Unlike the usual case, particularly under the US lemon laws, for example, direct producer liability (DPL) is not established throughout the EU. The CSD implementation communication completed the preliminary evaluation work of the *Consumer Law Compendium* in this regard and added a number of Member States to the list of jurisdictions that already (at least to some extent) had introduced DPL tools.[49] Overall the DPL evaluation remained undecided, in particular regarding the likely impact on the internal market. Simply put, the predominant assumption was that DPL might work as a 'safety net' for buyers, in the sense that it could increase the chances of their expectations of receiving conforming goods being satisfied.[50] The introduction of a region-wide DPL scheme could furthermore turn out to be beneficial for sellers other than the manufacturer, because it would eliminate the necessity for those sellers to seek redress against the respective manufacturer. At the same time, however, the communication pointed out that a number of policymakers advised caution by arguing that DPL could place too heavy a burden on manufacturers and lead to unclear liability chains.[51] To date no concrete steps have been taken to install a region-wide DPL mechanism in the EU. But the basic interest expressed in the documents might indicate that the topic is not off the table yet.

[45] European Commission, Communication on the implementation of Directive 1999/44/EC on certain aspects of the sale of consumer goods and associated guarantees including analysis of the case for introducing direct producers' liability, 24 April 2007, COM(2007) 210 final.

[46] With respect to the latter, the *Consumer Law Compendium* concluded as follows: 'It is apparent that all options have been used by some of the member states, but in no instance has there been an overwhelming tendency to use, or to disregard, any of the options given in the Directive.'

[47] Schulte-Nölke et al (eds), n 39, 430 (on second-hand goods) and 432 (on the notification requirement).

[48] European Commission, Communication on the implementation of Directive 1999/44/EC, 10.

[49] See Schulte-Nölke et al (eds), n 39, 441–42, mentioning the examples of France, Belgium, Portugal, Latvia, Lithuania, Spain and Slovenia. The CSD implementation communication adds Finland and Sweden to that list—see European Commission, Communication on the implementation of Directive 1999/44/EC, 11.

[50] European Commission, n 49, 11.

[51] ibid, 11–12.

ii. The Situation in the Member States

As indicated already, the CSD has achieved a relatively high degree of standardisation within the EU. Nevertheless, important differences remain. It is not the purpose of this chapter to offer a conclusive summary of the national implementation of the Directive. But a brief look at three major jurisdictions—England,[52] France and Germany—will illustrate some of the challenges national legislators faced when integrating the CSD requirements into long-established national warranty regimes.

Modern English warranty and sales law has a long history that dates back to the nineteenth century. Being a common law jurisdiction, it comes as no surprise that, at least initially, case law shaped the framework. *Jones v Just*, for example, helped to craft the concept of implied warranties of merchantability.[53] In *Hadley v Baxendale*, on the other hand, the court dealt with the recoverability of consequential damages and focused on the foreseeability of the damage at the time of the formation of the contract.[54] These and other early decisions led to the introduction of the 1893 Sale of Goods Act, consolidated in 1979 (now the Sale of Goods Act (SoGA) 1979). With the purpose of collecting existing rules developed by the courts, it led—as an example—to a certain degree of predictability with respect to US warranty questions too. One of its (international) merits was that it paved the way for the warranty concept as introduced by the UCC in the US.

To a certain extent English warranty law still shows parallels with the UCC approach. However, over the decades the SoGA has been subject to a number of revisions, partly as a result of case law developments, at later stages partly due to EU legislation—most notably the CSD. Amendments have concerned, for example, the professional buyer's right to reject non-conforming goods: in the event of breach of an implied term with respect to the description, quality or fitness of a good or sample of a good, he or she would lose this remedy if the low degree of the breach would make it unreasonable for a professional buyer to reject the good.[55] Switches from 'merchantability' to 'satisfactory quality' to assess the conformity of a good, and the introduction of mandatory rules for consumer transactions, most notably with respect to implied terms, constitute additional examples of SoGA revisions.

The CSD was implemented with a delay of over one year by the Sale and Supply of Goods to Consumers Regulations 2002.[56] From a legal policy point of view, it is noteworthy that the national legislator decided to go beyond the CSD regime. Unlike in most other cases of EU consumer law implementation—one of the authors has

---

[52] For the sake of simplicity, we shall—where not explicitly stated otherwise—use the term 'English law' to refer to pertinent legislation available in the UK. The reason for this is that key laws, such as the Sale of Goods Act, do not necessarily apply the same rules to all the constituent parts of the UK. In particular with respect to Scotland, differences remain.

[53] *Jones v Just* (1868) LR 3 QB 197.

[54] *Hadley v Baxendale* [1854] EWHC J70.

[55] SoGA 1979, s 15A, differentiating between conditions, ie terms breach of which makes it reasonable to reject the good, and mere cases of warranty, ie terms breach of which does not make it reasonable to allow rejection.

[56] Sale and Supply of Goods to Consumers Regulations 2002, SI 2002/3045.

commented on this issue elsewhere[57]—policymakers decided to exceed the minimum standard directive to a considerably large extent. The CSD rules on consumer transactions were integrated into the SoGA in an attempt to leave the then existing national framework widely untouched. Where possible, the legislator went beyond the parameters of the CSD. The decision not to enshrine the two-year period set out in Article 5(1) CSD but to keep the general limitation period of six years for contractual breaches is a good example.[58] The possibility to have recourse to the remedies of repair or replacement (in implementation of Article 3(2) CSD), or alternatively to SoGA remedies already available prior to the CSD is a further example of how the legislator tried to maintain the then existing rules.[59]

France is arguably one of the Member States with the longest tradition in specific consumer protection. Several of its sectoral consumer laws had been introduced years before the EU policymakers started with the first draft projects in the field of consumer law.[60]

With a delay of more than three years, the French implementation of the CSD was effected significantly late. As was the case in England, the French legislator tried to leave long-established national non-conformity rules widely untouched. The incorporation of the CSD rules into the French Consumer Code had the effect that the already complex French warranty regime became even more multi-layered.[61]

Traditionally, two regimes were applied to answer cases of non-conformity. Article 1604 of the French Civil Code (*Code civil*; CC) included a general delivery rule that (at least) initially was used in a number of contractual non-conformity cases. More specific rules dealing with contractual (non-)conformity can be found in Articles 1641 and 1642 CC.

This originally two-fold mechanism was heavily debated in legal academia and subject to extensive case law. Eventually, priority was given to the more specific rules in warranty-relevant cases, ie to Articles 1641 and 1642 CC.[62] The French approach to implementing the CSD in a separate piece of legislation—the French Consumer Code—added an extra layer. Non-professional buyers might now be able to base potential claims alternatively on the new, CSD-influenced regime enshrined in the French Consumer Code, or on the older CC rules.[63] Depending on the particular circumstances, the consumer's choice and chances might differ.

In contrast to England and France, Germany belongs to the group of Member States that opted for a comparatively broad reform of their warranty regimes.

---

[57] S Wrbka, 'The Faces and Implications of Legal Certainty in Contemporary Private Law—A Comparative Law Perspective' in M Fenwick et al (eds), *The Shifting Meaning of Legal Certainty in Comparative and Transnational Law* (Oxford, Hart Publishing, 2017) 135, 153.

[58] Limitation Act 1980, s 5.

[59] See, eg, MG Bridge, *The Sale of Goods*, 3rd edn (Oxford, Oxford University Press, 2014) 557, fn 426.

[60] Two earlier examples are rules on doorstep selling, introduced in 1972 (via Law No 72-1137 of 1972) and the introduction of a general consumer law—the French Consumer Code (FCC)—in 1978 (Law No 78-23 of 1978).

[61] Arts L 211-1 et seq French Consumer Code.

[62] For examples, see HW Micklitz et al, *Cases, Materials and Text on Consumer Law* (Oxford, Hart Publishing, 2010) 326–27 with further references.

[63] ibid, 325, with reference to Art L 211-13 French Consumer Code.

The timely implementation of the CSD formed part of the 2001 Law of Obligations Reform (*Schuldrechtsmodernisierung*).[64] Unlike in some other jurisdictions—see the French example, or Italy, which introduced a completely new Consumer Code[65]—the German legislator decided to incorporate the new rules into its Civil Code (*Bürgerliches Gesetzbuch*; BGB). The new regime (§§ 434–445 BGB) contains generally applicable warranty rules and is complemented by more specific special rules available in B2C cases only. One of the most noteworthy consequences of the German implementation is that the warranty limitation period was basically—ie irrespective of whether the case involves a non-consumer buyer or not—extended from six months to two years (for movables).[66] Although the German warranty regime was comprehensively revised, it must not be forgotten that the rules are (as a minimum standard) mandatory in B2C cases only. The possibility to limit warranty rights and remedies, in particular in B2B transactions, basically remains.[67]

iii. Further Harmonisation Endeavours at the EU Level

Attempts to standardise warranty and contract law comprehensively have been on the agenda for decades.[68] Two of the more recent contributions are the 2009 Draft Common Frame of Reference (DCFR) and the 2011 Proposal for a Regulation on a Common European Sales Law (CESL Regulation Proposal).

The DCFR—designed by collaboration between different research groups, most notably the Study Group on a European Civil Code and the Research Group on EC Private Law (Acquis Group)—aimed to introduce (non-binding) principles, definitions and model rules of European Private Law. It contains both general rules on non-conformity and more specific provisions applicable in B2C cases only.[69] In principle, the mechanisms built upon the then-existing, predominantly used concepts, although it should be noted that in some respects there are considerable differences. Most notably, the period of limitation follows a general (subjective)[70] three-year rule set out Article III.-7:201 DCFR—at least in B2C transactions.[71] Another case is the basic elimination of the two-tiered remedy regime that was introduced by the CSD. Price reduction, for example, is put on the same level as repair and replacement.

---

[64] BGBl I 2001, 3138.

[65] Legislative Decree no 206 of 6 September 2005.

[66] § 438(1)(3) BGB (in general two years) as against former § 477(1) BGB (in general six months).

[67] § 444 in combination with § 475 BGB.

[68] Projects can be dated back at least to the Principles of European Contract Law (PECL) with their roots in the late 1980s. The PECL were crafted by the Commission on European Contract Law, commonly known as the 'Lando Commission' (named after its chairman Ole Lando) and had the aim of introducing model rules on contract law to guide future attempts in harmonising European contract law.

[69] With a focus on sales transactions, see, in particular, chs 3 ('Remedies for non-performance') and 7 ('Prescription') of Book III and the more specific sales rules in ch 2, s 3 ('Obligations of the seller'—'Conformity of the goods') and ch 4 ('Remedies') of Book IV (Part A) DCFR.

[70] See Art III.-7:301 DCFR ('Suspension in case of ignorance').

[71] See the special, differentiating notification obligation regime for B2B in Arts III.-3:107 and IV.A-4:302 DCFR.

The CESL Regulation Proposal on the other hand, is narrower, because it applies only to cross-border transactions, and only if they can be classified as either B2C or—as long as they involve at least one small or medium-sized enterprise (SME) as defined by Article 7(2) CESL Regulation Proposal—B2B contracts.[72] Simply put, the CESL scheme widely follows its main model—the DCFR. One notable exception relates to the time limit for possible claims. Pursuant to Article 179(1) of Annex I to the CESL Regulation Proposal, a shorter period of two years should generally apply.

Thus far, however, neither the DCFR nor the CESL has led to a new European warranty regime. The strong opposition of Member States to further interference with their national approaches—as, for example, openly voiced in the context of the CRD negotiations that finally led to the removal of new warranty rules from the final directive—has succeeded in preventing the introduction of any truly comprehensive warranty regime in the EU.

This being said, things might change sectorally over the next couple of years. In the framework of its Digital Single Market Strategy (DSM Strategy), touched upon earlier in this book, the Commission presented a directive proposal on the distance sale of goods (including, in particular, online sales) in 2015.[73] The proposed instrument is based on the idea that the different levels of warranty law found at Member State level are a main obstacle to the growth of the internal market, and that further efforts have to be made to standardise the picture at the EU level. To achieve this, the proposal aims to comprehensively revise the regime of the CSD by presenting a maximum harmonised mechanism.[74]

At the time of writing, the instrument was still being discussed by the relevant institutions. Given the strong position Member States traditionally occupy, it remains doubtful whether the scheme (in its proposed form) will become a reality, in particular because it would lead to significant consequences for some jurisdictions—its standardised two-year limitation period is just one example.[75] Its limitation to distance sales might add further issues, because it could lead to a fragmentation of warranty regimes with different legal conditions and consequences for distance and non-distance sales. In any event, all these examples indicate the unabated interest of policymakers in establishing more comprehensive and standardised international (or at least cross-border) warranty concepts.

---

[72] Provisions relevant in the present context can be found in ch 10, s 3 ('Conformity of the goods and digital content'), ch 11 ('The buyer's remedies'), ch 16, s 1 ('Damages') and ch 18 ('Prescription') of Annex I to the CESL Regulation Proposal.

[73] Proposal for a Directive on certain aspects concerning contracts for the online and other distance sales of goods, COM(2015) 635 final. See ch 1, 'Consumer Law'. For background information see, eg, European Commission, 'Commission proposes modern digital contract rules to simplify and promote access to digital content and online sales across the EU' (2015), europa.eu/rapid/press-release_IP-15-6264_en.htm. For comments on the DSM Strategy, see ch 7, 'E-Commerce Law'.

[74] Art 3 of the proposal puts it as follows: 'Member States shall not maintain or introduce provisions diverging from those laid down in this Directive including more or less stringent provisions to ensure a different level of consumer protection.'

[75] See Art 14 of the proposal.

C. Warranty Law in Other Selected Jurisdictions

i. General Remarks

Although jurisdictions share some common understanding regarding contractual non-conformity and its regulation, the landscape remains—as already noted—diverse and fragmented. It would go beyond the scope of this project to give a conclusive overview of the global situation. But a short excursion into some additional examples will help to make this point a little more clear.

ii. Warranty Law in the People's Republic of China

One of these examples refers to Chinese warranty law. Its principles are enshrined in two statutes—the 1999 Contract Law of the People's Republic of China (Contract Law) and the 1993 Law of the People's Republic of China on the Protection of Consumer Rights and Interests (Consumer Rights and Interests Law) (more recently revised in 2013). While the Contract Law offers a generally applicable warranty framework, the Consumer Rights and Interests Law adds some specific provisions for use in B2C transactions.

The relevant Contract Law rules are scattered throughout the statute. They include a statutory, general rescission right (for cases where the contractual breach is of a fundamental nature),[76] a list of special remedies (including claims for repair, replacement, price reduction, damages),[77] a general right to claim damages for consequential loss (capped by the foreseeability of the damage)[78] and provisions specifically applicable to sales contracts. The last of these contain rudimentary definitions of contractual conformity (which basically follow the express/implied warranty divide),[79] as well as a special, yet arguably vague, inspection and notification scheme.[80] Generally speaking, the framework of the Chinese Contract Law leaves ample room for interpretation.

The key rules with respect to consumer transactions are embedded in Articles 23 and 24 of the Consumer Rights and Interests Law. With its revision in 2013 the Law adopted a six-month, partially reversed burden of proof rule, modelled after Article 5(3) CSD.[81] It is, however, narrower in scope and only applies to 'durable' goods.[82] Based on the *san bao* ('three guarantees') concept, which dates back to

---

[76] Art 94(iv) Contract Law uses the term 'frustration of the purpose of the contract' (authors' translation).

[77] Art 111 Contract Law. Art 111 does not prioritise any remedy but requires the exercise of the 'most reasonable' one on a case-by-case basis.

[78] Arts 112 and 113 Contract Law.

[79] See Arts 153 and 154 with (partial) reference to Arts 61 and 62(i) Contract Law. With respect to the group of implied warranties, Art 62(i) refers to state or industry standards as a primary source for determining the expectability of certain qualitative standards. In their absence, customary standards and any other (in the particular case) obvious standards should be taken into consideration.

[80] Art 158 Contract Law.

[81] Art 23(3) Consumer Rights and Interests Law.

[82] J Binding and L Jiang, 'Die Revision des chinesischen Verbraucherrechts—Beruhigungspille oder Drops gelutscht?' (2013) 20 *Zeitschrift für chinesisches Recht* 191, 197, where the authors point out that the Consumer Rights and Interests Law lists some examples that include, eg, cars, computers and refrigerators.

the 1980s,[83] Article 24 extends the right to return defective goods within seven days of their receipt to any consumer good that falls under the scope of the Consumer Rights and Interests Law, without the need to ask for repair or replacement. After the expiration of the seven-day period, consumers can return goods (and rescind the contract) only if the general conditions of the Contract Law are met.[84]

iii. Warranty Law in South Korea

South Korea falls into the category of those jurisdictions that regulate warranty issues statutorily only in a rudimentary way. The Korean Civil Code (KCC) briefly touches upon defect-related contractual non-conformity in its Articles 580–582.

Articles 580 and 581—with reference to Article 575 KCC—list a number of remedies that are available to answer such issues. Buyers may choose between receiving a non-defective good (which implies demanding repair or replacement), compensation (which in practice functions also as the basis for a possible price reduction) and (if the 'contract's objective cannot be realised')[85] rescission.[86] The KCC fails to provide for a precise definition of what would constitute non-conformity. But as a basic rule one would have recourse to both the party agreement and objective criteria. One remarkable difference from the other jurisdictions discussed in this chapter is the unique termination period of sixth months from the date the seller first becomes aware of the defect.[87] Once expired, the seller can merely exercise his or her general (culpability based) right to damages under Article 390 KCC.[88] In particular, regarding the latter option, one should note that the general prescription system under the KCC is considerably complex and based on a detailed separation into different categories that take account of the particular facts of the case.[89]

iv. Warranty Law in Australia

Our third example, Australia, represents attempts to comprehensively regulate warranties, in particular with respect to B2C transactions. Until 2011, the year that the

---

[83] The concept refers to an interplay between repair, replacement and the return of goods—for details see YY Yang, 'Consumer Protection Policies and Practice of Automobile Industry in China: Explanations and Findings', legalstudies.berkeley.edu/wp-content/uploads/2013/07/You-You-Erica-Yang-Sp13.pdf, 5–6; Binding and Jiang, n 82, 194.

[84] Z Liao, 'The Recent Amendment to China's Consumer Law: An Imperfect Improvement and Proposal for Future Changes' (2014) 5 *Beijing Law Review* 163, 166. Other available warranty remedies are not affected by this rule.

[85] Art 575(1) KCC (authors' translation). Note that the translation available on the website of the South Korean Government (www.moleg.go.kr/english/korLawEng?pstSeq=52674) obviously contains an error when it provides 'only if the objective of the contract is not *un*attainable' (emphasis added). Note further that Art 581 (which is the basis for the right to demand a non-defective good) merely mentions obligations in kind, not obligations in respect of specific goods. The right to demand repair should, however, apply mutatis mutandis to the latter category as well.

[86] Art 581 KCC.

[87] Art 582 KCC.

[88] For details on the interplay between culpability-based damage claims and warranty law in South Korea, see, eg, S Seong, 'Die Entwicklung des Leistungsstörungsrechts und die Rezeption der westeuropäischen Rechtstheorien in Korea—mit Bezügen zum japanischen Recht' (2011) 15 *Journal of Japanese Law* 199.

[89] See Arts 162 et seq KCC.

Australian Consumer Law (ACL) came into effect, the Australian jurisdictions generally regulated warranty issues autonomously.[90] The common understanding was that non-conformity issues should lead to certain warranty remedies. But the respective rules were considerably flexible (in particular in B2B cases) and—even where mandatory (*note*: this was the case with respect to some B2C issues)—not necessarily homogeneously regulated. The ACL brought a partial change, because it widely harmonised the then existing B2C frameworks and comprehensively enshrined a strict, buyer-friendly warranty regime.[91] Section 64 ACL stipulates that the respective rules are mandatory.[92]

Part 3-2 Division 1 ACL ('Consumer guarantees') includes a broad list of statutory criteria that relate to the supply of goods and services, in principle reflecting the ideas behind implied and express terms as defined earlier in this chapter.[93] Part 5-4 Division 1 contains a catalogue of remedies a non-professional buyer may exercise against the professional seller. The buyer usually has the right to have the good repaired or replaced.[94] The choice rests, however, principally with the seller.[95] If neither of these remedies is of help, a buyer can return the good or ask for a price reduction.[96] The ACL further generally allows for seeking damages from the seller 'for any loss or damage suffered by the consumer because of the failure to comply'.[97] Possible claims are capped by the foreseeability of the damages.

Overall, the ACL introduces a relatively generous warranty scheme. In cases where consumers are entitled to reject the good, they can do so within a reasonable time of the date the failure would be expected to become apparent.[98] The term 'reasonable' is not defined further. In practice, courts decide what is reasonable on a case-by-case basis.[99] Another noteworthy feature is the safety net of manufacturer liability enshrined in section 271 ACL. It allows the buyer to seek damages in the event of breaches of a certain category—the 'acceptable quality' category under section 54 ACL—directly from the manufacturer if 'the guarantee is not complied with'.[100] Likely actions against manufacturers are subject to a period of three years, calculated from 'the day on which the affected person first became aware, or ought reasonably to have become aware, that the guarantee to which the action relates has not been complied with'.[101]

---

[90] Australian Government, 'The Australian Consumer Law—A Guide to Provisions' (2010) ix. The ACL was adopted as sch 2 to the Competition and Consumer Act 2010.

[91] For the sake of simplicity, the term 'warranty' is used here to refer to non-conformity issues. It should be noted, though, that the ACL differentiates between different non-conformity schemes and uses different terms depending on the particular issue, including guarantees, warranties and conditions.

[92] For details, see s 64(1) ACL.

[93] With respect to the supply of goods, see ss 54 to 59 ACL.

[94] s 259(2) ACL.

[95] s 261 ACL.

[96] s 259(3) ACL.

[97] s 259(4) ACL.

[98] s 262(2) ACL defines this period as 'the period from the time of the supply of the goods to the consumer within which it would be reasonable to expect the relevant failure to comply with a guarantee ... to become apparent'.

[99] Australian Government, 'The Australian Consumer Law—A guide to provisions' (2010) 52.

[100] s 271(1)(b) ACL.

[101] s 273 ACL.

D. Attempts to Harmonise Warranty Law at a Global Level—the Example of the United Nations Sales Convention on Contracts for the International Sale of Goods

The differences that can be found at the national level might be particularly problematic in transnational scenarios, especially if the stakeholders involved are not familiar with the respective conflict-of-law rules. To overcome possible trade obstacles caused by different warranty regulations, initiatives were taken to standardise the rules at a global level.[102] Arguably the most important project was completed in 1980 when the United Nations Convention on Contracts for the International Sale of Goods was signed (CISG; frequently also referred to as the 'Vienna Convention').

The CISG came into effect on 1 January 1988 and is relatively popular with national legislators. By late 2017 the Convention was ratified by nearly 90 parties, and only a handful of economic powers, including the UK and India, have not shown willingness to join.[103] With 101 articles, the CISG introduced a relatively broad way to deal with sales contracts.

Three important, general caveats have to be issued. First, the Convention enjoys national legislative status and must be explicitly excluded by the contractual parties if they do not want it to govern the transaction in question. Second, the framework only applies in cross-border cases. Third, it does not apply in B2C cases, but only in cases where both the seller and the buyer are professionals.

When it comes to material non-conformity issues, Article 35 CISG is the key basis for possible claims. The criteria generally follow the non-conformity elements adopted by most modern warranty regimes. The starting point for determining the conformity of the delivered good is whether it meets the specifications as outlined in the contract.[104] The provision adds objective criteria that can be compared with the implied warranty concepts used at the national level.[105]

Largely because the CISG was crafted as a B2B instrument, the regime differs from most mechanisms discussed earlier. Article 38(1) CISG, for example, obliges the buyer to 'examine the goods, or cause them to be examined, within as short a period as is practicable in the circumstances'. Pursuant to Article 39(1), the

> buyer [furthermore] loses the right to rely on a lack of conformity of the goods if he does not give notice to the seller specifying the nature of the lack of conformity within a reasonable time after he has discovered it or ought to have discovered it.

---

[102] For an early attempt, see, eg, the 1964 Hague Convention relating to a Uniform Law on the International Sale of Goods and its provisions on the breach of contracts.

[103] For a full status list, see treaties.un.org/pages/ViewDetails.aspx?src=TREATY&mtdsg_no=X-10&chapter=10&lang=en.

[104] Art 35(1) CISG.

[105] It does not use the term 'merchantability' though (as known in particular from the UCC). But it is the common understanding that the implied warranty phrase of Art 35(2)(a) CISG—which is generally followed by Art 2(2)(c) CSD—resembles the merchantable idea—see GW Jones, 'Warranties in International Sales: UN Convention on Contracts for the International Sale of Goods Compared to the US Uniform Commercial Code on Sales' (1989) 17 *International Business Lawyer* 497, 498.

The remedial system of the CISG principally comprises repair, replacement, price reduction, rescission and (culpability detached) compensation claims (limited by the foreseeability of the damage).[106] Conceptually there are, however, certain differences compared with traditional schemes. For example, the CISG prioritises repair over substitution and makes the latter (at the buyer's request) available only in cases of 'fundamental breach[es]'.[107]

One might be tempted to argue that the broad approval of the CISG by the vast majority of industrial powers has considerably improved the situation for professional sellers and buyers. Obviously, it is thus far the furthest-reaching result of standardisation of warranty-relevant questions. But this cannot hide the fact that the potential of the CISG is limited.

First—depending on the particular jurisdictions involved—the more or less significant differences in comparison with conventional regimes make it necessary for parties to examine the possible advantages and disadvantages of the CISG carefully before concluding a contract—something that some parties might want to avoid by excluding the applicability of the CISG.

Second, the framework only applies to cross-border transactions. This means that traders could (in cases where the CISG is available) benefit from a standardised statutory set of rules for (non-consumer) cross-border sales, but they would have to comply with a different set of rules in purely domestic cases—both (admittedly), of course, only on condition that the respective professional is not able to push his or her standardised terms and conditions through.

Third, the CISG does not affect B2C sales transactions. Hence, in particular, retailers might not be able to enjoy the standardisation effect of the CISG. Here, special mandatory rules would apply—regardless of whether the contract constitutes a domestic or cross-border transaction.

Fourth, the CISG is a non-mandatory instrument. Parties can exclude its application and rely on alternative (in practice arguably most likely on conventional) national sales law regimes, or autonomously create their own rules (mostly via their terms and conditions).[108] Actually, the reliance on the CISG is not as widespread as it might seem in practice.[109]

Nearly 30 years have passed since the CISG came into effect. Looking at the still widespread opposition of businesses to its regime, the Convention has still not realised its full potential. Only time will tell if the increasing significance of transnational transactions will bring about a change. However, the exclusion of B2C sales from its regime might require different or (at least) supplementary solutions.

---

[106] Arts 45–52 CISG.

[107] Art 46(2) and (3) CISG. But see also Art 48 with some special rules to remedy (inter alia) non-conformity. See further the limitation with respect to rescission in Art 49.

[108] One caveat has to be noted in this context. Parties who want to exclude the applicability of the CISG have to do so explicitly, bearing in mind that the rules enjoy the status of a national law—see Art 99(2) CISG. If, eg, a seller coming from country A wants to make the conventional sales law applicable and buyer B agrees then the contract should state this in a way comparable to the following: 'The law applicable to this contract is the law of country A with the exclusion of the CISG.'

[109] For comments, eg, from a German perspective, see F Ferrari (ed), *The CISG and Its Impact on National Legal Systems* (Munich, Sellier, 2008) 143, 147.

IV. The Phenomenon of Planned Obsolescence— a Contemporary Challenge for Warranty Law

A. What is Planned Obsolescence?

It is notable that, in more recent times, the sustainable use and usability of goods have gained importance in technological, socio-political, environmental, economic and general policy discussions. Some key questions are as follows. First, do technological advancements have—or should they have—an impact on the lifetime of products? Second, what are the consequences for the environment of a growing consumer society, and what can be done to balance interests in producing, selling, using and consuming goods, on the one hand, and protecting the environment for the sake of future genera- tions, on the other? Third—and arguably most heavily debated—is there a tendency to shorten the lifecycle of goods and, if so, what (from a legal perspective) can be done to respond to this? This third pillar is commonly referred to as the phenomenon of 'planned obsolescence'. To borrow the words of one of the present authors, it relates to 'strategies and techniques of premature product aging applied by producers and sellers for the purpose of making end users replace old products with new ones faster than they ordinarily would by shortening the time of their use'.[110]

Our short excursion in this section will focus on the second part of the third question—the legal dimension. We do not aim to answer the question whether planned obsolescence really exists. What we mean to do in this and the following subsections is to discuss the likely relevance of warranty law in responding to potential cases of planned obsolescence. Before we turn to this legal question, though, a brief outline of planned obsolescence follows.

The planned obsolescence debate originated (at the latest) in the 1920s with the break-up of the Phoebus cartel, which concerned the deliberate limitation of the life- cycle of light bulbs as agreed by leading manufacturers. Over the next few decades obsolescence discussions were primarily held in the US and—to a far lesser degree—in Europe.[111] Mainly as a result of environmental concerns (occasionally intensified by consumer protection concerns), calls to prevent—or, where prevention was not pos- sible, remedy—damage that was claimed to be the result of planned obsolescence have been growing ever since. The legal debates have clearly broadened and begun to tran- scend competition law considerations. The French example of 2015, of a revision of the national Consumer Code with an insertion of a specially designed penal provision to answer proven cases of planned obsolescence, can be named in this context to show

---

[110] Wrbka, n 3, 67.
[111] Early key publications in the field of planned obsolescence include B London, *Ending the Depression through Planned Obsolescence* (New York, 1932); V Packard, *The Hidden Persuaders* (New York, D McKay Co, 1957); V Packard, *The Waste Makers* (New York, D McKay Co, 1960).

how (some) legislators seek to broaden the regulatory framework beyond antitrust instruments.[112]

Roughly around the time the French policymakers discussed their anti-planned obsolescence strategy, the debate reached a broader stage in Europe when both the European Commission and the European Economic and Social Committee (EESC) voiced concerns that supported the critique. These two sources are of particular interest in the present context, because they were behind two of the first attempts to explicitly and comprehensively address warranty law as a possible answer to planned obsolescence.

In its 2013 comment on sustainable product use, the EESC shared the view that shortened product lifecycles might create environmental risks. To counter this, the EESC commented on possible tools, which explicitly included warranty claims.[113]

The Commission has traditionally shown great interest in crafting legislation that will support the sustainable, environmental-friendly development of the internal market.[114] In 2011 the Commission went one step further, when it had to respond to a series of parliamentary questions regarding planned obsolescence. It expressly mentioned the significance of warranty law in this context, and arrived at the conclusion that warranty law could be a primary safeguard.[115]

Compared with the 'popularity' of the planned obsolescence topic at the policy-making level, comments from within legal academia are—at the time of writing—still few and far between, in particular with respect to warranty law.[116] Looking at modern warranty regimes, it seems to be important to answer two questions in particular, in an attempt to comment on the positive views of the EESC and the Commission. First, do planned obsolescence cases, where proven, constitute potentially warranty law-relevant scenarios of contractual non-conformity? Second, and provided that the first question can be answered in the affirmative, would the existing warranty regimes be of any help in asserting the buyer's interests?[117]

---

[112] Art L213-4-1(I) and (II) of the French *Code de la consommation* reads as follows: 'Planned obsolescence is defined as any measure with the intent to conceptually reduce the operating life of a good for economic considerations'; 'It is punishable with two years of imprisonment and a fine of euro 300,000' (authors' translation).

[113] European Economic and Social Committee, 'Towards more sustainable consumption: industrial product lifetimes and restoring trust through consumer information' [2014] OJ C67/23 at point 1.9.

[114] See, in particular, Directive 2002/96/EC, [2003] OJ L37/24; Directive 2008/98/EC, [2008] OJ L312/3; Directive 2009/125/EC, [2009] OJ L285/10; Directive 2010/30/EU, [2010] OJ L153/1.

[115] Commission reply to Parliamentary questions nos E-001284/2011, E-002875/2011 and E-004273/2011, www.europarl.europa.eu/sides/getAllAnswers.do?reference=E-2011-004273&language=EN.

[116] For notable exceptions, see H Koziol, *Obsoleszenzen im österreichischen Recht* (Wien, Jan Sramek Verlag, 2016); R Gildeggen, 'Vorzeitiger Verschleiß und die Verjährung von kaufrechtlichen Mängelgewährleistungsansprüchen' in T Brönneke and A Wechsler (eds), *Obsoleszenz interdisziplinär—Vorzeitiger Verschleiß aus Sicht von Wissenschaft und Praxis* (Baden Baden, Nomos, 2015) 269; G Wortmann and P Schimikowski, 'Geplanter Produktverschleiß und bürgerliches Recht' (1985) 16 *ZIP—Zeitschrift für Wirtschaftsrecht* 978; Wrbka, n 3.

[117] On a different occasion one of the present authors commented on these questions from an Austrian perspective—Wrbka, n 3, 68–75. The following subsections are based on the general observations made therein and add a comparative perspective to outline the potential of and challenges for warranty-based approaches towards planned obsolescence.

B. Warranty Law and Planned Obsolescence

i. Planned Obsolescence as a Potentially Relevant Warranty Case?

At the outset of every warranty analysis stands the question whether the delivered good is in conformity with the contractual obligation.[118] As a basic common principle one can conclude that the decisive contractual criteria would usually either be explicitly stated in the contract, or could be derived from the particular purpose of the contract. We commented on these two issues further in section III.A.i of this chapter, in the context of express and implied terms. For the purpose of simplicity, we shall refer to warranty-relevant contractual non-conformity issues as 'warranty-relevant defects'.

Looking at the phenomenon of planned obsolescence, one should note that the concept is remarkably broad. Classifying possible lifecycle-shortening strategies into different groups might be necessary to identify those activities that might constitute warranty-relevant defects. There is no common agreement on the concrete categories, but the early three-fold categorisation introduced by Vance Packard, 'obsolescence of desirability', 'obsolescence of function' and 'obsolescence of quality', might help to enhance understanding of the underlying considerations.[119] Obsolescence of desirability refers to cases in which users replace goods with new ones, 'persuaded' by successful marketing strategies that do not touch upon qualitative issues. One example might be purchasing a new car (although the current car still runs flawlessly) only because a famous singer drives that model in a commercial.

Obsolescence of function more closely relates to qualitative features and can be explained with objective arguments. However—unlike in our third category, outlined below—the purchased good still functions without any problems. Here the reason why users would replace goods is that the newer goods (at least allegedly) contain advanced features. A built-in camera of a new generation mobile phone might, for example, have higher resolution than its predecessor. From a warranty perspective, neither desirability nor function-related obsolescence cases could be of relevance. The purchased good would still be in conformity with the contract and not show any material defect.

Things might look different, however, when it comes to obsolescence of quality. This group comprises scenarios in which the lifecycle ends as a result of product aging. The million-dollar question is whether a particular defect relates to ordinary wear and tear, ie to the use of a good for such time and intensity as is generally to be expected. Only if this is *not* the case, ie if the lifecycle ends prematurely, could the end of the good's fitness for use be of relevance in the context of a warranty, because in such a case the good could not be used for as long as one might reasonably expect. In practice, determining whether the usability of a good comes to an end at a time that can be generally expected is a complicated endeavour. Nevertheless, applying objective criteria that take into account subjective circumstances, such as the intensity of use,

---

[118] See, eg Art 2(2) CSD: 'The seller must deliver goods to the consumer which are in conformity with the contract of sale.'

[119] Packard, n 111, 66–67.

can reveal the actual warranty relevance of the qualitatively caused end of use of a good (where given). In the majority of cases the particular assessment involves technical expertise, as well as comparative data on what must be considered as ordinary wear and tear, on the one hand, and unusual, ie warranty-relevant, wear and tear, on the other. One would have to look at a group of comparable goods, and also take into account technological advancements. Furthermore, as shown elsewhere, a decline in the overall (quality-related) lifetime of goods is not necessarily justifiable.[120] Eventually a holistic analysis of the particular circumstances might be needed to draw a firm conclusion.

ii. Planned Obsolescence and the Issue of Time

Cases of planned obsolescence represent a special group of material defects. Bearing in mind that obsolescence cases relate to the shortening of product lifecycles, relevant scenarios fall within the category of latent defects, ie defects that cannot be detected at the time of delivery, but which manifest in the course of time. Even technical experts would usually not be able to predict the exact life of a good at the time of its delivery.[121]

Arguably the most significant challenge in any attempt to utilise warranty mechanisms to respond to cases of planned obsolescence is linked to the issue of time prescription. When it comes to capping the possibility to exercise warranty rights, the underlying general question is how to preserve the possible defendant's interest in having certainty, while giving the possible claimant sufficient time to clarify the situation and prepare for a possible claim. Traditionally, legislators have taken different approaches. Prior to the implementation of the CSD, some EU Member States, such as Austria and Germany, for example, prioritised the seller's position by applying a considerably shorter warranty period of only six months for movables, while other jurisdictions adopted longer periods. To satisfy the wish for increased foreseeability Article 5(1) CSD and (most of) the implementing jurisdictions link the commencement of the warranty period to the delivery of the good (or—where relevant—the passing of risk).

From a practical perspective, one of the key problems of nearly every planned obsolescence case is that the defect might manifest relatively late. Whether or not the buyer can exercise possible warranty remedies depends on the particular solution available under the contract-governing jurisdiction. In particular, from a transnational perspective, arguably the most complicating factor is the diversity of the possibly applicable rules. Let us, for example, recall Article 5(1) of the minimum harmonised CSD, which states as follows:

> The seller shall be held liable ... where the lack of conformity becomes apparent within two years as from delivery of the goods. If, under national legislation, the rights ... are subject to

---

[120] S Wrbka, *Geplante Obsoleszenz aus Sicht des Gewährleistungsrechts* (Graz, NWV, 2015) 59.
[121] Submitting the particular good to a stress test might provide an answer. But it would bring the lifetime of the good to an end without the buyer being able to use it anymore. Hence, requiring such a test would not be justifiable.

a limitation period, that period shall not expire within a period of two years from the time of delivery.

This two-year period leaves room for both interpretation and leeway. As a general rule, national legislators are obliged to allow for the launching of possible actions (at least) for two years from the time of delivery. In practice Member States have taken different approaches. Some Member States apply a basically strict rule via the introduction of a two-year period (for claiming warranty rights)—at least with respect to movables.[122] Others offer a buyer-friendlier solution. One approach is to enshrine longer periods. Both the Irish and the English sales regimes, for example, apply a longer, general period of six years also in cases of contractual non-conformity.[123] A different approach is taken by a handful of Member States that link commencement of the limitation period to the detectability of defects.[124] A particularly complicated solution can, for example, be found in Austria. Under the default rule of its Civil Code, the warranty period would commence with the delivery of the good in the case of material defects, and at the moment the buyer becomes aware of the defect in case of rights-related defects.[125] Commentators explain this differentiation with the argument that rights-related defects usually cannot be detected when using the good.[126] Case law, in principle, extended this rule and now also applies the detectability rule, in a slightly modified way, to latent material defects in cases where the non-conformity relates to product specifications on which the parties have explicitly agreed.[127] Latent material defects relating to implied terms would, however, still follow the default 'delivery rule'.

Harmonisation attempts that go beyond the CSD have largely failed. Both the DCFR and the CESL allowed for a certain amount of flexibility. The DCFR enshrined a basic three-year prescription period, but took account of some subjective conditions that might ultimately lead to an extension of the time within which it would be possible to claim warranty rights.[128] The CESL generally followed this example, but returned to a shorter general period of two years, which—via Article 180 CESL—was linked to subjective commencement criteria similar to those found in the DCFR counterpart.[129] However, as explained earlier, neither the DCFR nor the CESL was put into practice.

---

[122] See, eg, § 933(1) of the Austrian Civil Code (*Allgemeines Bürgerliches Gesetzbuch*, ABGB).

[123] Statute of Limitations 1957, s 11(1) and Limitation Act 1980, s 5. (The situation is slightly different in Scotland, where a five-year limitation applies pursuant to the Prescription and Limitation (Scotland) Act 1973, s 6.) For some non-EU examples of longer periods, see, eg, Gildeggen, n 116, 279.

[124] Schulte-Nölke et al (eds), n 39, 445, where the authors point out that Belgium, Finland, Hungary and the Netherlands are among those countries that utilise later commencement events.

[125] § 933(1) sentence 3 ABGB.

[126] R Welser and B Jud, *Die neue Gewährleistung* (Vienna, Manz, 2000) § 933 ABGB Recital 5, with reference to H Krejci, *Reform des Gewährleistungsrechts* (Vienna, Verlag der österreichischen Staatsdruckerei, 1994) 136.

[127] The main difference from the rights-related defect rule is that under the first, it is the point of objective detectability that triggers the period, whereas in rights-related cases it is the actual, ie subjective, point of becoming aware of the non-conformity.

[128] Arts III-7:201 and III-7:301 DCFR. Art III-7:307 adds an absolute limitation by unconditionally capping the warranty at 10 years.

[129] Arts 179 and 180 CESL.

Unlike other instruments, the CSIG is considerably reserved when it comes to the prescription of time limits for possible claims. The most significant exception relates to notification of defects. Article 39 CISG provides as follows:

(1)   The buyer loses the right to rely on a lack of conformity of the goods if he does not give notice to the seller specifying the nature of the lack of conformity within a reasonable time after he has discovered it or ought to have discovered it.

(2)   In any event, the buyer loses the right to rely on a lack of conformity of the goods if he does not give the seller notice thereof at the latest within a period of two years from the date on which the goods were actually handed over to the buyer, unless this time-limit is inconsistent with a contractual period of guarantee.

However, as long as buyers comply with this notification obligation, possible warranty remedy claims are still preserved under the CISG regime. Whether or not buyers could still submit a claim would be answered by the relevant time limitation rule of the applicable national regime.[130]

Overall one has to note that bringing an action might prove significantly difficult in cases of planned obsolescence. Many jurisdictions apply time limitation schemes, under which the materialisation of a warranty-relevant obsolescence defect might come too late to allow the buyer to assert his or her position.

V. Concluding Remarks on the Challenges for Warranty Law from a Transnational Perspective

Contractual breaches, in the particular case of qualitative non-conformity issues, undeniably represent a highly relevant area of law in practice. Professional sellers commonly aim to limit their potential liability in their terms and conditions. This strategy might—unless mandatory rules apply—make sense, in particular in a transnational context. As we have pointed out in this chapter, though, the existing national warranty frameworks are fragmented. Issues such as the availability of remedies, limitation periods, possible claims for damages (which might include consequential damages) and the range of potentially liable parties are among those matters that are regulated in significantly different ways.

Endeavours to harmonise national regimes have been of assistance only to a very limited extent. The CSD, for example, introduced a number of minimum common denominators. However, its scope—it only affects B2C transactions—and its incompleteness, coupled with its underlying minimum harmonisation approach, leave ample room for national discretion. The CISG, on the other hand, is of direct significance only with respect to B2B transactions. But, just like the CSD, the CISG does not

---

[130] In a similar vein, eg, I Saenger, 'CISG Art. 45' in F Ferrari et al (eds), *Internationales Vertragsrecht*, 2nd edn (Munich, CH Beck, 2012) CISG Art 45, Recital 11.

provide for a conclusive scheme. As pointed out earlier, clarification of questions relating to the time limits applicable to possible claims, for example, is left to the applicable private international law rules in the particular case. Furthermore, contractual parties are free to derogate from the rules of the CISG, or to exclude the regime altogether. Looking at the legislative interests of national legislators, further-reaching standardisation of warranty schemes might—at least for the time being—be extremely difficult.

From a transnational business perspective, sellers and buyers have also to be aware of the fact that in B2C scenarios, warranty law is usually highly characterised by the mandatory nature of the respective rules, in the sense that the standard enshrined cannot be deviated from to the non-professional buyer's detriment. In practice, this might further increase the need, in particular, for professional sellers to familiarise themselves with a complex system of fragmented laws and conflict-of-law rules. The need to clarify the particular situation with regard to the applicable rules in the case at hand might arguably overly challenge not only the average seller, but also the average lawyer. In light of this complex situation, it is fair to consider transnational warranty law as one of those areas that would benefit from comprehensive support from stakeholders with considerable expertise in transnational warranty law. To achieve the desired effect, this third-party support should ideally be offered in plain, simple and intelligible language, being easily and promptly available to parties who seek to gather information. This would clearly improve the overall level of legal certainty in any situation.

Last, but not least, as far as planned obsolescence is concerned, we can partly confirm that warranty law could generally be of significance to answer those cases that we refer to as involving 'obsolescence of quality'. However, depending on the applicable jurisdiction, having recourse to warranty rules might be of greater or lesser effect—regardless of the primary question of proving the existence of a warranty-relevant instance of non-conformity. Arguably the biggest issue relates to the time limitation of possible claims. In many instances warranty-relevant defects would manifest too late to allow for a legal action. Detailed overviews of existing schemes, with respect to the limitation of warranty claims in cases of latent defects, might be helpful to clarify the true potential of warranty law.[131]

Selected Further Reading

Bradgate, R and Twigg-Flesner, C, *Blackstone's Guide to Consumer Sales and Associated Guarantees* (Oxford, Oxford University Press, 2003)

---

[131] Possible bases to build on are the more general, but geographically limited overviews of the situation in the EU in the *Consumer Law Compendium* and in ECC-Net, 'Commercial Warranties: Are They Worth the Money?—Summary' (2014) 16–17, www.europe-consommateurs.eu/fileadmin/user_upload/eu-consommateurs/PDFs/PDF_EN/REPORT-_GUARANTEE/Summary-report_tableaux_EN.pdf. Neither of them, however, explicitly deals with the issue of latent defects.

Brönneke, T and Wechsler, A (eds), *Obsoleszenz interdisziplinär: Vorzeitiger Verschleiß aus Sicht von Wissenschaft und Praxis* (Baden-Baden, Nomos, 2015)

Bucher, S, *Gewährleistung im Gemeinsamen Europäischen Kaufrecht* (Baden-Baden, Nomos, 2016)

Carter, CL, Van Alst, JW, Sheldon, JA and De Armond, E, *Consumer Warranty Law: Lemon Laws, Magnuson-Moss, UCC, Manufactured Home, and Other Warranty Statutes*, 5th edn (Boston, MA, National Consumer Law Center, 2015)

Di Matteo, LA and Hogg, M (eds), *Comparative Contract Law: British and American Perspectives* (Oxford, Oxford University Press, 2016) 347–78

Graziano, TK, *Comparative Contract Law: Cases, Materials and Exercises* (Basingstoke, Palgrave MacMillan, 2009) Case 6

Kruisinga, SA, *(Non-)Conformity in the 1980 UN Convention on the International Sale of Goods: A Uniform Concept?* (Antwerp, Intersentia, 2014)

Leisinger, BK, *Fundamental Breach Considering Non-Conformity of the Goods* (Munich, Sellier, 2007)

Pridgen, D and Marsh, GA, *Consumer Protection Law in a Nutshell*, 4th edn (St Paul, MN, West Academic, 2016)

Reitz, JC, 'A History of Cutoff Rules as a Form of Caveat Emptor: Part I—The 1980 UN Convention on the International Sale of Goods' (1988) 36 *American Journal of Comparative Law* 437

Reitz, JC, 'History of Cutoff Rules as a Form of Caveat Emptor: Part II—From Roman Law to the Modern Civil and Common Law' (1989) 37 *American Journal of Comparative Law* 247

Rohwer, CD, Skrocki, AM and Malloy, MP, *Contracts in a Nutshell*, 8th edn (St Paul, MN, West Academic, 2017)

Schwenzer, I, Hachem, P and Kee, C, *Global Sales and Contract Law* (Oxford, Oxford University Press, 2012)

Tepper, PR, *The Law of Contracts and the Uniform Commercial Code*, 3rd edn (Boston, MA, Cengage Learning, 2014)

Twigg-Flesner, C, *Consumer Product Guarantees* (Aldershot, Ashgate, 2003)

White, JJ and Summers, RS, *Uniform Commercial Code*, 6th edn (St Paul, MN, West Academic, 2000)

Wrbka, S, *Geplante Obsoleszenz aus Sicht des Gewährleistungsrechts* (Graz, NWV, 2015)

Zhou, Q and DiMatteo, LA, 'Three Sales Laws and the Common Law of Contracts' in LA Di Matteo and M Hogg (eds), *Comparative Contract Law: British and American Perspectives* (Oxford, Oxford University Press, 2016) 347

4

Compensatory Collective Redress and Alternative Dispute Resolution

I. Outline

Commercial actions and transactions inherently bear the risk of leading to legal disputes. In most cases, disputes revolve around two parties only. In modern times litigation has traditionally dominated the landscape to resolve such conflicts. However, conventional litigation might not always be in the best interests of injured parties who wish to get their legal claims enforced. Cases could be complex and affect more than two stakeholders, or involve comparatively low amounts that bear no reasonable relation to the costs of litigation. In this sense, at least two of Adrian Zuckerman's three justice cornerstones—time and cost—could be seen as obstacles to rights enforcement.[1]

More recently, additional mechanisms have gained momentum in an attempt to simplify the process and to answer to concerns and social developments, which include mass consumption and the wish to save time and money. The underlying rationale for the introduction of special procedures and devices can be seen in the fact that traditional litigation can be of help whenever (only) few parties are affected and the litigants are confident enough to take the case to a court. There are, however, scenarios that might require a different solution. For example, things could become more complicated in cases where a greater number of people are affected (and a conventional joinder of parties makes no sense or is technically not possible). Reviewing every single case individually might put a too heavy burden on the judiciary. This in return would have a negative effect on other cases that are waiting to be resolved,

---

[1] AAS Zuckerman, 'Justice in Crisis: Comparative Dimensions of Civil Procedure' in AAS Zuckerman (ed), *Civil Justice in Crisis, Comparative Perspectives of Civil Procedure* (Oxford, Oxford University Press, 1999) 31, 47, where Zuckerman summarises 'the three dimensions of justice—truth, time and cost'.

because court resources are limited. Practical issues could also arise in situations in which the amounts in dispute are too low to make it worthwhile to launch an action. Furthermore, even if it made sense to pursue a claim, parties might still refrain from using the ordinary courts for different reasons. Enforcement-seeking stakeholders might be too inexperienced or too afraid of resorting to conventional litigation. They might lack the financial resources required to go to court or to instruct a lawyer. They could be sceptical of the often time-consuming resolution process, or of the possible lack of special and/or non-legal expertise of career judges. Eventually, the lack of confidentiality in litigation might add to parties' reservations.

As a result of this, various instruments have been crafted to answer some of the concerns surrounding conventional litigation. This chapter outlines and discusses two of the more popular forms—compensatory collective litigation and non-litigious mechanisms, ie alternative dispute resolution (ADR). Both aim to remedy some of the alleged shortcomings of conventional litigation and have been designed and refined in many different ways around the globe. The examples set out in this chapter will help to facilitate understanding of the mechanisms, their likely advantages and possible disadvantages.

The analysis will be divided into two main parts—one focusing on compensatory collective actions and the other on ADR. Both parts will discuss the development of pertinent mechanisms in general, before commenting on some features and trends in different jurisdictions. The chapter ends with a discussion of pending issues, challenges and possibilities, in particular with respect to cross-border scenarios.

II. Collective Actions

A. Collective Actions and the Access-to-Justice Project

In the 1970s an international group of legal scholars, led by Mauro Cappelletti and Bryant Garth, conducted research on access to justice at the University of Florence and the European University Institute in Florence, Italy. The research focused on mechanisms to get legal interests enforced more efficiently and effectively. The Florence Access-to-Justice Project (Florence Project) identified three 'waves of access to justice'. These waves chronologically defined the instruments implemented and utilised in different jurisdictions to facilitate dispute resolution.

The first access to justice wave discussed financial obstacles, examining procedures to enable the poor to go to court. This can be considered the most genuine form of achieving access to justice. Cappelletti and his colleagues did not stop at this point, however. They realised that enforcement issues are more complex, and in many cases go beyond monetary barriers (in a narrow sense).

The second wave looked at the group of 'diffuse interests', a term that the Florence Project defined as 'collective or fragmented interests, such as those in clean air or consumer protection'.[2] The research showed that stakeholders who suffered damage refrained from going to court not primarily because of purely financial concerns, but as a result of a mix that—in addition to a lack of financial resources—most notably comprised factors such as a lack of time and insufficient legal experience. Individuals might think that it was not worth going to court because the amount in dispute did not stand in justifiable relation to the time that needed to be spent in seeking a lawyer's advice. They might have reservations regarding the courts, because of a lack of legal knowledge and experience. Furthermore, even if individuals were willing to launch proceedings, they could be better off if they formed groups and joined with other affected stakeholders who had suffered similar harm.

The third access to justice wave added one more layer. The Florence Project grouped more recent attempts to ease the burden for right-seeking parties under the 'access-to-justice approach'.[3] This term referred to methods that went beyond financial support and collective redress. Prominent examples include specialised courts, accelerated procedures and non-litigious forms of dispute settlement—ADR. We shall return to the last of these in the second half of this chapter.

B. Collective Redress in General

The Florence Project confirmed the suggestion that conventional litigation failed to serve the purpose of achieving access to justice in certain situations. One of these scenarios concerned cases in which a multitude of individuals suffered comparable damage. Substantiated claims could stay unpursued, in particular if the thresholds for launching individual actions were too high.

At the beginning of the new millennium, Rachael Mulheron published a comparative study on one of the prototypes of compensatory collective redress—class actions in common law countries. In the course of her analysis, she delved deeper into the subject and pointed out that collective actions, in general, served a number of functions that would add value to ordinary litigation. Mulheron showed that collective redress (also within the group of common law jurisdictions) could take different forms, but that they all principally rested on five interrelated, common 'objectives'. In addition to enhanced access to justice—the second wave of the Florence Project—she identified the objectives of 'principle and predictability', 'proportionality, not perfection', 'judicial economy' and 'balancing judicial activism and personal autonomy'.

Mulheron's analysis breaks the most widely known collective redress characteristic, access to justice, into four sub-pillars. The first sub-pillar—'provid[ing] the substantive law with teeth'—is a commonly found argument in any attempt to improve the enforcement of substantive law. Anthony Ogus, for example, uses the same rationale in the context of the EU's 'better regulation' approach, as do Geraint Howells

---

[2] M Cappelletti and B Garth, 'Access to Justice' in M Cappelletti and B Garth (eds), *Access to Justice— A World Survey, Book 1* (Alphen aan den Rijn, Slijthoff and Noordhoff, 1978) 1, 18.

[3] ibid, 49.

and Stephen Weatherill with respect to consumer law.[4] Simply put, even the best substantive laws would not be of help if parties did not comply with them and if there were no instruments to remedy that. The second access to justice sub-pillar refers to the key argument of the second Florence Project wave—reducing individual costs (understood as partial costs in relation to collective rights enforcement). It can be understood as comprising strategies to optimise the balance between prospective wins and the financial burden in taking legal steps. Mulheron's third characteristic adds a psychological argument—strengthening the plaintiffs' negotiation power. Individual claims grouped together would weigh stronger than if one individual had to act alone. Fourth, courts could decide parallel cases in one single procedure. Hence, the judiciary would be disburdened and plaintiffs could expect faster decisions.

Some of Mulheron's additional, complementing main objectives of collective redress can be understood as more precise expressions of her 'access to justice' subcategories. Enhanced judicial economy, for example, stands for an improved, more effective and efficient judiciary as a consequence of bundling individual claims into one single procedure. This, according to Mulheron, would have the positive effect of going easy on judicial resources. Courts would not be paralysed by an abundant number of separate claims. The German Telekom case, with close to 17,000 shareholders having taken individual action, discussed further in section II.D.ii, can be understood as a prime example in this regard. In particular in scenarios where the respective case is final and would not allow for subsequent litigation by other affected parties—we shall discuss this further in section II.C in the context of 'opting out'—court efficiency could have a positive effect even for the defendants, because they would not have to fear (much) additional time-consuming litigation.

Collective actions are widely believed to balance the wish for 'perfection' with proportionality and appropriateness considerations. In this sense, Mulheron explains that collective redress requires compromises to be made. With separate, individual actions, defendants would have the opportunity to voice their arguments directly. This, however, as explained with regard to court efficiency, negotiation power and cost issue concerns, comes at a price it does not always make sense to pay. Joining a collective action complaint, on the other hand, puts most group members into the role of spectators. Nevertheless, it increases the chances of receiving compensation that, in terms of lawsuit effectivity and efficiency, can be considered proportionate and appropriate (enough), and thus outweighs the possible disadvantages of staying argumentative and litigation passive.

Lastly, collective actions follow principles that serve the wish for overall predictability, both in terms of procedural steps and with respect to the possible outcome of the particular case. Additionally, comparative research and the exchange of experience between jurisdictions have allowed for the establishment of clear procedural rules

---

[4] A Ogus, 'Better Regulation—Better Enforcement' in S Weatherill (ed), *Better Regulation* (Oxford, Hart Publishing, 2007) 121, where the author argues that '[d]evising "better regulation" without sufficient attention to the enforcement dimension is unsatisfactory'. G Howells and S Weatherill, *Consumer Protection Law*, 2nd edn (Aldershot, Ashgate, 2005) 660, where Howells and Weatherill conclude that '[c]onsumer rights are only as effective as their enforcement'.

to guide the stakeholders through the different phases of a collective action lawsuit. This has the positive effect of preventing the misuse of collective redress.

It has to be noted, though, that not all commentators agree on these collective action objectives. The phenomena of 'blackmail settlements' and 'fake group actions', for example, can be used as counter-arguments against (at least) some forms of collective redress—we shall return to both in a moment. Nevertheless, collective actions have increasingly enjoyed popularity around the globe, and although they have not been implemented exhaustively, they have become of greater significance over the past few decades. With the following examples, we first focus on selected common law jurisdictions—the birthplace of class actions. Subsequently we discuss trends in the EU, in particular because of the heavy debates pursued there more recently.

C. Collective Redress in Common Law Countries

Modern compensatory collective redress has its roots in the common law. More precisely, the US-style class action, as enshrined in Rule 23 of the Federal Rules of Civil Procedure (FRCP), can be considered the first modern, comprehensive collective redress scheme.

Dating back to the 1930s, but substantively revised in 1966, Rule 23(a) FRCP lays out the underlying framework and ideas behind US-style class actions. In principle, four conditions have to be fulfilled to allow for a class action: numerosity, commonality, typicality and adequate representation. In a very simplified way, these can be outlined as follows:

— The group of affected individuals must be large enough not to allow for a joinder of parties, a scenario in which all group members would enjoy party status.
— The claims have to be similar in a sense that they are bound together by common questions of law or fact.
— The claim(s) of the representative party/parties has/have to be typical of the group claims.
— The representative party/parties should be competent enough to 'fairly and adequately protect the interests of the class'.

Rule 23(b) to Rule 23(h) FRCP refine the class action procedure. This includes provisions on different types of class actions ((b)), on how to certify the actions and notify class members ((c)), on how to conduct the action ((d)), on possible settlements ((e)) and appeals ((f)), the class counsel ((g)), and fees and costs ((h)).

Rule 23 FRCP has served as a basis for federal and State class actions in the US,[5] and as a model for collective redress schemes in many other common law jurisdictions. Australia and some Canadian provinces (with Ontario and British Columbia

---

[5] See, eg, the reference in the context of private securities class litigation pursuant to 15 USC § 78u-4(1): 'The provisions of this subsection shall apply in each private action arising under this chapter that is brought as a *plaintiff class action pursuant to the Federal Rules of Civil Procedure*.' (emphasis added)

leading the way) have followed, with revised systems in the early 1990s. Although the mechanisms (to a greater or lesser extent) differ from one another, they rest on similar ideas that basically incorporate the common objectives mentioned earlier. Most notably—and in contrast to, for example, most European jurisdictions—common law collective redress tools are mainly based on opting out. This means that claims that are found to be common are bound together and form part of the same class and lawsuit, unless notified class members submit a notice (usually to the competent court) that they mean to drop out of the class and preserve the right to take action individually. Opting out has to be understood as the opposite to opting in, the predominant (but as we shall see shortly, not necessarily exclusive) approach taken by those European jurisdictions that have implemented collective action schemes. Under the latter regime, ie opting in, individual claims are litigated as part of the class only if the affected parties agree to join. Put differently, while allegedly harmed individuals have to become active to have their claims litigated in a collective/class action lawsuit under an opting-in scheme, in an opting-out scenario they have to take action (only) if they do not want to join.

Common law jurisdictions chose opting out as their underlying class formation scheme arguably because it can be considered the more authentic form of effective and efficient group action. With the help of opt out, a greater number of similar claims can be grouped together, which can have some positive effects for plaintiffs. Most notably, it helps to litigate cases that otherwise might stay unpursued due to passive individuals. The plaintiff advantages might, however, pose a significant risk to defendants—and in some cases could even impair the plaintiffs' interests.

Two scenarios in particular should be pointed out in this context. In the literature, one can find the term 'blackmail settlements' to refer to the first of these. Commentators note that US-style class actions lower the motivational threshold to launch actions, while allowing for aggregated amounts that (in particular in combination with occasionally excessive punitive damages—a type of punishment for non-compliance with the law) would (irrespective of the substantive merits of the plaintiffs' arguments) put disproportionate pressure on businesses to settle cases to avoid higher costs. Christopher Hodges summarises the business side's concerns as follows:

> Blackmail settlements are said to occur where claims that have poor or uncertain merit are settled because it is commercially cheaper for a defendant to do so, in order to avoid the unrecoverable costs of defence, business disruption, adverse publicity and damage to shareholder value.[6]

In similar vein, Roger Van den Bergh and Sonja Keske claim that 'class actions might be launched with the aim to harm the reputation of a company'.[7]

'Fake collective actions' stand at the opposite side of the spectrum. Businesses afraid of high compensation claims could 'cooperate' with the lead plaintiff in a way

---

[6] C Hodges, *The Reform of Class and Representative Actions in European Legal Systems—A New Framework for Collective Redress in Europe* (Oxford, Hart Publishing, 2008) 132, fn 5.
[7] R Van den Bergh and S Keske, 'Rechtsökonomische Aspekte der Sammelklage' in M Casper et al (eds), *Auf dem Weg zu einer europäischen Sammelklage?* (Munich, Sellier European Law Publishers, 2009) 17, 31 (authors' translation).

that would reduce the amounts to be paid below a justifiable amount. Willem van Boom and Marco Loos refer to such actions as having 'the hidden purpose of failing the claim, thus freeing the tortfeasor from otherwise successful individual claims'.[8] In particular in the case of opting out, where the number of group members is usually larger than in opt-in cases, the number of poorly-compensated individuals could be significantly high, with only very few (if any) individuals having the possibility to launch separate actions (namely, only those who dropped out).

To minimise the risk of abuse of collective actions, common law jurisdictions have introduced a number of instruments that, in most cases, put the courts in a prominent position. The mechanisms differ regionally, but in most instances they include the following: an initial claim-screening process ('certification'), court approval of settlements, court-appointed class counsel and comprehensive notification procedures with respect to class members. Nevertheless, criticism against opt out remains strong. In particular in civil law countries, policymakers and legislators have remained sceptical of the possible advantages of opt out over opt in.

D. Collective Redress in the EU

i. Collective Redress at the Pan-EU Level

In the EU, compensatory collective redress is a rather more recent item on the political agenda. This does not mean, however, that collective redress is not of significance in the EU. Actually, the EU serves as a prime example in discussion of contemporary collective redress, as European commentaries have been dominating the debate more recently.

At the pan-EU level, collective redress has been used for roughly two decades, primarily in the form of non-compensatory—at least not directly compensatory— tools. In this sense, the 1998 Injunctions Directive[9] can be viewed as the first, more comprehensive attempt to benefit harmed individuals as a group. It tried to introduce a mechanism to stop unlawful business behaviour in business-to-consumer (B2C) situations by allowing specially designated bodies—the Member States could choose between mandating public bodies or private institutions, or opt for both—to seek the end of unlawful practices with the help of injunctions.[10] The instruments were, however, of limited effect, largely because they did not include compensation claims. Stakeholders who suffered damage as a result of unlawful business practices could, of course, try to get individual compensation. But this is/was not part of the proceedings offered under the non-compensatory redress schemes.

---

[8] W van Boom and MBM Loos, 'Effective Enforcement of Consumer Law in Europe; Private, Public, and Collective Mechanisms' in W van Boom and MBM Loos (eds), *Collective Enforcement of Consumer Law: Securing Compliance in Europe through Private Group Action and Public Authority Intervention* (Groningen, Europa Law Publishing, 2007) 229, 242.

[9] Directive 1998/27/EC, [1998] OJ L166/51.

[10] Comparable yet narrower instruments can be found in sectoral legislation. The Unfair Contract Terms Directive (Directive 93/13/EEC, [1993] OJ L95/29), eg, included the possibility of answering the use of illegal contractual provisions.

Over the years debates on the possible introduction of compensatory collective redress mechanisms have intensified. At the time of writing, there is no pan-EU compensatory collective redress scheme, but compensatory collective redress has—as will be seen in the next subsection—been implemented autonomously by several Member States, although in different ways. The differences between the national approaches are sometimes massive, which makes it difficult to deal with the collective redress situation in the EU without making some underlying observations.

Put simply, one can differentiate between three larger categories of collective redress (when focusing on the basic composition on the plaintiff side): group actions, representative actions and test cases. The first two basically follow the same idea: individual claims are bundled together and brought to court in one single procedure. Schemes might vest private bodies, public authorities and/or private individuals with the standing to sue. The decisive difference between group and representative actions is to be seen in the enforcement procedure of successful litigation. While it is for the (lead) plaintiff to enforce a judgment in the case of group actions, group members can individually enforce their shares in the representative action scenario. In the instance of test cases, one case is singled out and litigated while the others wait for a decision in the test case procedure. It should be noted that in most jurisdictions, a test case ruling does not have a directly binding effect in parallel cases and can 'only' be used as a supporting argument.[11]

Generally speaking, compensatory collective redress in the EU is—in particular compared with US-style class actions—a more recent phenomenon. Over the years, more than half of the EU Member States have developed national compensatory collective redress schemes. At the pan-EU level, however, compensatory collective redress has not yet been implemented, although the topic has been heavily discussed at both the political and the academic levels.

Pertinent discussions originated in the field of antitrust law. The wish was to guarantee and stimulate fair competition with the help of additional, collective devices that would allow for skimming off unlawfully gained profits. Soon after the publication of the Green Paper on damages actions for breaches of EC antitrust rules in 2005,[12] the European Commission expanded its focus and included consumer issues in the compensatory collective redress debate.[13] In 2008, the Commission presented both a White Paper on damages actions for breaches of EC antitrust rules and a Green Paper on consumer (compensatory) collective redress.[14] Parallel to these political developments, compensatory collective redress has gained more and more attention in legal academia, where an abundant number of events and publications have been the consequence.[15]

---

[11] For an exception in the form of a semi-lateral effect (ie binding only if the test case is successful), see, eg, the Greek test case model.

[12] European Commission, Green Paper on damages actions for breach of the EC antitrust rules, 19 December 2005, COM(2005) 672 final.

[13] European Commission, EU Consumer Policy Strategy 2007–2013—Empowering consumers, enhancing their welfare, effectively protecting them, 13 March 2007, COM(2007) 99 final, 5 and 11.

[14] European Commission, White Paper on damages actions for breach of the EC antitrust rules, 2 April 2008, COM(2008) 165 final; European Commission, Green Paper on consumer collective redress, 27 November 2008, COM(2008) 794 final.

[15] See S Wrbka, *European Consumer Access to Justice Revisited* (Cambridge, Cambridge University Press) 102–49 with further references.

Opinion remained divided between the factions. Legal academia and consumer representatives were basically in favour of a possible pan-EU initiative. The business sector, on the other hand, remained sceptical, and voiced concerns that the market and the economy in general would be unreasonably impaired if the main features of US-style class actions were adopted in the EU. Four US characteristics in particular remained heavily disputed—punitive damages, pre-trial discovery, US-style contingency fees and opt-out mechanisms.

Likely because of the considerable influence of business interest representation at the EU level, the European Parliament eventually responded with reservations regarding the introduction of a pan-EU compensatory collective instrument. In 2012 it issued a resolution on collective redress that mirrored the concerns expressed by the business sector.[16] The Commission made its response one year later with its Recommendation on common principles for injunctive and compensatory collective redress mechanisms in the Member States concerning violations of rights granted under Union law (2013 Collective Redress Recommendation).[17] Taking a rather passive approach, the Recommendation addressed—amongst other things—the aforementioned features of US-style class actions, and confirmed the view that (at the political level) comprehensive, strong instruments were still viewed with scepticism.[18]

ii. Collective Redress at the EU Member State Level

The (temporary) passiveness of the EU legislator can be seen as a victory for critics of transnational (EU) compensatory collective enforcement. It is, however, not the end of attempts to comprehensively implement the second access to justice wave of the Florence Project—the search for accompanying diffuse interests. A couple of Member States—eg Austria and France—had already put in place certain compensatory collective redress schemes before 2000, but have recently been debating options to expand or 'renovate' these devices. In the case of France, this has more recently (applicable since 1 January 2015) led to the adoption of a refined mechanism to collectively answer infringements. The 'Hamon Law' (*loi Hamon*) introduced, inter alia, a new collective redress scheme applicable in antitrust and consumer disputes.[19] With the help of this mechanism, selected consumer organisations may launch a compensatory collective action, initially without the need to identify the victims. If and once the defendant is found liable, injured consumers have the chance to 'opt in', ie to receive compensation based on the court decision.

Since the early 2000s in particular, academic and political debates at the Member State level have intensified and led to the introduction of a variety of new instruments

---

[16] European Parliament, Towards a Coherent European Approach to Collective Redress, 2 February 2012, INI(2011) 2089.

[17] European Commission, Recommendation on common principles for injunctive and compensatory collective redress mechanisms in the Member States concerning violations of rights granted under Union law, [2013] OJ L201/60.

[18] See, in particular, paras 13 (on the loser-pays principle/US-style contingency fees), 21 (on opt in/opt out) and 31 (on punitive damages).

[19] Law no 2014-344 on consumer rights, 17 March 2014. For details, see, eg, Overview of Class/Collective Actions and Current Trends, www.lw.com/thoughtLeadership/class-actions-france.

in Member States that previously had no—at least no comparable—mechanisms in place. Sweden (2003), the Netherlands (2005), Finland, Greece and Italy (all in 2007), Denmark (2008), Hungary (2009), Poland (2010), Malta (2012) and Belgium (2014) can be listed in this context.[20]

In some cases, the introduction of specially designed laws was a reaction to practical issues. Germany serves as an interesting example. In 2005, the German legislator adopted the Capital Markets Model Case Act (*Kapitalanleger-Musterverfahrensgesetz*; 2005 KapMuG). It was the reply to a massive amount of litigation with respect to allegedly misleading prospectus information provided by Deutsche Telekom. More than 16,000 investors brought individual actions against the company. The regional court in Frankfurt, the competent court in these cases, was—in absence of a procedural tools that would have allowed it to group them—clearly overburdened. With the 2005 KapMuG Germany tried to allow for more efficient and effective case handling by introducing a special two-stage device that combined the use of test cases with opt-in compensatory collective redress. In 2012 the KapMuG was revised. The 2012 KapMuG takes a different approach from its 2005 counterpart. It integrates opt out by allowing for a comprehensive settlement to be negotiated at the test case stage (and approved by the court).

Generally speaking, the instruments crafted at the Member State level considerably vary with respect to their comprehensiveness and procedural characteristics. Opting in has been the preferred basis in most Member States. But the examples of the Netherlands, Portugal, (partially) Denmark and (with the 2012 KapMuG also partially) Germany show that the opt-out concerns voiced at the EU level are not necessarily shared at the domestic level.[21]

iii. On the Possible Future of Compensatory Collective Redress in the EU

In the European collective redress debate the fronts have remained hardened. Commentators have taken positions either in favour of or against US-style class actions. The discussions have mostly focused on the permissibility and feasibility of introducing opt-out tools. In general, the debate has been led in a comparatively one-dimensional way, in the sense that the contributions clearly favoured either opt in or opt out. On some occasions, however, the approaches have been more subtle and distinguished between different types of collective damage.

To understand the arguments more easily, it makes sense to break down the interests possibly involved (harmed) into three categories that, as a whole, might be called 'multilayer interests'.[22] A distinction can be made between (private) individual, (private) collective and public interests in enforcing collective damage claims.

---

[20] For a comprehensive list of commentaries on these instruments, see Wrbka, n 15, 103–04.

[21] J Stuyck et al, 'An Analysis and Evaluation of Alternative Means of Consumer Redress' (2007), www.eurofinas.org/uploads/documents/policies/OTHER/POLICY/ISSUES/comparative_report_en.pdf, 291–93.

[22] See already S Wrbka, 'European Consumer Protection Law: Quo Vadis?—Thoughts on the Compensatory Collective Redress Debate' in S Wrbka et al (eds), *Collective Actions: Enhancing Access to Justice and Reconciling Multilayer Interests?* (Cambridge, Cambridge University Press, 2012) 23, 24–27.

The first group—individual interests—does not differ from those found in 'ordinary', ie purely two-party, conflicts. Here, one party (allegedly) harms the other party's legal interests. Put differently, the harmed party would—as an individual—have an interest in being compensated.

If the wrongdoer were to harm more than one party in a similar way, a greater number of stakeholders would be affected. In such a situation, parallel individual compensation interests would exist. The harmed parties could have a collective interest in taking joint action. This would be the case if collective steps increased the chances of receiving compensation. Collecting evidence more easily or efficiently, splitting (at least) the preparatory costs, saving time in taking actions and a possibly stronger appearance as a group might encourage harmed parties to become active.

Lastly, not only directly affected parties, but also the state and not directly affected stakeholders could have an interest in rights enforcement. Bundling individual actions into one collective proceeding could, for example, have a positive impact on the efficiency and effectivity of the courts. It could save court resources and time, which in return could speed up litigation as a whole, because the waiting time for cases put on hold would be shortened. Likewise, there could be scenarios where collective actions would have public expenditure-saving effects. One could think, for example, of state-financed payment of damages for the loss of profits if parties temporarily or permanently remain unable to earn money as a consequence of damnification. Further, lowering the burden for substantiated litigation could have market-stimulating effects, because it would indirectly benefit business stakeholders that comply with the legal framework.

The relevance of individual, collective and public interests is not always equally balanced. Depending on the circumstances, individuals might have a greater or smaller interest in pursuing individual claims or in joining a possible collective action. In the relevant literature, one can find terms such as rational apathy (*rationale Apathie*) and rational disinterest (*rationales Desinteresse*) referring to the phenomenon of dispute avoidance.[23] In particular in cases in which the individual damage is comparatively minor, injured parties would often decide not to take action against wrongdoers. At least, the vast majority would not invest time in going to court.

This 'unwillingness to sue theory' has been the subject of numerous EU studies since the late twentieth century. While some studies indicate that the willingness of consumers, in particular, is generally low irrespective of the individual amounts in dispute, most related studies reveal that this phenomenon is of greater significance the lower

---

[23] For the use of the term 'rational apathy', see, eg, C Meller-Hannich, 'Einführung. Auf dem Weg zu einem effektiven und gerechten System des kollektiven Rechtsschutzes' in C Meller-Hannich (ed), *Kollektiver Rechtsschutz im Zivilprozess* (Baden-Baden, Nomos, 2008) 13, 14; C Michailidou, *Prozessuale Fragen des Kollektivrechtsschutzes im europäischen Justizraum* (Baden-Baden, Nomos, 2007) 49; G Wagner, '"Kollektiver Rechtsschutz"—Regelungsbedarf bei Massen- und Streuschäden' in Casper et al (eds), n 7, 41, 53; R Van den Bergh, 'Should Consumer Protection Law Be Publicly Enforced? An Economic Perspective on EC Regulation 2006/2004 and Its Implementation in the Consumer Protection Laws of the Member States' in van Boom and Loos (eds), n 8, 177, 183; for the use of the term 'rational disinterest' see, eg, Janssen, 'Auf dem Weg zu einer europäischen Sammelklage?' in Casper et al (eds), n 7, 3, 5.

the involved amounts are.[24] Earlier research arrived at the conclusion that particularly amounts below €2,000 could not be considered 'motivating' enough for individuals to go to court. The time and money that need to be spent in launching actions in these cases do not bear rational relation to the possible level of reimbursement.

Overcoming the rational apathy against taking individual action has been the subject of various procedural law initiatives, most notably of the European Small Claims Procedure (ECSP).[25] The ESCP initially set the amount of €2,000 as the upper limit for simplifying the judicial steps for compensation-seeking parties, but more recently it is available for claims up to €5,000.[26] Although the ESCP might have improved the situation in some instances, problems remain in scenarios in which the value of the damage is considerably lower. These cases have been regularly commented on, in particular in the German literature. Commonly referred to as types of damage with low and very low amounts in dispute (low-value and lowest-value damage; *Bagatellschäden*), individual claims not exceeding €100 to €200 are usually grouped under this pillar.[27] Here, the financial risk of losing the case arguably significantly outweighs the likely chance of winning.[28]

The cost risk—inherent in litigation systems that rest on the 'loser pays' principle—can be of additional demotivating significance in cases in which the damage suffered is greater. This is basically the consequence of the fact that court costs and attorney fees are usually higher, the greater the amount in dispute. Nevertheless, related research indicates that the rational apathy against litigation is comparatively lower than in cases of low-value and lowest-value damage. As long as there is a realistic chance of receiving compensation, it might be thought worthwhile to pay the higher amount. This could create a different issue. If 'too many' stakeholders decided to sue individually, courts could be overloaded with claims and hearings if the cases could not be grouped into multiparty proceedings.

---

[24] On consumers' general unwillingness to sue, see, eg, The Gallup Organization Hungary, 'Attitudes towards cross-border sales and consumer protection' (2010), ec.europa.eu/commfrontoffice/publicopinion/flash/fl_282_en.pdf, 102. For studies on the interrelationship between the individual damage and the willingness to go to courts see, in particular, H von Freyhold et al (eds), 'Cost of Judicial Barriers for Consumers in the Single Market' (1995), www.freyvial.de/Publications/egi-2.pdf; von Freyhold, Vial & Partner Consultants, 'The Cost of Legal Obstacles to the Disadvantage of Consumers in the Single Market' (1998), www.freyvial.de/Publications/egii-42.pdf, 276–77; European Opinion Research Group, 'European Union Citizens and Access to Justice' (2004), www.medsos.gr/medsos/images/stories/PDF/eurobarometer_11-04_en.pdf, 28; TNS Opinion & Social, 'European Small Claims Procedure' (2013), ec.europa.eu/public_opinion/archives/ebs/ebs_395_en.pdf, 44.

[25] Regulation (EC) 861/2007, [2007] OJ L199/1.

[26] Regulation (EU) 2015/2421, [2015] OJ L341/1.

[27] See, eg, HW Micklitz and A Stadler, *Unrechtsgewinnabschöpfung: Möglichkeiten und Perspektiven eines kollektiven Schadenersatzanspruches im UWG* (Baden-Baden, Nomos, 2003) 92; A Stadler, *Bündelung von Interessen im Zivilprozess: Überlegungen zur Einführung von Verbands- und Gruppenklagen im deutschen Recht* (Heidelberg, CF Müller, 2004) 13; A Stadler, 'Erfahrungen mit den Gewinnabschöpfungsansprüchen im deutschen Wettbewerbs- und Kartellrecht' in M Reiffenstein and B Pirker-Hörmann (eds), *Defizite kollektiver Rechtsdurchsetzung* (Vienna, Verlag Österreich, 2009) 93, 107 with further references; A Stadler, 'Group Actions as a Remedy to Enforce Consumer Interests' in F Cafaggi and H-M Micklitz (eds), *New Frontiers of Consumer Protection: The Interplay between Private and Public Enforcement* (Antwerp, Intersentia, 2009) 305, 327.

[28] Wagner, n 23, 53, where the author explains that the cost risk of suing for €100 is numerically nearly three times higher than the suffered damage of €100.

In the literature two terms were created to discuss these scenarios. Low-value damage and lowest-value damage that occur in parallel are grouped under the term 'scattered damage' (*Streuschäden*). In this category of multiple damage, it is the public interest in overall legal compliance that is particularly strong, while individual and collective interests in receiving compensation might be of significantly low actual importance. The term mass damage (*Massenschäden*), on the other hand, represents those cases in which the individual and collective interests in receiving compensation are considerably high—usually high enough to encourage individual actions. As explained above, public interests remain strong.

Looking at both concepts, one could arguably say that facilitating collective actions serves different ideas depending on the scenario in question. With respect to scattered damage, collective actions could predominantly be utilised for the sake of deterrence and business compliance with the law, rather than for satisfying the wish to receive compensation ('principle of deterrence'; *Präventionsfunktion*). In the case of mass damage, however, it is not only the search for deterrence and compliance that argues for the increased use of (substantiated) collective actions. In addition, collective redress could allow for simplified compensation. This is commonly referred to as the 'principle of remediation' (*Ausgleichsprinzip*) in the collective redress literature.[29]

The identification of different types of diffuse interests, with scattered damage at one end of the spectrum and mass damage at the other, creates challenges for European legislators that want to retain their underlying procedural principles, first and foremost the right to be heard—or, in other words, the opportunity to decide about the fate of one's own damage. In this respect, commentators have repeatedly voiced concerns that in particular the comprehensive introduction of an opt-out mechanism could be incompatible with Article 6 of the European Convention on Human Rights.[30] However, these concerns should be put into a wider context. The biggest practical issue with unexceptionally upholding the right to self-determination to the largest possible extent might be seen in the fact that, especially in cases of scattered damage, ie in cases of individual low and lowest amounts, harmed stakeholders would still remain passive. Hence, compensatory collective redress mechanisms that rest on opting in would in the large majority of cases fail to show effect. Although the threshold for pursuing individual claims would be lower than in the case of ordinary litigation, time and money-related factors might still discourage individuals from joining. As a consequence, wrongdoers might still manage to keep large portions of their illegally gained profits (ie those that relate to the unpursued interests).

---

[29] ibid, 50, where Wagner discusses both the principle of remediation and the principle of deterrence (*Präventionsfunktion*).

[30] German Bundesrat, Resolution on the Green Paper from the Commission of the European Communities on Consumer Collective Redress, 13 February 2009, No 951/08, para 23; D Haß, *Die Gruppenklage: Wege zur prozessualen Bewältigung von Massenschäden* (Munich, VVF, 1996) 326; H Koch, 'Alternativen zum Zweiparteiensystem im Zivilprozeß' (1989) 4 *Kritische Vierteljahresschrift für Gesetzgebung und Rechtswissenschaft* 323, 337; GE Kodek, 'Collective Redress in Austria' (2009) 622 *The ANNALS of the American Academy of Political and Social Science* 86, 89; W Lüke, *Die Beteiligung Dritter im Zivilprozess: Eine rechtsvergleichende Untersuchung zu Grundfragen der subjektiven Verfahrenskonzentration* (Tübingen, Mohr Siebeck, 1993) 94.

Arguably the biggest challenge might be to reconcile the interests in fostering the right to self-determination and lowering the risks of abuse, on the one hand, and in maximising legal compliance and satisfying the principle of remediation, on the other. Looking at the underlying issues of rights enforcement in the cases of scattered damage and mass damage, and taking further account of the arguments in favour and against opt in/opt out, it may be seen that a two-tiered approach might best accomplish this goal. We do not go into detail here: this has already been treated elsewhere.[31] It should be noted, though, that—if one is willing to make compromises—it might be possible to accommodate both sides' interests. In principle, legislators could introduce opt-in-based collective actions for cases of mass damage, ie for cases where it can realistically be expected that individuals are willing to become active. Already conducted research—if updated—might serve as a basis to determine the amounts that would have to be in dispute to prompt harmed parties to act. For cases of individual claims that are too small for it feasibly to make sense to pursue them for the sake of individual remediation, one might prioritise opt-out-based (or even mandatory participation in) collective redress over the wish to satisfy the right to self-determination. This could even go as far as allowing public entities or private representative bodies to keep possible winnings to fund further actions to maximise legal compliance.

E. Concluding Remarks: Jurisdictional Issues in a Transnational Context

The development of collective compensatory redress remains in a state of flux in many parts of the world, in particular in European jurisdictions and those that have not followed the US example. One can expect new initiatives to be taken over the next few years. In this section, we want briefly to highlight some issues as seen from a cross-border perspective. Initiating a lawsuit in a transnational or cross-border context necessarily poses certain challenges. Of legal interest in particular are questions of the applicable substantive law and the place of jurisdiction, ie of identifying the competent court. A brief look at the situation in the EU will serve as an example of the complications that may arise regarding the latter question.

The Brussels I Regulation on jurisdiction and the recognition of judgments in civil and commercial matters[32] is, in principle, the primary source of law to clarify jurisdictional issues when it comes to litigation against persons residing in an EU Member State. It simplifies the identification of the competent court in a cross-border scenario. In particular in comparison with cases in which there are no clear international or transnational rules, this is of considerable practical importance. However, a slightly closer look at the Brussels I regime reveals that in the case of compensatory collective redress, the actual merits are not that significant.

---

[31] Wrbka, n 15, 132–42.
[32] Regulation (EC) No 44/2001 [2001] OJ L12/1 replaced by Regulation (EU) No 1215/2012 [2012] OJ L351/1 (Brussels I Recast).

As a basic principle, litigation should take place in the Member State in which the defendant is domiciled.[33] The Brussels I regime introduces a number of exceptions to this rule that aim to facilitate the pursuit of claims in special circumstances. Although the Brussels I regime does not include any explicit provisions on collective redress, some regulations, such as Article 18(1) Brussels I Recast (which covers consumer claims and allows consumers to alternatively sue in their home country) could serve as a sectoral basis for enhancing collective actions.

There are, however, certain limitations and complications that might require future clarification. Two bigger issues should be pointed out in this respect. In cases in which the individuals affected come from different Member States, the favourable rule under Article 18(1) might not help in practice if the harmed parties want to launch a collective lawsuit. Article 18(1) only allows the choice between the plaintiff's and the defendant's home countries. If the plaintiff's side is composed of consumers from different Member States, the only available choice would be the defendant's Member State, because there is not (only) one consumer home country. This would restrict the choice of jurisdiction to the default setting of suing in the courts of the defendant's domicile. One option would be to revise or reinterpret Article 18(1) in way that would—in line with the rationale behind it—allow one of the following to be chosen as an alternative to the defendant's Member State. In cases of collective redress, one could, for example, allow the Member State in which most group members are domiciled as an alternative place of jurisdiction. One could even go one step further and allow for any group member's Member State to serve as a possible place of litigation. Admittedly, however, taking into account that the compensatory collective redress schemes available in the Member States fundamentally differ in terms of the formation of classes, procedure and enforcement—one can, for instance, distinguish between opt in and opt out, representation by public bodies and private organisations—this would open the door to forum shopping. Nevertheless, if the special provisions of the Brussels I regime were really intended to simplify litigation, plaintiff-friendly jurisdictional choices would be the logical consequence.

Comparable considerations can be found in the context of designating possible plaintiffs. In many European jurisdictions, the legislators have crafted their collective redress instruments in a way that allows public entities and/or private organisations to act on behalf of harmed individuals. The existing jurisdictional framework under the Brussels I regime might, however, be ill-equipped to achieve the goal of true simplification. Research carried out in particular in the context of the Injunctions Directive (both with respect to the original 1998 version and its 2009 replacement) shows that representative bodies are reluctant to take action in a foreign country. Article 4 of the Injunctions Directive, which allows for injunctions in the case of intra-community (now intra-EU) infringements to be launched by qualified entities in the wrongdoer's home country, has largely remained without effect. Instead, the vast majority of qualified entities have chosen to launch proceedings in their home countries.

---

[33] Art 4(1) Brussels I Recast.

Financial concerns, a lack of experience with foreign procedure and language issues have featured high on the list of obstacles.[34]

The Brussels I regime does not offer much relief for representative actions. Case law of the Court of Justice of the European Union (CJEU) shows that Article 18(1) Brussels I Recast is understood in a narrow way. As ruled, for example, in *Shearson Lehmann Hutton Inc v TVB Treuhandgesellschaft für Vermögensverwaltung und Beteiligungen mbH* (*Shearson Lehmann Hutton*), the plaintiff-friendly choice should only be available in cases in which the consumers themselves bring proceedings.[35] Following this understanding, Article 18(1) would not be of help in cases in which public entities or private bodies litigate on the affected consumers' behalf. This is the consequence of the fact that the plaintiff in such a case, ie the private entity or private body, did not conclude the contract(s) that form(s) the basis of the case. The picture is not entirely clear, however, because in some instances national courts have adopted a more flexible understanding of the Brussels I regime and have accepted jurisdiction in comparable cases.[36] Further clarification is surely needed.

III. Alternative Dispute Resolution

A. Alternative Dispute Resolution in General

Simply put, ADR can be defined as comprising non-litigious forms of dispute resolution. It comprises a wide variety of tools that range from negotiation to mediation, from conciliation to arbitration.[37] Modern ADR can generally be considered a

---

[34] European Commission, Report concerning the application of Directive 98/27/EC of the European Parliament and of the Council on injunctions for the protection of consumers' interests, 18 November 2008, COM(2008) 756 final 17–27.

[35] Case C-89/91, *Shearson Lehmann Hutton Inc v TVB Treuhandgesellschaft für Vermögensverwaltung und Beteiligungen mbH* [1993] ECLI:EU:C:1993:15, para 28.

[36] Relevant cases are reported, eg, in Portugal, where the courts have accepted jurisdiction with respect to cross-border actions taken by the Portuguese Association for Consumer Protection, DECO (see L Tortell, 'Country Report Portugal' (2008) 10—file with the authors). For further examples, see, eg, R Geimer, 'Art 15 EuGVVO' in R Geimer and RA Schütze (eds), *Europäisches Zivilverfahrensrecht*, 3rd edn (Munich, CH Beck, 2010) Art 15 EuGVVO, para 20 (with references at fnn 75 and 76); H Koch, 'Internationaler Kollektiver Rechtsschutz' in Meller-Hannich (ed), n 23, 53, 54–55; J Kropholler and J von Hein, *Europäisches Zivilprozessrecht*, 9th edn (Frankfurt am Main, Verlag Recht und Wirtschaft, 2011) Art 15 EuGVO, para 12 (with references at fn 48).

[37] Note the conceptual nuances of these four approaches. Negotiation is usually carried out directly between the parties concerned, without the involvement of a third-party intermediary. Mediation is hosted by a mediator who would aim to facilitate the solution-finding process without giving substantive feedback or advice. A conciliator would take a more active role and might suggest solutions, without possessing decision-making competences. The strongest and most litigation-like of these four ADR examples is arbitration. Here an arbitrator (or an arbitral tribunal) would be granted decision-making powers. Unlike judges in litigation, however, arbitrators are freer to design the overall procedure and decision-making process. Furthermore, in most cases arbitrators would be experts in the substantive field in question, often coming from legal practice (and not being career judges).

more recent method of resolving disputes without needing to undertake conventional litigation. It is widely believed to offer an attractive alternative for parties who prefer fast decision making, informal and confidential proceedings, and cost-effective dispute resolution over traditional means of redress that rely on and involve career judges and an oftentimes complex judicial apparatus.

Just as is the case with compensatory collective redress, modern, institutionalised (commercial) ADR originated in the US, where it has been widely used since the 1970s and 1980s. Although ADR has enjoyed popularity predominantly in business-to-business (B2B) scenarios, more recently it has risen in importance with respect to B2C disputes too. This is largely the result of the digitalisation of dispute resolution. We shall return to this issue later in this chapter.

The significance of ADR in a transnational context is highlighted in particular by the introduction of the UNCITRAL Model Law in International Commercial Arbitration (UNCITRAL Arbitration Model Law) in 1985.[38] Over the years the UNCITRAL Arbitration Model Law has risen in practical relevance, and has served as the basis for many national arbitration laws around the world. Amended in 2006 to reflect modern contractual practices, eg with respect to arbitration agreements, the UNCITRAL Arbitration Model Law has been adopted by more than 70 countries, and has undeniably contributed to the rise in popularity and use of arbitration. Nevertheless, it should be pointed out that the UNCITRAL Arbitration Model Law has not (yet) been adopted comprehensively in the sense that it enjoys extensive worldwide acceptance. For example, most African and South American jurisdictions have yet to show their willingness to follow the rules of the Model Law. Different levels of acceptance can also be found in the EU, with a considerable number of Member States (including France, Italy, Sweden, Finland, Poland and Portugal) not having adopted the UNCITRAL Arbitration Model Law as of early 2017.[39]

The following subsections provide a brief, non-exhaustive overview of ADR developments in selected jurisdictions. We begin with a look at the US, before switching to Asia, Africa and the EU. Subsequently the focus will be on online ADR (ODR), which arguably might be the fastest developing form of ADR in more recent years.

B. Traditional Alternative Dispute Resolution in the US

Alternative dispute resolution (in principle) enjoys a long history that dates back to the early second millennium BCE, when types of informal negotiation were used to settle inter-kingdom disputes in Mesopotamia. Since then, non-litigation forms of dispute resolution have been implemented in virtually every period and around the globe, initially with the focus on settling disagreements between different jurisdictions.[40]

With the rise of modern states, endeavours intensified to utilise ADR to restore and secure domestic peace. Examples from the US, where ADR helped to end the Civil

---

[38] www.uncitral.org/uncitral/en/uncitral_texts/arbitration/1985Model_arbitration.html.

[39] www.uncitral.org/uncitral/en/uncitral_texts/arbitration/1985Model_arbitration_status_map.html.

[40] For a brief summary of the development of ADR, see, eg, the 'ADR Timeline' in JT Barrett and JP Barrett, *A History of Alternative Dispute Resolution: The Story of a Political, Cultural and Social Movement* (San Francisco, Jossey-Bass, 2004) xxv–xxx.

War in 1865 and to resolve slave labour issues shortly thereafter, can be understood as primary expressions thereof. In the late nineteenth century and at the beginning of the twentieth century, debates on the possible adoption of pertinent legislation proliferated. Initially the primary focus of ADR was not necessarily on resolving commercial disputes between two businesses or businesses and consumers, but rather on achieving a social balance by ending employment disputes and preventing social unrest.[41]

The first real shift to and rise in commercial ADR took place with the increased economic interest of US States and the federal Government in raising the level of institutionalised arbitration in the 1920s. The Federal Arbitration Act of 1925 and the first State statute, New York's Arbitration Law of 1920, sounded the bell for this new era of ADR. These instruments included provisions on the validity of contractual arbitration clauses, rules on appointing arbitrators and—arguably most notably—rules on enforcing arbitral awards with the help of the courts. Further impetus followed in 1926, when the American Arbitration Association was formed to support arbitrators and parties to arbitration with information and overall guidance.

For some decades, however, ADR did not significantly rise further in popularity. It was a presentation delivered by Frank Sander at the Roscoe Pound Conference in 1976 that triggered a turnaround in the US.[42] Frequently called the 'Big Bang' of modern ADR, Sander's speech on the 'Varieties of Dispute Processing' inspired stakeholders who were—for different reasons—looking for alternatives to litigation. His vision of a 'multi-door' courthouse that promoted a multitude of additional dispute resolution mechanisms (that went beyond litigation and arbitration and included in particular mediation, conciliation and ombudsman services) was well received by representatives from the judiciary, as well as by many other interest groups. The US Supreme Court, for instance, had previously lamented the heavy burden on ordinary courts that resulted from an increasing amount of litigation (with the majority of actions being of a commercial/economic nature). The court hoped that ADR could help to unburden the judiciary. Other stakeholders had occasionally been sceptical as regards the appropriateness and competence of career judges and conventional litigation. While the courts' legal expertise was not the key issue, the inflexibility of the court system and the alleged lack of non-legal expertise nurtured the wish and search for alternatives.

Sander's speech raised the overall awareness of and motivation to cultivate and enhance ADR. This included the launch of new institutions that offered ADR funds, training and research, as well as governmental initiatives to encourage parties to have recourse to ADR institutions. Further, it paved the way towards accepting and utilising new technologies to speed up ADR. We shall return to this issue in section III.E.

---

[41] See, eg, M McManus and B Silverstein, 'Brief History of Alternative Dispute Resolution in the United States' (2011) 1 *Cadmus* 100, 101, where the authors summarise as follows: 'At this stage of ADR's development, it was perceived of less as an alternative to litigation and more as a tool to avoid unrest, strikes, and the resultant economic disruption.'

[42] For a transcript of the speech, see F Sander, 'Varieties of Dispute Processing' (St Paul, MN, West Publishing, 1976).

C. Traditional Alternative Dispute Resolution in Asia and Africa

In many Asian countries and African regions, some forms of ADR similarly have a long history. Mediation in particular has been playing a significant role in these parts of the world.

In Buddhist societies, for instance, Confucian doctrine, which places a high value on harmony, peace and the making of compromises, has been considered a key reason why parties traditionally have recourse to non-litigious forms of dispute settlement. Another, but arguably to some extent related, difference is that, compared with most Western market economies, leading Asian industrial nations have a lower attorney per capita ratio.[43] Although this might be explained by a variety of factors, the lesser 'need' for barristers (as a consequence of favouring ADR over litigation in many Asian countries, regardless of the religious background) is arguably one of them. Japan is a good example: disputes are usually avoided by relying on networks that include third party intermediaries—*shoukai-sha/shoukai-jou* ('introducers') or *chuukai-sha* ('middle-meeting-persons')—who facilitate negotiations via 'trust' building and fostering. In cases where disputes arise, the *chuukai-sha* would alternatively function as mediators. It is the broad understanding that in Asian societies in particular, compromises are generally preferred over lengthy, 'one party takes all' litigation.

Historically, mediation also plays an important role in many parts of Africa, in particular when it comes to intra-community disputes. To secure tribal solidarity, tribal elders would aim to support dispute resolution. A logistic issue enhances the use of ADR: ordinary, institutionalised courts would be found only in bigger cities. In particular for remote villages and communities, accessing the courts would not be a feasible alternative.

Unlike mediation, arbitration has a shorter history in both Asia and Africa, especially when it comes to institutionalised forms. Occasionally, as was the case in Japan, for example, with its (since revised) arbitration rules set out in the Civil Procedure Act of 1890, arbitral legislation had it roots in the late nineteenth century. However, and for the most part, institutionalised arbitration has, until recently, not played a significant role in most Asian societies, including Japan. Things started to change slightly at the beginning of the new millennium, when a considerable number of Asian jurisdictions decided to introduce national arbitration laws based on the UNCITRAL Arbitration Model Law. The trend towards such institutionalised UNCITRAL arbitration has been sustained ever since, with the more recent examples of South Korea and Mongolia having adopted pertinent legislation in 2016 and 2017 respectively.[44]

In Africa to date, the UNCITRAL Arbitration Model Law has, generally speaking, not been implemented in a comparatively extensive, 'harmonised' way.

---

[43] See, eg, www.statista.com/statistics/224787/number-of-lawyers-in-china/ (for China), www.law.harvard. edu/programs/olin_center/papers/pdf/Ramseyer_681.pdf (for Japan), www.nichibenren.or.jp/library/ja/ bar_association/word/data/Korea.pdf (for South Korea), www.nomikosodigos.info/en/articles/824-over-population-of-lawyers-in-greece (for the US and the EU).

[44] www.uncitral.org/uncitral/en/uncitral_texts/arbitration/1985Model_arbitration_status_map.html.

Fewer than a dozen jurisdictions have introduced domestic arbitration laws based on the UNCITRAL Arbitration Model Law and, with the exception of Rwanda (which adopted such a law in 2008), those African countries which have, took that step in the last decade of the twentieth century (or in the year 2000).[45] Nevertheless, commentators on African arbitration argue that older European models and more recent economic developments have contributed to a rise in the use of arbitration in Africa too.[46]

D. Traditional Alternative Dispute Resolution in the EU

In general, several European jurisdictions first introduced statute-based ADR in the late nineteenth century. The UK Conciliation Act of 1896 is a good example. However, with few exceptions, ADR was dormant for some decades in Europe. It was only roughly around the time that Sander presented his multi-door court vision in the US that European jurisdictions generally showed increased interest in broadening dispute resolution beyond ordinary litigation.

By the end of the twentieth century ADR (sectorally) entered discussions at the pan-EU level. With a view to strengthening the internal market by enhancing procedural consumer laws, the Commission issued a series of policy papers in the 1990s. The 1993 Consumer Access to Justice Green Paper drew on the recommendation of the third access to justice wave of the Florence Project to foster the use of ADR.[47] Five years later, in 1998, the Commission launched two projects. It published both a (general) communication on the use of non-litigious B2C dispute resolution, which introduced a standardised complaint form, and a recommendation of principles to guide ADR institutions through the process.[48] A couple of initiatives followed over the next few years, with a Council resolution in 2000 on a Community-wide network of national bodies for the extra-judicial settlement of consumer disputes and a more comprehensive ADR Green Paper in 2002 on the likely introduction of ADR for civil and commercial matters in general. The ADR Green Paper resulted in an (non-binding) European Code of Conduct for Mediators and a Mediation Directive Proposal (again covering civil and commercial matters in general), both in 2004.

It took the EU legislator another four years to respond with the first piece of legislation—the Mediation Directive of 2008.[49] Compared with later instruments, the

---

[45] ibid.

[46] See, eg, W Kidane, *China-Africa Dispute Settlement: The Law, Economics and Culture of Arbitration* (Alphen aan den Rijn, Kluwer Law International, 2012) 367.

[47] European Commission, Green Paper on access of consumers to justice and the settlement of consumer disputes in the single market, 16 November 1993, COM(93) 576 final 56 asking for the introduction of 'specific out-of-court procedures for the settlement of consumer disputes'.

[48] European Commission, Communication on the out-of-court settlement of consumer disputes, 30 March 1998, COM(1998) 198 final; European Commission, Recommendation on the principles applicable to the bodies responsible for out-of-court settlement of consumer disputes, [1998] OJ L115/31. The latter Recommendation was complemented by a set of recommended principles for ADR instruments that—as is the case, eg, in mediation—leave the parties more freedom in the process: see European Commission, Recommendation on the principles for out-of-court bodies involved in the consensual resolution of consumer disputes, [2001] OJ L109/56.

[49] Directive 2008/52/EC, [2008] OJ L136/3.

Mediation Directive is wide in its application, in the sense that it covers many forms of civil and commercial disputes. Its broad application is limited, however, by the fact that it applies only to cross-border disputes and fails to make the earlier Code of Conduct (as well as any other qualitative standards) mandatory. More than that, the Mediation Directive merely recommends the introduction and use of mediation, but does not require Member States to take any concrete action. Overall, the Mediation Directive can be understood as a reflection of the slower development of ADR in the EU when compared with the US.

With the Mediation Directive, the EU legislator fell short of true innovation. In particular, the limitation to mediation, combined with the lack of both the mandatory introduction of mediation institutions and binding minimum standards of mediation, must be considered unsatisfactory. The picture with regard to the availability, speed and costs of ADR and the quality of related institutions remained widely uneven throughout the EU. For a long time, the Member States failed to agree on a common plan for more stringent rules. The reluctance of several European jurisdictions to adopt the UNCITRAL Model Law, as noted in section III.A, indicates that (still to date) differences of opinion regarding the most suitable ADR approach continue to cause significant issues for comprehensive pan-EU utilisation of ADR.

In the early 2010s, the attempt to institutionalise non-litigious dispute resolution gained some momentum, however, when the EU crafted two more ADR laws. Supported by data and research on the shortcomings of then-existing tools at the Member State level, proponents of ADR succeeded in implementing the idea to establish further-reaching rules. The underlying conviction was that a well-functioning internal market needed well-functioning enforcement rules to enable individuals seeking justice to access easy dispute settlement. The decision to introduce a framework of mandatory ADR for disputes—mandatory in the sense that Member States have to make sure that ADR is available when required—mainly rested on two further findings. Experience showed that efforts to enhance the litigation environment by installing special procedures—most notably small claim litigation—and offering special assistance (eg legal aid) did not significantly change the picture. Consumers, in particular, remained passive as regards litigation. Looking at other forms of dispute resolution, it became obvious that more ambitious steps had to be taken to offer a true alternative. Generally speaking—arguably with the exception of larger B2B disputes that involved financially stronger enterprises and those that placed value on the flexibility and confidentiality of arbitration—ADR had remained widely unused in the EU. The blame lay not only in insufficient quality standards and unsatisfying cost schemes, but also in a lack of ADR awareness.

In 2013, the EU legislator responded with the ADR Directive.[50] Although its scope is limited to B2C disputes—more precisely to consumer-initiated B2C redress—it offers a potentially comparatively strong regime that goes well beyond the framework of the Mediation Directive. Not only does the ADR Directive apply irrespective of whether the dispute is of a cross-border or merely domestic nature; it also adds some ADR devices formerly not covered at the pan-EU level—most notably arbitration—and obliges Member States to install tools that fulfil certain procedural and qualitative criteria.

---

[50] Directive 2013/11/EU, [2013] OJ L165/63 (ADR Directive).

In terms of establishing ADR as a viable option, the ADR Directive was a land-mark event. Provided that one finds and implements effective awareness-raising strate-gies, the combination of obliging Member States to provide for ADR and a catalogue of mandatory principles might indeed encourage consumers to have recourse to alter-natives to litigation. For example, under the new regime, efforts should be made to resolve disputes within 90 days after submission of a complaint. When compared with the average time spent in obtaining a binding decision—available data suggest up to three to four years with respect to dispute resolution in general[51]—accomplishing this would mean a considerable improvement. The enforcement-enhancing effect might be maximised by the requirement that ADR should come 'free of charge or ... at a nominal fee for consumers'.[52] With these two decisions the EU legislator obviously intended to answer two key concerns we encountered earlier: the time and cost to be invested in dispute resolution.

The examples discussed in this and the previous subsections show that over the last few decades, ADR has been the subject of considerable developments around the globe. We saw that policymakers are of the strong belief that ordinary litigation might not be the most suitable or appropriate form for resolving disputes. The refinements introduced by various countries and regions all aim at simplifying rights enforcement in terms of time-related and monetary concerns. The following subsection will go one step further and explain how technology can be used to enhance dispute resolution to an even greater extent.

E. Online Dispute Resolution

The rise of information and communication technology (ICT) and e-commerce over the last few decades has added significant potential to ADR by introducing a special redress layer: online (alternative) dispute resolution (ODR (or OADR)). Some authors consider ODR as one of the core factors necessary to boost e-commerce. Faye Wang, for example, states that 'ODR may become one of the possible and most efficient channels to enhance trust and confidence in doing business online'.[53]

The Internet having been invented in the late 1960s, the World Wide Web in the late 1980s and the first Internet Service Provider having been introduced in the early 1990s, ODR is a comparatively new phenomenon. Relevant debates started in the mid-1990s, when stakeholders began to realise that cyberspace offered both challenges and new opportunities for ADR. Challenges, because it was not clear which substantive and procedural laws should apply when parties from different jurisdictions interacted in an environment that could hardly be tied to one particular country. New opportuni-ties, because ICT developments allowed for the use of new tools to enhance dispute resolution, regardless of the location of the parties seeking redress.

---

[51] Stuyck et al, n 21, 324.
[52] Art 8(c) ADR Directive.
[53] FF Wang, *Law of Electronic Commercial Transactions: Contemporary Issues in the EU, US and China* 2nd edn (Abingdon, Routledge, 2014) 5.

A number of initiatives have emerged ever since, in particular in Western industrial societies, where financial resources and advanced economies have fostered the debates. Prominent examples included university-affiliated research and ODR-facilitating institutions, as well international exchanges, for instance at the annual International ODR Forum, which was first hosted by the UN Economic Commission for Europe in Geneva in 2002.[54] Parallel to these mostly academic or state-run projects, several start-up companies jumped at the chance to launch tailor-made ODR services. By the end of the twentieth century, ODR, in particular in the US, saw its first increase, which, however, was initially limited to disputes that stemmed from online transactions, as they were considered the most closely related basis for possible inter-party disputes.

Over the years, the ODR market has grown further, and in many cases is now available for settling disputes regardless of whether they originate in an online or offline activity. In particular, the simplified accessibility of ODR, best illustrated by its detachedness from physical anchorage, has constituted an attractive alternative. Looking at regional developments, one can, however, once again identify differences. Comparing, for example, the situation in the US and the EU, one will see that—just as was the case with conventional ADR—the US took a lead role, that being where most leading (in particular privately run) service providers started their businesses.

Despite its advantages, most obviously in terms of speed and easy, universal accessibility, ODR has led to several practical, inherent issues. One of the biggest challenges thus far has been to strike the appropriate balance between utilising new technologies (ie ICTs) to maximise the speed/minimise the costs of ODR and strengthening the parties' trust in ODR. Ethan Katsh, one of the early and prominent commentators on ODR, summarises the situation as follows: 'Rather than finding disputes that can utilise ODR, the new challenge is finding tools that can deliver trust, convenience, and expertise for many kinds of conflict.'[55] Put differently, from a purely technical perspective, it was relatively easy to implement ODR; all that was needed was—in simplified terms—cyberspace and an ODR service provider capable of creating, hosting and running an ODR scheme that would allow the parties easy access to the tool. However, to be successful and to sustain a place on the ODR market, ODR instruments had to work on their underlying technologies and improve their reliability, not only in terms of technical dependability, but also when it came to the question of whether a particular service was genuinely and truly trustworthy.

One of the more recent examples of efforts to ensure the trustworthiness of ODR services can be found in the EU. The 2013 ADR Directive earlier outlined was accompanied by a specifically designed law to deal with the issue of stakeholder

---

[54] University-linked examples include the Center for Information Technology and Dispute Resolution/ National Center for Technology and Dispute Resolution, launched by the University of Massachusetts, and the ADR Hub supported by Creighton University's Werner Institute—for details see E Katsh, 'ODR: A Look at History' in MS Abdel Wahab et al (eds), *Online Dispute Resolution: Theory and Practice—A Treatise on Technology and Dispute Resolution* (The Hague, Eleven International Publishing, 2012) 11; or the initiative's respective websites: odr.info (National Center for Technology and Dispute Resolution) www.adrhub.com (ADR Hub). For information on the International ODR Forum, see odr.info/international-odr-forum/.

[55] Katsh, n 54, 13.

trust in ODR—the ODR Regulation of the same day.[56] For many years, policymakers in the EU had remained sceptical of ODR. Concerns were voiced particularly with respect to due process issues.[57] Furthermore, parties had to rely on the usability, availability, security and dependability of ICT. A complicating factor was that—compared with ordinary ADR and litigation—ODR lagged behind in terms of having the actual opportunity to interpret facial expressions and body language—even in those cases where video conference tools were available. This was the logical consequence of not being able to physically interact with the other stakeholder(s) involved, ie not being able to communicate with the opposite party/parties in person but merely via email, telephone, live chats or (at best) video conferences. As this conceptual difference naturally remains unchanged even today, it becomes all the more obvious that it is extremely important to take ancillary steps if one wants to foster party trust in ODR. This was one of the main ideas behind the ODR Regulation.

The ODR Regulation is tightly interlinked with the ADR Directive. Most notably, it builds on the mandatory quality standards introduced by the Directive. At the same time, it should be noted that the two instruments differ in terms of their scope. While the ODR Regulation also applies to cases launched by traders, its scope is limited to online sales only. In this respect, it takes a narrower approach than the ADR Directive and most already existing ODR mechanisms, including many of the schemes introduced by ODR service providers mentioned earlier, which are available regardless of whether a dispute originates in an online or offline activity.

The main body of the ODR Regulation is composed of provisions that aim to establish a smooth procedure. The ODR scheme offered under the Regulation rests on a central entry point, the free-of-charge accessible 'Online Dispute Resolution' website run by the European Commission and launched in February 2016. This European ODR Platform is designed in a way that allows persons seeking redress to make use of ODR services offered in the Member States in any of the official languages of the EU.[58] When accessing the website, parties can choose their preferred language and proceed to fill in a standardised complaint form in that particular language. The services can be used in either direction in domestic and cross-border B2C disputes, ie by traders who want to file a complaint against a consumer or vice versa. To improve the user-friendliness of the complaint form and to facilitate the ODR process, the Commission summarised and developed the relevant practical parameters of the ODR Regulation further in 2015 with its ODR Implementing Regulation.[59]

Since its launch in February 2016, the ODR Platform has been gradually consolidated and refined to help as many likely parties as possible. Ensuring that parties seeking redress have easy access to practical assistance by neutral intermediaries rests on the idea that several of the privately-run schemes had not been perceived as

[56] Regulation (EU) 524/2013, [2013] OJ L165/1.
[57] See, eg, L Edwards and C Wilson, 'Redress and Alternative Dispute Resolution in EU Cross-Border E-Commerce Transactions' (2007) 21 *International Review of Law Computers & Technology* 315, 321–23.
[58] See webgate.acceptance.ec.europa.eu/odr/main/.
[59] Implementing Regulation (EU) 1051/2015, [2015] OJ L171/1.

being sufficiently objective and user-friendly. Pablo Cortes, for example, praised the technically high standards of private initiatives launched earlier, but claimed that 'they have been proven not to be consumer-friendly as yet'.[60] Before launching a complaint, individuals seeking redress can inform themselves by reading brief pieces of information on the ODR process directly on the ODR Platform. The procedure itself is divided into four stages: (i) filing a complaint, (ii) agreeing on an ODR body, (iii) the handling of the dispute by the ODR body, and (iv) the result stage. Mutually choosing an ODR body is facilitated primarily by two means. First, the ODR Platform contains a list of designated bodies, grouped by their location. Information about the bodies includes the area of expertise and contact details. Second, for further questions of any relevant kind, ie with respect to choosing a suitable ODR body, but also questions that might arise earlier (at the complaint filing stage) or later (eg in the context of the actual dispute resolution process), national contact points advise the parties. (One should note, however, that the advice does not include any feedback with regard to the merits of cases.)

In terms of visibility, the Commission has been trying to raise awareness, in particular by requesting businesses that either principally accept the use of ODR schemes or which are obliged under national legislation to commit to ODR tools, to provide a link to the ODR Platform on their websites. Provided that online businesses comply with this requirement and that the implementation of it is realised appropriately, that is follows the Commission's linking policy, which offers specifically designed banners,[61] this strategy might indeed result in positive effects. At the same time, however, it has to be regretted that the Commission—at the time of writing—has not yet included any information about or a link to ODR and its platform on the European e-Justice portal, the Commission's central legal and judicial information portal.[62] Nevertheless, as of January 2018, the ODR Platform had already been used relatively frequently, with a total number of roughly 66,000 complaints filed (of which approximately one-third were of cross-border nature).[63]

F. Concluding Remarks: Pending Issues and Challenges for ODR

Alternative dispute resolution, in particular in its cyberspace version—ODR—is undeniably on the rise. It arguably offers an easily accessible, cheap, fast and confidential alternative to conventional, litigious dispute resolution. However, certain questions deserve closer attention.

[60] P Cortes, *Online Dispute Resolution for Consumers in the European Union* (Abingdon, Routledge, 2011) 223.

[61] See europa.eu/youreurope/promo/odr-banners/index_en.htm.

[62] It should be noted, however, that according to the e-Justice Portal Team, the Commission is working on possible integration into the portal's platform (email answer dated 21 April 2017, on file with the authors).

[63] Data as of 27 January 2018. Total number of complaints filed: 29,395. Percentage of national disputes: 38.6%; percentage of cross-border disputes: 61.44%. For details (including a list of affected sectors), see ec.europa.eu/consumers/odr/main/index.cfm?event=main.statistics.show.

As indicated in the section III.E, building and maximising trust in ADR/ODR might be one of the prime challenges for the future. This can be understood in many, complementary ways, which include the following issues. First, it has to be ensured that ADR/ODR schemes fulfil minimum quality standards that meet those found at the level of litigation. Substantive, specialised non-legal knowledge, for example, is clearly one of the advantages claimed for arbitration. But one should strive to ensure that this does not come at the cost of legal expertise. Career judges have to undergo extensive educational and professional training to guarantee an appropriate level of legal expertise. Although many jurisdictions have introduced ADR/ODR licensing procedures for arbitrators, mediators, etc (which include legal training modules), one can find considerable differences. In particular in cases in which there is a significant party imbalance in terms of legal knowledge, or an increased need for further substantive protection of legal interests, a proper balance between legal and non-legal expertise needs to be struck to allow potential parties to rely on the ADR/ODR services offered.

Second, actual impartiality and procedures to guarantee this need to be introduced and applied extensively. Unlike litigation, with its opportunity to appeal decisions, not all ADR/ODR schemes necessarily come with a (default) appellate option. Admittedly, due process issues might open the way to review by ordinary courts. But even in some of the cases where this option exists, parties might not be sufficiently informed/instructed about this option.

Third, when it comes to ODR, the existence of many parallel schemes might confuse potential claimants (and defendants as well). Depending on the region, there might be a couple of publicly or privately run schemes, or even both at the same time. Choosing a suitable mechanism can pose a challenge, and in some instances claimants might be persuaded (by the other party) to agree on a certain scheme that might not be in their best mutual interests but strongly favours one side only.

Maximising awareness and designing ADR/ODR schemes in a way that encompasses the 'right' cases are two additional challenges. As already explained elsewhere, the need to raise awareness is a general issue, in the sense that it can be found in the context of any procedural mechanism.[64] Crafting and introducing workable schemes is, of course, desirable, but the public needs to be properly informed about the existence and at least some basic operational features of the particular device. In this respect, one can only await relevant data on more recent initiatives, eg on the requirement to include a link to the ODR Platform, as seen earlier in the context of ODR in the EU. It will be interesting to see whether more potentially affected persons can be reached than with other, non-ADR mechanisms, about which, particularly in the beginning, there were very low levels of awareness.[65]

With respect to ODR in particular, one can further note that there are conceptually different approaches when it comes to the cases covered. For instance, while the ODR Regulation focuses on online transactions only, schemes introduced under different umbrellas often can be used irrespective of whether the dispute has online

---

[64] Wrbka, n 15, 271–73.
[65] ibid, 270 and 273.

or offline roots. To reach a wider audience, to go with the general trend of expanding ODR and to level differences that could be seen as practical obstacles, particularly in a cross-border context, ODR services might want to aim at encompassing not only online, but also offline cases.

Language naturally is one of the biggest not necessarily law-related reasons why cross-border disputes are difficult to resolve. Online dispute resolution might have an advantage over offline redress in this context, because it allows for technical solutions that could be of practical help. The ODR Platform launched in 2016 might serve as an example of how to utilise software and language services to simplify the process in this regard. It can be used in any of the official EU languages. Parties and dispute resolution bodies that do not share a common language are supported by automatic translation. In addition, professional translators are available to translate the final outcome of a procedure.[66]

Technological considerations might add further issues. A challenge for ODR in particular is its dependence on ICT. Although ODR can generally be considered a fast and uncomplicated alternative to litigation, measures need to be taken to prevent technical disturbance to the greatest extent possible.

Last but not least, two intrinsically legal issues will—particularly with the expected further increase in ODR—need to be dealt with more closely in the near future. Ensuring the 'correct' use of substantive law is not limited to ODR. Depending on the circumstances and interests involved, disputes might require different solutions that range from a relatively discretional use/choice of law to compulsory compliance with certain mandatory minimum rules. An interesting further question is raised with regard to ODR in the context of the enforceability of the outcome of online arbitration. In contrast to conventional (offline) ADR, ODR is not (explicitly) covered by the pivotal New York Convention on the Recognition and Enforcement of Foreign Arbitral Awards (New York Convention). This leaves us with the question whether arbitral awards created by an online procedure (ODR arbitral awards) are enforceable in the sense of the New York Convention. In legal academia, there is a widespread belief that one can apply the framework of the Convention analogously to ODR arbitral awards. However, it has to be pointed out that this issue has not yet been answered decisively. Pertinent case law is still lacking.[67] Possible due process concerns might necessitate the introduction of explicit criteria that would have to be met by the respective ODR institutions, for an award to qualify as enforceable under the New York Convention regime. Standards as introduced, for example, under the ADR Directive/ODR Regulation regimes should be considered convincing enough to allow ODR arbitral awards to be included within the New York Convention framework.

---

[66] See ec.europa.eu/consumers/odr/main/?event=main.help.faq at 'Which language can I use on this site?'.

[67] In a similar vein, see, eg, Cortes, n 60, 112, who claims that '[t]o date, online arbitration awards have not been fully tested in the courts'; and C Liebscher, 'Article V' in R Wolff (ed), *New York Convention on the Recognition and Enforcement of Foreign Arbitral Awards—Commentary* (Munich, CH Beck, 2012) Art V, para 408, noting that '[n]o actual case has yet been presented on this issue'.

Selected Further Reading

Collective Redress

Anderson, B and Task, A, *The Class Action Playbook* (Oxford, Oxford University Press, 2010)

Backhaus, JG, Cassone, A and Ramello, GB (eds), *The Law and Economics of Class Actions in Europe*: *Lessons from America* (Cheltenham, Edward Elgar, 2012)

Cafaggi, F and Micklitz, HW (eds), *New Frontiers of Consumer Protection*: *The Interplay between Private and Public Enforcement* (Antwerp, Intersentia, 2009)

Cashman, P, *Class Action Law and Practice* (Sydney, The Federation Press, 2007)

Greenwood, J and Aspinwall, M (eds), *Collective Action in the European Union*: *Interests and the New Politics of Associability* (London, Routledge, 1998)

Hodges, C, *The Reform of Class and Representative Actions in European Legal Systems*: *A New Framework for Collective Redress in Europe* (Oxford, Hart Publishing, 2008)

Mulheron, R, *The Class Action in Common Law Legal Systems*: *A Comparative Perspective* (Oxford, Hart Publishing, 2004)

Nuyts, A and Hatzimihail, NE (eds), *Cross-Border Class Actions*: *The European Way* (Munich, Sellier European Law Publishers, 2014)

Steele, J and van Boom, W (eds), *Mass Justice*: *Challenges of Representation and Distribution* (Cheltenham, Edward Elgar, 2011)

van Boom, W and Loos, M (eds), *Collective Enforcement of Consumer Law*: *Securing Compliance in Europe through Private Group Action and Public Authority Intervention* (Groningen, Europa Law Publishing, 2007)

Wrbka, S, Van Uytsel, S and Siems, M (eds), *Collective Actions*: *Enhancing Access to Justice and Reconciling Multilayer Interests?* (Cambridge, Cambridge University Press, 2012)

Alternative Dispute Resolution

Abdel Wahab, MS, Katsh, E and Rainey, D (eds), *Online Dispute Resolution*: *Theory and Practice—a Treatise on Technology and Dispute Resolution* (The Hague, Eleven International Publishing, 2012)

Balthasar, S (ed), *International Commercial Arbitration* (Munich, CH Beck, 2016)

Barrett, JT and Barrett, JP, *A History of Alternative Dispute Resolution*: *The Story of a Political, Cultural and Social Movement* (San Francisco, CA, Jossey-Bass, 2004)

Cortes, P, *Online Dispute Resolution for Consumers in the European Union* (Abingdon, Routledge, 2011)

Cortes, P (ed), *The New Regulatory Framework for Consumer Dispute Resolution* (Oxford, Oxford University Press, 2016)

Ferrari, F (ed), *Forum Shopping in the International Commercial Arbitration Context* (Munich, Sellier European Law Publishers, 2013)

Grenig, JE, *Alternative Dispute Resolution*, 4th edn (New York, Thomson Reuters, 2016)

Haloush, H, *Online Alternative Dispute Resolution: A Solution to Cross-Border Electronic Commercial Disputes* (Saarbrücken, VDM Verlag Dr Müller, 2008)

Hodges, C, Benöhr, I and Creutzfeldt-Banda, N (eds), *Consumer ADR in Europe* (Oxford, Hart Publishing, 2012)

Hörnle, J, *Cross-border Internet Dispute Resolution* (Cambridge, Cambridge University Press, 2009)

Moffitt, ML and Bordone, RC (eds), *The Handbook of Dispute Resolution* (San Francisco, CA, Jossey-Bass, 2005)

Nolan-Haley, J, *Alternative Dispute Resolution in a Nutshell*, 4th edn (St Paul, MN, West Academic, 2013)

Ware, S, *Principles of Alternative Dispute Resolution*, 3rd edn (St Paul, MN, West Academic, 2016)

5

Corporate Governance

I. Outline

Putting in place the right organisation and governance structures is crucial to the long-term prospects of any business. This is particularly true for any business that has aspirations to be globally successful. Moreover, identifying a regulatory framework that can incentivise firms to adopt the right organisation and governance is a key challenge facing policymakers responsible for stimulating business growth and economic development.[1]

And yet a great deal of uncertainty surrounds what 'good governance' actually means in a contemporary business context, and how, from a regulator's point of view, we might go about achieving it. Complicating matters, an increasing anti-corporate sentiment means that a significant degree of public suspicion now surrounds corporations and the very possibility of 'good' corporate governance.[2]

Such scepticism is hardly surprising. Contemporary corporate governance frameworks developed in the early 2000s in response to the Enron and other corporate scandals.[3] And yet the new rules did little to prevent the 2008 financial crisis. Nor do they seem to have positively affected the performance of listed companies post-2008. The number, scale and effects of corporate scandals do not appear to be diminishing.[4] Think Volkswagen, Olympus or Wells Fargo for recent examples of large-scale corporate scandals involving high-profile multinational firms.

The difficulty in finding effective organisation and governance structures is compounded by the economic context in which all firms now operate. We live in a hyper-competitive, global economy, where innovation cycles are becoming ever shorter.

---

[1] See, eg, M Maher and T Andersson, *Corporate Governance: Effects on Firm Performance and Economic Growth* (Paris, OECD, 1999).

[2] See C Mayer, *Firm Commitment: Why the Corporation is Failing Us and How to Restore Trust in It* (Oxford, Oxford University Press, 2013).

[3] See BR Cheffins, 'Delaware and the Transformation of Corporate Governance' (2015) 40 *Delaware Journal of Corporate Law* 11.

[4] See CJ Milphaut and K Pistor, *Law and Capitalism: What Corporate Crises Reveal About Legal Systems and Economic Development Around the World* (Chicago, IL, University of Chicago Press, 2010).

Younger, more agile companies with few assets and employees are constantly emerging to disrupt incumbents, further adding to the pressures.[5]

In this chapter, we first review traditional debates within corporate governance, before turning to a discussion of important recent initiatives. Specifically, the chapter focuses on post-2000 (i) attempts at improving the performance of the board of directors and (ii) efforts designed to encourage investors, particularly institutional investors, to take a more long-term and engaged approach to their firms. The focus of the discussion is on the largest firms, specifically publicly listed corporations.

II. The 'Agency Cost Problem'

'Corporate governance' refers to the structures and procedures within an organisation that aim at ensuring that authority, responsibility and control flow downwards from investor-shareholders—the economic, legal, and moral *owners* of the company— through a board of directors to management and, finally, to the employees.[6] The extant corporate governance framework is built around the idea of a settled and well-defined corporate hierarchy. In particular, corporate governance rules are designed to protect those at the pinnacle of the hierarchy, namely, the investor-shareholders.

As such, the dominant view of corporate governance has traditionally focused on the maximisation of shareholder value.[7] According to the dominant view, the goal of a firm should be to increase the financial interests of the investors; and by doing so, the firm can maximise opportunities to be successful. Thus good governance is defined primarily in terms of shareholder primacy, ie the goal of governance is to put in place structures and processes that maximise the financial interests of the shareholders as represented by the share price.

In this model of corporate governance, governance mechanisms are primarily aimed at curtailing various agency problems, notably those that arise between self-serving executives and the owners or, alternatively, self-serving managers and executives. In each case, the risk is that the agent acts in his or her own self-interest and not in the best interests of the company. The result is that everyone suffers the negative consequences of firm underperformance (and possible bankruptcy). The control of agents via regulations that are designed to align the incentives of agents has been the primary focus of corporate governance discourse and regulation.

---

[5] M Fenwick and EPM Vermeulen, 'The New Firm: Staying Relevant, Unique and Competitive' (2015) 16 *European Business Organization Law Review* 595.

[6] For the classic statements, see A Berle and G Means, *The Modern Corporation and Private Property* (New Brunswick, Transaction Publishers, 1932); MC Jensen and WH Meckling, 'Theory of the Firm: Managerial Behavior, Agency Costs *and* Ownership Structure' (1976) 3 *Journal of Financial Economics* 305.

[7] See FH Easterbrook and DR Fischel, *The Economic Structure of Corporate Law* (Cambridge, MA, Harvard University Press, 1991).

In this way, increasing shareholder control over other actors within the firm has become the declared objective of modern corporate governance rules.[8] In practice, this shareholder primacy model means adopting measures that aim to ensure that all of the other actors/stakeholders within a firm act as if they were investor-shareholders. By aligning the interests and incentives of the various actors in this way, firm performance—again, as measured by the share price—can be improved. If the corporate governance is right then shareholder value will naturally follow. Such an outcome is of benefit to *all* of the stakeholders in a firm, as well as the public, who benefit from the goods and services that a successful firm provides.

Nevertheless, there are important differences in corporate governance debates in different jurisdictions, and to a large extent these differences reflect differences in the history and composition of the different securities markets.[9]

In those markets that are characterised by smaller and more widely dispersed shareholdings—ie liquid trading markets, such as the US or UK—the focus of the corporate governance discussion has been on creating mechanisms intended to curtail agency problems that arise between self-interested management and passive investors.[10] These problems are usually explained by the 'vertical agency relationship', in which the managers are the agents and the shareholders are the principals. This type of agency problem stems from shareholders' being disengaged from the task of monitoring and, when necessary, disciplining management. A clear separation of ownership and control provides management with the opportunity to take advantage of their informational advantage regarding a company's strategies, policies and prospects, without the risk of being detected.

In the concentrated ownership—or blockholder—systems found in different forms in Europe, Asia and other economies, the scale of the 'vertical agency problem' is mitigated because some investors tend to hold a disproportionately larger stake in listed companies.[11] By virtue of their stake in the company, such blockholders have both the incentive and capacity to monitor and discipline management. In such a case, institutional investors, families and sometimes even the state control a majority of shares and voting rights. This creates a potential three-way conflict between controlling shareholders, managers and minority shareholders. However, since the blockholders usually mitigate the problems related to managerial opportunism, it is not surprising that policymakers and regulators focus on possible conflicts that may occur in the 'horizontal agency relationship' between the blockholders (and the managers who have an incentive to respond to their demands) and the minority investors.[12]

In this context, the problems also vary depending on the type of blockholder and, in particular, the distinction between companies controlled by institutional

---

[8] See, eg, J Fox and JW Lorsch, 'What Good Are Shareholders?' (2012) July–August, *Harvard Business Review*.

[9] See WW Bratton and JA McCahery, 'Incomplete Contracts, Theories of the Firm and Comparative Corporate Governance' (2001) 2 *Theoretical Inquiries in Law* 745.

[10] See L Stout, *The Shareholder Value Myth: How Putting Shareholders First Harms Investors, Corporations and the Public* (Oakland, CA, Berret Koehler, 2012).

[11] See CG Holderness, 'A Survey of Blockholders and Corporate Control' (2003) 9 *Economic Policy Review* 1.

[12] LA Bebchuk and RJ Jackson Jr, 'The Law and Economics of Blockholder Disclosure' (2011) *Harvard John M Olin Discussion Paper Series No 702*.

investors (so-called 'outside blockholders') and those subject to family control ('inside blockholders').

It is also worth noting that in modern more global securities markets, which are typically characterised by high-frequency trading and rapid and continuous changes in share ownership, institutional investors are inclined to focus on short-term returns. The short-term stance of the 'outside' blockholders' investment strategy exposes the minority shareholders to opportunistic behaviour. The fact that outside blockholders have increasingly used derivative instruments and short-selling techniques in order to make profits, merely serves to compound the horizontal agency problem between these outside blockholders and minority investors.[13]

Second, there are those listed companies, such as the many family-owned—and sometimes even state-owned—companies, with inside blockholders, who actually hold management positions or serve on the board of directors of the companies in which they invest. Again, vertical agency problems are much less relevant in this context, but horizontal agency problems are a major concern in listed companies with sizable inside blockholders of this type.[14]

Despite efforts at controlling the various agency problems via corporate governance reform, the perception of problems remains. In an attempt to remedy these problems, several recent policy initiatives have been adopted. The following discussion focuses on recent efforts to improve the performance of the board of directors and attempts at encouraging shareholders—and particularly institutional shareholders—to adopt a more engaged role in firm governance.

III. Improving the Board of Directors

The board of directors of a company can be crucial to corporate success and, as such, can be seen as one of the most important institutions in modern capitalism. The core function of the board is to mediate the relationship between shareholders (who own the company) and the managers (who, on a daily basis, run the company). This task is achieved by (i) selecting the top managers (ie the Chief Executive Officer (CEO) and other senior executives), (ii) offering strategic advice in developing a business plan or acquiring competitors, and (iii) monitoring for managerial incompetence or fraud.

The performance of boards, however, has often been disappointing and, historically, boards have had a bad press, being accused of everything from gross incompetence to corruption.[15] More recently, the Enron and WorldCom scandals of 2000–02 and

---

[13] See LR Strine, 'Ordinary Investors of the US and EU Unite: A Reflection on Sound, Sustainable Wealth Creation' (2013) *DSF Policy Paper Series No 34*.

[14] See Holderness, 'A Survey of Blockholders and Corporate Control'.

[15] SM Bainbridge, *Corporate Governance After the Financial Crisis* (Oxford, Oxford University Press, 2012) 50.

the financial crisis of 2008 revealed a systemic failure of many boards to adequately perform their monitoring and policing roles in particular.[16]

Clearly, this represents a missed opportunity. The potential strategic benefits of a well-functioning board seem clear. A board has the capacity to help companies gain a competitive advantage. Such a board can help build connections with government, society and other stakeholders. It can assist company leaders in making better decisions and avoid tunnel vision by providing them with relevant information on the current state of the business environment in which they operate. Boards can also facilitate the identification of new business opportunities, or provide a better sense of their peers and competitors. Lastly, pro-active board members with relevant expertise can help business leaders in identifying expertise gaps on their executive teams. It is in this more collaborative context that boards can have an impact on a company's business strategies and capacity for innovation, and maximise opportunities for success.

The dynamics and functioning of the board are key in this regard. In order for a company to grow, thrive and reach its full potential, corporate boards are expected to be committed, alert and inquisitive. More importantly, they should be pro-actively engaged in the company's business and affairs. Only board members who prepare for meetings and frequently attend them are able to add value to the discussions. On the other hand, board members also need to ask hard questions and challenge the strategic assumptions of management. And they can only do this effectively when they possess the relevant capacities and a willingness to devote energy to the tasks of both monitoring *and* strategy building.

Unfortunately, however, board members often complain that there is simply not enough time to discuss strategy developments, innovation and value creation. In large part, this is because so much time is now taken up with discussing compliance issues. In such a context, the ability of board members to add genuine strategic value is limited.

This reflects the post-2000 emergence of a so-called 'monitoring model' of the board.[17] One effect of Enron and other corporate scandals was a much greater emphasis on compliance post-2000. An important and unintended side-effect of this focus on oversight, supervision and risk management, and the subsequent lack of time for boards to adequately perform the advisory-strategic function, has been a one-sided, compliance-oriented board. Commentators suggest that if the balance of a board is tilted towards those with compliance expertise, it is hardly surprising that the agenda and time of that board are devoted to such issues.

Again, this is not intended to understate or dismiss the compliance function. Obviously, in a contemporary regulatory context it is vital that a board devotes energy to monitoring compliance. The multiple legal risks—often complex and transnational in character—that have been created by the contemporary regulatory environment mean that monitoring of compliance is essential.[18]

---

[16] See WA Dimma, *Tougher Boards for Tougher Times: Corporate Governance in the Post-Enron Era* (Mississauga, Wiley, 2006).
[17] See Bainbridge, n 15, ch 2.
[18] M Fenwick, 'The New Corporate Criminal Law and Transnational Legal Risk' in M Fenwick and S Wrbka (eds), *Flexibility in Modern Business Law: A Comparative Assessment* (Tokyo, Springer, 2016) 149.

However, it is equally important to stress the value of board diversity and, in particular, the importance of board members who can help a firm develop new business strategies in collaborative partnership with senior executives. After all, such strategies are crucial to the long-term success—possibly even the very survival of any firm, particularly in the context of globalisation and hyper-competitive global markets. And in the absence of such success or survival, questions of compliance (obviously) become less important.

How, then, to achieve this type of board? The past decade has seen several attempts to make boards more effective. In the US, for example, the Sarbanes-Oxley Act (2002) and the Dodd-Frank Act (2010) forced companies to appoint more independent directors and disclose more information about board compensation, and other jurisdictions followed.[19] But much of this drive towards independent directors was conducted within the framework of developing a monitoring model, ie the belief that independent directors are better able to perform the monitoring function than those with a pre-existing relationship to the company. Therefore, this chapter will focus on another more recent regulatory trend related to improving the quality of board effectiveness, namely, measures designed to encourage better board evaluation.

A. Board Evaluation

In this context, board evaluation can be understood in a broad sense to refer to any mechanisms that are institutionalised within a company to gather information on board performance. Board evaluation has recently attracted increased attention from regulators, investors and other stakeholders.[20] The reason for this seems fairly straightforward. When done properly, board evaluation can provide a vital tool for directors to review and improve their own and their company's performance. Evaluation provides a potentially important resource that can generate significant value-creation opportunities for all firms.

The performance and effectiveness of a board can be evaluated along multiple variables. Broadly speaking, these would include: (i) the quality of the monitoring and risk management (the monitoring function); (ii) the quality of the strategic and other business-related advice (the strategic function); (iii) board members' pro-active participation (board dynamism); and (iv) the diversity and independence of the board.

Of course, board evaluation is a not a new idea. Many boards have long recognised that it is important for them to frequently evaluate and assess the effectiveness of their performance. Nevertheless, regulators have come to recognise the value in firms' conducting such self-evaluation exercises. This has resulted in more and more attention to board evaluation across multiple jurisdictions. Moreover, international bodies have picked up on this issue. For example, the *G20/OECD Corporate Governance Principles* now recommend including a principle on regular board evaluations in a country's corporate governance framework.[21]

---

[19] See Cheffins, n 3.

[20] For a recent review, see T Griffin et al, 'Board Evaluations and Boardroom Dynamics' (2017) *Stanford University Graduate School of Business Research Paper No 17-22*.

[21] OECD, *G20/OECD Corporate Governance Principles* (Paris, OECD Publishing, 2015) Principle VI.F.

A comparative review of contemporary regulations regarding board evaluation reveals three different approaches. First, there are jurisdictions that currently have no specific measures on board evaluation. Such jurisdictions may require evaluation of individual directors, but not necessarily of the board as a whole. This does not mean, however, that boards in such jurisdictions are not subject to an obligation to implement some sort of evaluation. At a minimum, an implicit requirement to assess the functioning and operation of the board might be derived from the board members' obligation to pursue the welfare of the company and not their own self-interest. Moreover, since consultancy and other advisory firms seem keen to encourage companies to put the issue of board effectiveness on the corporate governance agenda, there is often real pressure to engage in some form of evaluation. This trend will only become more widespread as more consultancy firms start publishing research reports based on such board evaluations.

A second group comprises jurisdictions that encourage board evaluation by including an evaluation recommendation in their corporate governance codes. Many countries now provide for such a recommendation, based on a 'comply-or-explain' principle. Deviations from the recommendations to assess boards, committees and board members are thus possible, if explained in an accurate manner. Nevertheless, the pressure to comply seems to be quite compelling. Take Japan as an example. Japan's Corporate Governance Code contains a principle regarding the evaluation of board effectiveness: 'Each year, the board should analyse and evaluate its effectiveness as a whole, taking into consideration the relevant matters, including the self-evaluations of each director. A summary of the results should be disclosed.'[22]

Interestingly, the corporate governance codes of countries that fall within the German civil law tradition (and which have a very strong 'two-tier' corporate governance tradition), such as Germany, Austria and Hungary, only very generally describe the board evaluation and effectiveness requirements. The German Corporate Governance Code states that 'The Supervisory Board shall examine the efficiency of its activities on a regular basis.'[23] The evaluation of individual members is not prescribed. It is therefore not surprising that the assessment of members of supervisory boards is not common practice in Germany. The board evaluation provision in the Corporate Governance Code of Austria is slightly more detailed, specifying the frequency of the evaluation: 'The supervisory board shall discuss the efficiency of its activities annually, in particular, its organisation and work procedures (self-evaluation).'[24]

Of course, the risk with listed companies is that they will take a minimal approach to compliance when it comes to corporate governance, so that the impact of more detailed board evaluation principles is arguably more effective. The board evaluation principles in the UK, for example, are a good example of more detailed assessment requirements. General principles on board evaluation are followed by more detailed 'supporting principles' outlining the aim and purpose of evaluation.[25]

---

[22] Tokyo Stock Exchange, 'Japan's Corporate Governance Code' (2015) Principle 4.11.3.

[23] Regierungskommission Deutscher Corporate Governance Kodex, 'German Corporate Governance Code' (2017) s 5.6.

[24] Österreichischer Arbeitskreis für Corporate Governance, 'Austrian Corporate Governance Code' (2015) s 36.

[25] Financial Reporting Council, 'The UK Corporate Governance Code' (2016) s B.6.

Again, it appears that board assessments are more likely to be effective when the relevant corporate governance codes detail the objectives of the evaluation process, as well as the type of evaluation. In France, Italy, the Netherlands and the UK, the code provisions specifically recommend gaining insight into the composition and diversity of the board.

Unsurprisingly, the more detailed code provisions also cover the disclosure of the results of the evaluations. Many corporate governance codes now require publication of the results in the company's annual report.

Lastly, there are those jurisdictions that oblige regular board evaluation. India and the US are examples of countries that impose a legal obligation to conduct board evaluations annually.

Consider the US. Listed companies are required to conduct an annual performance evaluation of the board under the listing rules of the New York Stock Exchange. The rules state that the board should conduct a self-evaluation 'at least annually to determine whether it and its committees are functioning effectively'.[26] The audit, compensation and nominating and governance committees must also conduct an annual performance evaluation. What is interesting is that companies listed on Nasdaq are not required to engage in self-evaluation, but still do so as a matter of good practice. The evaluation process is now widespread in the US. Almost all of the boards of Standard & Poor's 500 (S&P 500) companies have disclosed annual performance evaluation results.[27]

The regulatory requirements in India are generally in line with the regulations and practices in the US. The Companies Act 2013 requires listed companies to disclose the annual evaluation process regarding the board, its committees and the individual directors. The nomination and remuneration committee is responsible for carrying out the evaluation of each director's performance. Moreover, the Listing Regulations require the evaluation of the performance of the independent directors on the board. The entire board must participate in the evaluation of each independent director, except, of course, for the director being evaluated. The mode, manner and evaluation criteria must be defined by the nomination and remuneration committee. The full board is required to monitor and review the evaluation framework for the board of directors.

So what has been the effect of these global regulatory efforts to promote board evaluation? As is often the case in a corporate governance context, the risk of regulatory initiatives aimed at compelling—or even just 'nudging'—a particular activity is that they merely encourage formalistic, box-ticking behaviour in which mitigating the costs and managing the appearance of compliance become the key objectives of regulated firms. In such a case, however, any resources devoted to projecting an image of meaningful evaluation are wasted and the potential strategic gains from self-evaluation are never realised.

The more general challenge raised by board evaluation, therefore, is how to build a genuine and effective evaluation culture inside a firm, and this is a complex issue.

---

[26] New York Stock Exchange Rule 303A.091.
[27] See Spencer Stuart, '2017 Spencer Stuart US Board Index' (2017), www.spencerstuart.com/research-and-insight/ssbi-2017.

So, what might policymakers and regulators do to ensure that boards get the most out of their evaluations? How can regulators help to promote a culture in which boards, committees and their members are all genuinely committed to implementing meaningful evaluation with a view to improving board effectiveness?

Take the issue of *when* to evaluate. Clearly, the most common practice is for company boards to evaluate themselves at fixed points in time, most typically on an annual basis. And from a regulator's point of view, specifying the frequency of evaluation seems to make sense. However, in considering this issue it is important to realise that there is no 'one-size-fits-all' blueprint for the evaluation of a board, and that the evaluation needs of any firm are inevitably going to be dynamic and firm-specific. Most obviously, they will vary enormously depending on the age of a specific business, or the particular sector in which the business operates. For instance, if a company is at a stage in its lifecycle when it is looking to expand its sphere of operations into new markets, board evaluation may be necessary in order to assess whether more international experience or local knowledge of the new markets is required. Companies and their boards also tend to evaluate and address board composition and diversity issues when they encounter problems of some kind. Lastly, the board of companies with a disappointing stock price performance may also find it valuable to implement an ad hoc evaluation of their current performance.

Such simple cases indicate that boards may need to conduct evaluations more than once a year. In this respect, board evaluation needs to be dynamic in nature and responsive to changes in the firm's operations and needs. As such, the most effective model may be to continuously assess board performance through a process of on-going evaluation. Of course, the reporting of evaluations may be necessary only once a year.

Equally, *what* to evaluate raises a number of difficult issues. Board evaluation clearly needs to move beyond a narrow compliance and risk-management perspective. Organisational design within large firms needs to be redirected to innovation, products and the people, and board evaluation can play a crucial role in this task. In a digital and globalised world, boards should facilitate an environment that offers the best chance for their companies to retain the best talent, deliver the best products, and maintain the capacity to constantly reinvent themselves in the face of rapid technological, economic and social change.

The key, then, is to identify and implement evaluation processes that maximise opportunities to deliver more meaningful and relevant strategic advice to management and other stakeholders in a company. This is not to suggest that compliance does not matter; rather, it is to note that a broader range of considerations needs to be incorporated into any evaluation exercise.

In conclusion, the current regulatory approach risks breeding an empty, formalistic style of compliance. This usually reveals little about the actual mechanics of the evaluation process and the results and takeaways from the most recent evaluation. This is a problem as it limits learning opportunities for other firms, but it also means that firms treat evaluation as an obligation to be fulfilled and not as a genuine opportunity for adding strategic value and communicating with the market.

There are some exceptions, however, and learning from such best practice seems vital. Some firms do embrace a more open style of communication regarding their evaluation procedures. Regulators need to make clear that adopting a detailed and open style of communication can improve a board's ability to provide more meaning-ful disclosure to stakeholders, inside and outside the firm. Regulators must make more effort to support, encourage and persuade boards to recognise the rewards that come from the open disclosure of the evaluation process.

And the potential rewards do seem clear. At the very least, open communication of evaluation can increase the commitment of board members to participate in the (future) evaluation process and their engagement with it, which will in turn improve the functioning and performance of the evaluation and of the board.

IV. Mobilising Institutional Investors

A second set of recent corporate governance initiatives has focused on promoting shareholder engagement, specifically encouraging institutional investors to adopt a more engaged relationship with their firms.

A. The Investment Landscape Today and the Need for Shareholder Engagement

When talking about investors it is helpful to begin with the distinction between institutional investors and retail investors. Over the course of the last few decades, there has been a significant increase in the number of shares owned by institutional investors. In the UK, for example, it is estimated that 90 per cent of shares are now held by financial intermediaries.[28] A similar trend can be seen in other major securities markets.[29]

Policy discussion has focused on encouraging these institutional investors—who are sophisticated market actors, at least in comparison to retail investors—to take a more active role in firm governance.[30] There is a consensus that firms can make strategic gains from such engagement. However, although studies on this issue have found that some institutions spend time and resources on active ownership, a significant number of institutional investors do not actively engage in the corporate governance of their portfolio companies.[31]

This recognition of the potential value of shareholder engagement also seems to reflect the prevailing view that the recent financial crisis was, at least in part, caused by

---

[28] JG Hill, 'Good Activist/Bad Activist: The Rise of International Stewardship Codes' (2017) *European Corporate Governance Institute Working Paper No 368/2017* 3.

[29] ibid.

[30] For an early discussion of this issue, see BS Black, 'Shareholder Passivity Re-examined' (1990) 89 *Michigan Law Review* 520.

[31] ibid.

a lack of shareholder intervention. 'Where were the shareholders?', as John Plender put it in a *Financial Times* article written in the early stages of the crisis.[32]

So, who are these institutional investors? There is no clear or settled definition of an 'institutional investor'. The only thing we can say with certainty is that an institutional investor is not a natural person; it is—by definition—organised as a legal entity. However, the precise legal form varies enormously among different institutional investors, covering everything from joint stock companies (for example, closed-end investment companies) to limited liability partnerships (like private equity firms), as well as incorporation by special statute, for example in the case of sovereign wealth funds. Institutional investors may also operate independently, or be part of a larger corporate group. Mutual funds, for example, are often set up as subsidiaries of banks or insurance companies.

It is often the case that institutional investors can be regarded as synonymous with 'intermediary investors', ie an institution that manages the money of other people. But there are exceptions. Sovereign wealth funds, for instance, can be seen as ultimate owners when they serve as financial stabilisation funds. There are also hybrid forms, such as private equity funds, where the managing partner co-invests, to varying degrees, with the external investors. Nevertheless, the rise of financial intermediation—what some commentators characterise as 'agency capitalism'—is a defining feature of the investment landscape today.[33]

Two categories of institutional investors need to be distinguished. The first category is traditional institutional investors, which comprises pension funds, insurance companies and investments funds. Traditional institutional investors can then be divided into several subcategories. For instance, we can distinguish between investors that have internal investment guidelines that includes policies on active long-term engagement and those investors that do not spend resources on active engagement.

The second group comprises the alternative institutional investors, such as hedge funds, private equity firms, exchange-traded funds and sovereign wealth funds. They tend to take a more aggressive and proactive approach.[34]

It is also important to note the increasingly complex investment chain that characterises investments today. Institutional investors often invest in instruments offered by other institutional investors. Pensions funds may, for instance, invest in private equity funds, and insurance companies may buy into mutual funds. The plethora of advisors, asset managers, brokers, bankers and other intermediaries only makes understanding the identity of shareholders in listed companies more complicated.

The enormous variety of institutional investors, their different investment strategies and the potential for conflicts of interest between them can lead to a profit-driven short-term investment approach. It is therefore significant that a number of new policy and regulatory measures in the area of corporate governance aim at encouraging institutional investors, their asset managers, advisors and other intermediaries to take a

---

[32] J Plender, 'Shut Out' *Financial Times* (18 October 2008).

[33] RJ Gilson and JN Gordon, 'Agency Capitalism: Further Implications of Equity Intermediation' in JG Hill and RS Thomas (eds), *Research Handbook on Shareholder Power* (Cheltenham, Edward Elgar, 2015).

[34] BR Cheffins and J Armour 'The Past, Present & Future of Shareholder Activism by Hedge Funds' (2011) 37 *Journal of Corporate Law* 51.

more responsible long-term ownership perspective when investing in a company. The belief is that by obliging or nudging institutional investors to adopt a longer-term perspective, a more effective and balanced corporate governance can be achieved, and that this is crucial to the creation of sustainable and long-term corporate value.

Given the important role of institutional investors in the contemporary corporate governance debate, the *G20/OECD Principles of Corporate Governance 2015* included a new chapter (Chapter III) on institutional investors, stock markets and other intermediaries, which 'addresses the need for sound economic incentives throughout the investment chain, with a particular focus on institutional investors acting in a fiduciary capacity'.[35] The *G20/OECD Principles* have therefore acknowledged the importance of long-term value creation and the special role of institutional investors in achieving this goal. This is based on the belief that shareholders/investors are best suited to appointing and monitoring directors, who have the obligation to represent the long-term interests of the company.

In pursuing this goal, it is important to understand that if shareholder engagement is not part of the investors' business model and investment strategy, promoting their active engagement may be ineffective (particularly if we believe that these investors are generally more concerned with a company's stock price and short-term performance). For instance, mandatory requirements for investors to engage by exercising their voting rights may again simply lead to a box-ticking approach. Moreover, the mandatory voting involvement of institutional investors is often mainly limited to voting their shares in line with the information provided by proxy advisors, giving the proxy advisory industry a crucial role in the corporate governance processes of listed companies.

Arguably, corporate executives, aware of the importance of the advisors' recommendations, proactively change their strategies in order to receive proxy advisors' support. If these voting recommendations are mainly based on corporate governance checklists without taking the long-term growth of companies into account, the proxy advisory industry will only further add to the short-term mentality of corporate managers, boards and shareholders.

A strict adherence to a corporate governance framework that protects the 'short-term' interests of these investors may, then, have the counterproductive effect of eroding long-term growth and innovation in listed companies. Unsurprisingly, therefore, regulators have attempted to fix the shortcomings of the corporate governance framework by promoting measures that encourage long-term shareholder engagement.

B. Regulatory Measures Designed to Promote Shareholder Engagement

Policymakers and regulators, convinced that the detached and short-term attitude of investors played a significant role in the 2008 financial crisis, have subsequently

---

[35] OECD, *G20/OECD Corporate Governance Principles*, n 21, 5.

attempted to fix the shortcomings of the corporate governance framework by promoting regulatory measures that encourage long-term shareholder engagement.[36]

Ideally, a 'stewardship' culture should emerge from such regulatory interventions. Such a culture is characterised by an engaged and long-term approach in which the institutional investor seeks to make an active and meaningful contribution to firm governance, management and performance. For these institutional investors, engagement involves more than just voting: it includes monitoring and entering into a purposeful dialogue with companies on matters such as strategy, performance, value creation, innovation, risk and corporate governance matters, including risk management, the composition of the board of directors and remuneration.

The *goals* of the current policy and regulatory interventions can therefore be identified more precisely:

— To encourage traditional institutional investors (who have, until now, adopted a 'no engagement' or 'reactive engagement' approach) to embrace a 'stewardship engagement' strategy towards firm performance and governance.
— To encourage alternative institutional investors to adopt a less event-driven or short-term strategy, and instead to behave more like those traditional institutional investors who have practised a stewardship-type of engagement.

A review of regulatory measures results in a typology of relevant regulatory and policy measures to encourage institutional investors' 'stewardship engagement'. Table 5.1 provides a summary. A brief review of these different types of measures follows.

Table 5.1: Regulatory Measures Designed to Promote Investor Engagement

Measures that 'enable' institutional investor engagement	1. General shareholder rights
	2. Measures that give investors holding above a certain percentage of shares special powers and rights
Measures that 'support' institutional investor engagement	3. Measures compelling disclosure of information on the ownership and control structure of a company
Measures that 'require' institutional investor engagement	4. Measures that require involvement on board composition
	5. Measures that require involvement on remuneration
Measures that 'encourage' institutional investor engagement	6. Measures related to voting
	7. Stewardship Codes and Corporate Governance Principles

[36] See, generally, SM Bainbridge, *Corporate Governance After the Financial Crisis* (Oxford, Oxford University Press, 2012).

i. General Shareholder Rights

Rules that give shareholders various rights can be found in all jurisdictions. The primary source of such rights is, typically, company law. Standard rights include the right to attend the general shareholders meetings, the right to speak at such meetings and the right to vote at meetings. The issues that can be voted on generally include issues and matters relating to the structure and organisation of the company. Examples are the election, appointment and removal of directors, the approval of annual reports, and the approval of significant changes to the structure of the company—notably mergers and acquisitions—or changes to the share capital structure. These rights can be thought of as a necessary precondition of any form of shareholder engagement.

ii. Measures Providing for Special Shareholder Rights

A more important category concerns measures that give various additional rights to those holding more than a certain percentage of shares or voting rights. For example, the right to convene meetings and have items put on the agenda. The key issues here are the thresholds of share ownership or voting rights that trigger the special powers, and the scope of the special powers themselves. Again, the primary source for these rights is usually general company law.

There are multiple differences with respect to the threshold and the procedure that shareholders have to follow. Consider Australia. The Corporations Act 2001 defines the level at 5 per cent for certain rights.[37] Acquiring 5 per cent or more of the outstanding shares confers rights to call a general meeting and propose resolutions.

We see a similar arrangement under Canada's corporate statutes. Under the Canada Business Corporations Act, registered shareholders holding 5 per cent or more of the outstanding shares of a corporation that carry the right to vote at a meeting may call a meeting.[38] A call for a meeting is required to state the business to be conducted at the meeting and must be sent to each director, as well as to the registered office of the corporation.

In China, under the Company Law, shareholders who solely or in aggregate hold more than 10 per cent of the total share capital of a company for at least 90 consecutive days may call for an extraordinary shareholders' meeting.[39]

In the US, the Delaware General Corporate Law (DGCL) is a good example, not least because Delaware is by far the most popular state for company formation.[40] With respect to Delaware corporations, under the DGCL, a company's certificate of incorporation or by-laws may authorise shareholders to call a special meeting of shareholders. The certificate of incorporation or by-laws would then set forth the procedural requirements for calling a special meeting, including the minimum holding requirements for a shareholder to call such a meeting.

---

[37] Corporations Act 2001 (Australia), s 249D(1).
[38] Canada Business Corporations Act, s 143(1).
[39] Company Law (China), s 39.
[40] Delaware General Corporate Law, s 211(d).

iii. Measures Requiring Disclosure of Ownership and Control Information

Possession of relevant information on the structure of a company is a necessary precondition for any kind of shareholder engagement. For instance, the articles of association and/or by-laws of the company need to be publicly available in order to help investors understand their specific rights. In order for an institutional investor to predict the impact of its actions, it is also necessary to have current and accurate information about the ownership structure of a firm. Access to the shareholders' register is often necessary to give institutional investors some insights into possible allies and support.

But knowing the identity of the other shareholders alone is clearly not sufficient. Information about the natural persons (or states) that actually have control over the shareholders is more important. Most jurisdictions have therefore implemented rules and regulations that require the disclosure of the beneficial owners, if a certain percentage threshold of ownership is exceeded. In most cases, this 'substantial ownership' threshold varies between 3 per cent and 5 per cent. These information rights are usually granted under both the company laws and securities regulations of the respective jurisdictions.[41]

What is particularly valuable is that online resources make this information readily available to shareholders and other stakeholders of the company. In the UK, for example, a company's constitutional documents, such as the articles of association, are available publicly and online at Companies House, the UK Registry of Companies. We see similar rules in many other jurisdictions.

Moreover, UK companies are generally required by the Companies Act to comply with any request from a shareholder to inspect or receive a copy of the company's shareholder register. This request can be denied only if it has not been made for a 'proper purpose' (which must be demonstrated in court). The Institute of Chartered Secretaries and Administrators has published non-binding guidelines that give more insights into what constitutes a 'proper purpose' (which normally include shareholders exercising their rights). A 'proper purpose' requirement is also common in most countries. As in the UK, exercising shareholders' rights is viewed as a proper purpose. Examples of 'improper purpose' include gathering information about personal wealth of a shareholder, or using the list for commercial purposes.

The UK Companies Act also gives shareholders the right to request information about the beneficial ownership of the shares. Companies are obliged to give any available information about the beneficial owners (again, if the request was made for a 'proper purpose'). Here it should be noted that many UK listed companies give an instruction to brokers to serve such notices on a monthly basis.

And there is more. Since April 2016, most UK companies are required to maintain a publicly available register of the beneficial owners (ie those with significant control) of the company. This information is freely available. 'Significant control' is given a broad definition. A person with significant control is an individual who holds more

---

[41] See M Fenwick and EPM Vermeulen, *Disclosure of Beneficial Ownership After the Panama Papers* (Washington, DC, International Finance Corporation, 2016).

than 25 per cent of the shares or voting rights in a company, has the right to appoint or remove the majority of the board of directors, or otherwise exercises significant influence or control.

This is different from most countries, where institutional investors (or other stakeholders) only have access to the list of registered shareholders. The information about holders of 'bearer shares' is usually not available. Also, the shareholder registers in most countries do not include information about the beneficial ownership of the shares. The identity of the beneficial owners only becomes available after they have acquired a substantial number of shares. Substantial ownership is usually defined in terms of 'percentage ownership'.

Lastly, another aspect of this issue concerns coordination between investors. The *G20/OECD Principles of Corporate Governance 2015* state that 'shareholders, including institutional shareholders, should be allowed to consult with each other on issues concerning their basic rights ...', subject to exceptions to prevent abuse'.[42] The *Principles* therefore oppose the implementation of rules and regulations that could hamper the ability of shareholders to coordinate their actions and communicate with each other. As such, communication among shareholders is generally considered to be good for the company, as long as their coordination is not used to manipulate markets or obtain control over a company without complying with takeover and disclosure laws and regulations.

iv. Measures Requiring Engagement on Board Composition

Shareholders have a right to receive information about matters relating to the structure of a company. The right to approve structural changes is usually also reserved to shareholders. These fundamental changes must be approved by either a simple majority or a supermajority (normally a 75 per cent majority) of the shareholders present at the shareholders meeting. Sometimes a specific quorum, ensuring sufficient representation at the shareholders meeting, is also required.

These general rules can be found in countries' company laws, and are usually repeated and described in more detail in a company's articles of association and/or by-laws. Yet company laws, securities regulations and corporate governance codes/guidelines have introduced special voting arrangements to facilitate the active and engaged participation of minority shareholders. These rules tend to focus on the composition and remuneration of the board of directors and/or senior executives.

To be sure, some jurisdictions allow cumulative voting for the election and appointment of directors. China even requires the use of cumulative voting when a controlling shareholder has more than 30 per cent of the voting shares. In a cumulative voting system, shareholders are entitled to cast their votes for multiple candidates. In effect, this gives them one vote per share multiplied by the number of directors to be elected. If more minority shareholders use their cumulative voting rights for the same director, they may be able to outvote the majority.

---

[42] OECD, *G20/OECD Corporate Governance Principles*, Principle II.C.6.d.

In order to give minority shareholders stronger rights, a number of jurisdictions have adopted special arrangements that require or allow minority shareholders to appoint one or more members of the board of directors. It is clear that these arrangements have the potential to 'activate' engagement (at least 'reactive engagement' strategies) in companies that are characterised by a low level of exposure to shareholder engagement, due to the influence of controlling shareholders.

Here it should also be noted that since early 2017, more than 50 per cent of the S&P 500 companies in the US included 'proxy access' in their by-laws due to the collective efforts of institutional investors. Usually, these proxy access provisions allow a shareholder or group of shareholders that has owned 3 per cent or more of the company's shares for three years to nominate 20 per cent of the board seats, without undertaking the expense of a proxy solicitation.[43]

v. *Measures Requiring Engagement on Remuneration*

What is particularly significant in the context of institutional investor engagement is the requirement that a company's remuneration policy must be discussed with the shareholders and, in many cases, also approved by the shareholders. This varies in different jurisdictions from a binding vote to an advisory, non-binding vote.

No matter whether the 'vote' is binding or advisory in nature, this mechanism provides institutional investors with a clear means to express their dissatisfaction with the performance of the managers and directors. This is particularly the case in the event of shareholders' being able to approve the implementation of the policy.

Many countries have therefore introduced mechanisms that allow shareholders to vote on the level and amount of remuneration. Yet the scope of these rules varies considerably among the jurisdictions (varying from the approval of the remuneration of individual directors/managers to the total remuneration of all the directors/managers). In the UK, for instance, the Companies Act requires that the board's remuneration policy be subject to a binding vote (which must be passed every three years).[44] This approval of the remuneration policy is coupled with an annual advisory/non-binding vote on the implementation report. This report provides information about how the remuneration policy has been implemented in the previous financial year.

Australia has also introduced an advisory and non-binding voting mechanism under which shareholders are allowed to cast votes against a proposal to approve the remuneration report.[45] In order to hold directors accountable for executive salaries and bonuses, a so-called 'two-strike' rule was introduced with regard to the remuneration arrangements for executives. Under this rule, if more than 25 per cent of the votes are cast against the remuneration report in two consecutive years, shareholders will have the opportunity to put the entire company board up for re-election. Even though the two-strike rule has not yet been used, it is clear that it provides institutional investors with a powerful means of engaging the company or other shareholders on broader corporate governance issues.

---

[43] See Council of Institutional Investors, 'Proxy Access' (2017) available at www.cii.org/proxy_access.
[44] Companies Act 1985, s 439.
[45] Corporations Act 2001, as amended, ss 250R(2) and 250U–250V.

vi. Measures Requiring Engagement over Voting

The regulatory measures discussed so far are all linked to the *governance of the company*. In contrast to such company-oriented governance measures, there is a recent trend to implement measures that directly target the institutional investors, and attempts to pressure them indirectly to be more actively engaged with firm governance.

The first type of measures concerns voting policies and mandatory voting. Such measures can, in turn, be split into three groups, depending on the origin and nature of the obligation. First, there are those measures that the institutional investors adopt themselves. Second, there are private initiatives—notably guidelines adopted on the part of industry bodies. Lastly, there are the public initiatives, in which the state requires action—via the law—on the part of the institutional investors.

Take Finland. Most Finnish institutional shareholders have guidelines and policies or codes of conduct on how to steer their investments, and more specifically guidelines on how to act as an engaged shareholder of a listed company. Institutional investors, such as major pension funds, insurance companies and Solidium Oy (an investment company owned by the state of Finland), are major operators in the Finnish market and have important shareholdings in several listed companies. Due to their unique and dominant position in the Finnish market, their guidelines arguably have a significant effect on the level of shareholder engagement by other institutional investors.

In the US, other primary sources of practices relating to shareholder engagement include the policy guidelines of proxy advisory firms (such as Institutional Shareholder Services (ISS) or Glass Lewis), large institutional investors (such as BlackRock, T Rowe Price and Vanguard) and of others in the investment community (such as the Council of Institutional Investors, TIAA-CREF and CalPERS). These sources are very influential in practice.

In contrast, in other jurisdictions private industry guidelines are used. In Italy, for example, the investor community has issued several non-binding guidelines and codes of best practice in this area. Guidelines issued by the Italian Asset Managers Associations are particularly noteworthy in this regard.

In Australia, the main industry body that regulates the activities of larger institutional investors is the Australian Financial Services Council (FSC). The FSC members include investment funds, pension funds and insurance companies, as well as a range of service providers supporting the industry, such as law or accountancy firms. In 2013, the FSC published a binding standard (Binding FSC Standard No 13), which requires all members to approve a formal 'voting policy' that sets out the principles and guidelines under which 'rights to vote' must be exercised. An institutional investor that is a member of the FSC may decide to abstain from voting, but must not fail to take any action. A 'no engagement' approach is not permitted under Standard No 13. Although the FSC Standards are compulsory, the nature of the FSC as an industry body limits its disciplinary powers with regard to any breaches by its members.

Lastly, there are those jurisdictions that adopt laws on this issue. Israel is interesting in this regard. Additional sources of regulations, relating to shareholder engagement for Israeli institutional investors, are the Joint Investments in Trust Law 1994; the Ordinance Supervision of Financial Services (Provident Fund) (Participation of Managing Company at a General Meeting) 2009; and the Circular for Financial Institutions of the Capital Market, Insurance and Savings promulgated by the Israeli

Ministry of Finance. These public sources require, among other things, that institutional shareholders have a duty to participate in general shareholders meetings and to invest adequate resources to monitor the companies in which they invest. The legal duty set forth in these rules and regulations derives from the institutional investors' ability not only to monitor, but also to influence the decision-making process at shareholders meetings, and from their obligation to ensure the highest possible return on their members' funds.

vii. Stewardship Codes and Corporate Governance Principles

The regulatory measures discussed so far mainly focus on corporate governance matters, particularly those focused on executive compensation and composition of the board. The problem, however, is that institutional investors required to act on board composition, remuneration or voting on other issues will often rely on the recommendations of proxy advisors. The proxy advisory industry thus plays a dominant role in the corporate governance process in listed companies. Such reliance on third parties can create a vacuum with respect to genuine discussion about long-term strategies, innovation and value creation.[46]

Yet policymakers, regulators, company directors and institutional investors increasingly believe that shareholder engagement should go beyond simply following proxy advisor recommendations. It should also include a purposeful, meaningful and constructive dialogue between a firm and the institutional investors. This dialogue can offer a competitive advantage for companies. Institutional investors can provide an outside view, assist in detecting blind spots in strategy, raise awareness of external risks and help connect to other stakeholders with the capacity to add value.

In order to encourage this kind of meaningful and constructive engagement, industries and countries have therefore promulgated and published so-called 'stewardship codes'. The distinctiveness of such codes lies in the attempt to create more general, responsible and purposeful investor engagement. In particular, they attempt to foster the view that institutional investors must be viewed as 'stewards' of a company.

The first country-based stewardship code was published in 2010 by the UK Financial Reporting Council. The UK Stewardship Code sets out good practice for institutional investors seeking to engage with the board and management of listed companies. It applies on a 'comply or explain' basis.

Rather than setting formal standards, the regulator has drafted a code, which institutional investors may either comply with or, if they do not comply, explain publicly why they do not. It is principles-based rather than rules-based, and provides recommendations rather than imposing rules. The Code was revised in 2012. It states that institutional investors should:

— Publicly disclose their policy on how they will discharge their stewardship responsibilities.

---

[46] See J Kay, 'The Kay Review of UK Equity Markets and Long-Term Decision Making—Interim Report' (July 2012), www.gov.uk/government/uploads/system/uploads/attachment_data/file/31544/12-631-kay-review-of-equity-markets-interim-report.pdf.

— Have a robust policy on managing conflicts of interest in relation to stewardship, which should be publicly disclosed.
— Monitor their investee companies.
— Establish clear guidelines on when and how they will escalate their stewardship activities.
— Be willing to act collectively with other investors where appropriate.
— Have a clear policy on voting and disclosure of voting activity.
— Report periodically on their stewardship and voting activities.

The Japanese regulator has also introduced a stewardship code, published in 2014. Historically, investor activism was rare in Japan, not least because of a system of cross-shareholding that protected management from outside shareholder supervision.[47] The Code was part of a package of corporate governance reforms introduced by Prime Minister Abe's administration, as part of an attempt to reinvigorate the economy after decades of stagnation. The hope was that the Code would create a more attractive environment for foreign institutional investors, and that their expertise would be of value to underperforming firms. As in the UK, the Japanese Code lays out a number of principles, which are not legally binding but are, nevertheless, influential, since they are issued by the state.

The Japanese Stewardship Code is modelled after the UK Code and provides, amongst other principles, that the institutional investor should establish and disclose its policy (i) to discharge its responsibility to facilitate the continuous growth of the invested company, and (ii) to try to increase the medium-term or long-term return of the beneficial owners and clients of the institutional investor. The Japanese Steward-ship Code also recommends constructive dialogue between the institutional investor and the company.

Nevertheless, there are some interesting differences between the UK and Japanese approaches. In particular, the language and tone of the Japanese Code seems to favour a more consensus-based form of engagement, whereas the UK Code directly pro-vides a framework of escalating action for institutional investors who are ignored by management. This escalating framework of measures range from expressing concern through to the removal of directors.

A number of other countries have followed and developed, or are developing, their own stewardship codes, particularly in Europe, but also in Brazil, Canada, Malaysia, South Africa, South Korea and Thailand.

An alternative approach is stewardship codes that are the result of private initia-tive at an industry level. An example of such a private, industry-based initiative is the Italian Stewardship Principles for the exercise of administrative and voting rights in listed companies by financial intermediaries (which provide a set of high-level best practices designed to promote discussion and coordination between financial interme-diaries and listed issuers).

In addition to stewardship codes introduced at a national level, there have also been attempts at a transnational level to offer more general guidance on shareholder

---

[47] See T Eguchi and Z Shishido, 'The Future of Japanese Corporate Governance & Development of Japanese Style External Governance' in Hill and Thomas (eds), n 33.

engagement and the promotion of a more long-term strategy. The Commonsense Principles of Corporate Governance provide a prominent example of the trend toward more responsible long-term value strategies in corporations.[48] Recognising that 'most everyone agrees that we need good corporate governance, there has been wide disagreement on what that actually means'. In July 2016, a group of leading corporate executives, asset managers and investors unveiled a report that examined the 'commonsense principles' for publicly listed companies, their boards of directors and shareholders. Although the Commonsense Principles of Corporate Governance focus particularly on publicly listed companies in the US, they aim to help policymakers in other jurisdictions assess and recalibrate corporate governance mechanisms.

The Commonsense Principles of Corporate Governance reflect the drafters' intention to encourage executives to take a long-term approach to the governance of their companies. A long-term approach under such principles can be accomplished by framing the required quarterly reporting for the company in the broader context of the company's articulated strategy, and by providing a company outlook for trends and metrics that reflect the company's progress, or lack thereof, on long-term goals. However, it is the sort of approach one might take if one owned 100 per cent of a company.

The focus on long-term value creation has become increasingly widespread. In 2016, the International Council of the World Economic Forum issued The New Paradigm: A Roadmap for an Implicit Corporate Governance Partnership Between Corporations and Investors to Achieve Sustainable Long-Term Investment and Growth (The New Paradigm).[49] Like the Commonsense Principles of Corporate Governance, The New Paradigm gives the board of directors a crucial role in implementing corporate strategies and a corporate culture that pursues sustainable long-term value creation. Similarly, in January 2017, a coalition of institutional investors and global asset managers issued the Corporate Governance Principles for US Listed Companies by the Investor Stewardship Group.[50] These Principles also focus on long-term value creation. They are based on the belief that shareholders/investors are best suited to appoint directors who represent the long-term interests of the company. The board of directors should monitor management and develop incentive structures that are aligned with these interests.

All of this activity again raises the question of whether the various measures described here have actually improved engagement between institutional investors and companies. What has been the effect of the different regulations, changes in regulations or other regulatory initiatives promoting engagement? Clearly, given the recent nature of these initiatives, it is too soon to say whether such measures will operate as intended.[51] After all, the stated goal of such measures is the promotion of long-term engagement. Nevertheless, if we take the example of stewardship codes, there are already some interesting developments.

---

[48] See www.governanceprinciples.org. For a commentary on the principles, see J McGregor, 'These Business Titans Are Teaming Up for Better Corporate Governance' *Washington Post* (21 July 2016).

[49] See corpgov.law.harvard.edu/2017/01/11/corporate-governance-the-new-paradigm/.

[50] See www.Isgframework.Org/Corporate-Governance-Principles/.

[51] For an early attempt at a more comprehensive evaluation, see Ernst & Young, 'Q&A on Stewardship Codes' (August 2017), available at www.ey.com/Publication/vwLUAssets/ey-stewardship-codes-august-2017/$FILE/ey-stewardship-codes-august-2017.pdf.

First, there seems to be a greater awareness of the risk of box-ticking and a new focus on the *quality* of disclosure of signatories. Consider the UK. Interestingly, traditional institutional investors seemed willing to sign up to the Stewardship Code's 'best practices'. However, although the UK Stewardship Code was successful in attracting signatories, the regulator still felt the need, in November 2016, to introduce a 'tiering system', evaluating public statements according to the quality of their Code statements. Nevertheless, we should perhaps recall that the UK is a country with traditionally high levels of exposure to investor engagement. As such, it may not necessarily be representative of countries with controlling shareholders and lower levels of institutional investor engagement. To assess the potential benefits of a stewardship code and its impact on investors' engagement in countries with a traditionally lower exposure to investor engagement and a lack of 'investor culture', it is helpful to consider Japan.

Partly as a result of adopting a stewardship code, a corporate governance code and other measures, Japan has risen in the Asian Corporate Governance Association rankings, up three places between 2014–16 to third overall.[52] Yet the Japanese Stewardship Code has undoubtedly faced challenges.[53] A number of corporate pension funds decided against adopting the Code. And even amongst those institutional investors that have endorsed it, many engage in minimal compliance. Research by the *Financial Times* used Secom's corporate pension fund as an illustrative example.[54] In a simple table of less than a half-page, the fund set out that it voted on 9,034 agenda items at the shareholders meetings of 2,269 companies. But it would go too far to suggest that the introduction of a stewardship code has been a failure in Japan. There seems to be much greater interest in Japanese firms amongst foreign (especially US) institutional investors, and—at least in part—the new Code has contributed to this trend.[55]

Recent events involving the Japanese company Seven & I Holdings, operators of the Seven Eleven convenience store franchise in Japan, also reveal something about engagement strategies post-Stewardship Code. Over several decades, the Seven & I Holdings group enjoyed huge success under the charismatic and visionary leadership of Toshifumi Suzuki. But in April 2016, Suzuki resigned as Chairman and CEO after being defeated in a boardroom struggle over succession. An opposing faction on the board supported the views of an activist US hedge fund that wanted to replace Suzuki and restructure Seven & I Holdings. This change in governance was generally heralded by analysts as being a good thing. There were increasing concerns that Mr Suzuki's autocratic and top-down style of leadership, as well as his openly stated wish for his son to succeed him, was hurting the long-term prospects of the company.

Lastly, we need to distinguish between the different types of 'stewardship codes': private or industry-based codes, and public or country-based codes. The question naturally arises as to which approach is preferable.

Although industry-based guidelines are theoretically better able to address industry specific problems and issues, thereby promoting performance and professionalism, country-based codes can ensure that the principles are more suitably designed

---

[52] See www.acga-asia.org/upload/files/CG_Watch_2016_Press_Conference_ppt.pdf.
[53] L Lewis, 'Companies Fail to Buy into the Stewardship Code' *Financial Times* (23 October 2016).
[54] L Lewis, 'Secom Breaks Ranks to Highlight Reform Failures of Japan Inc' *Financial Times* (23 May 2017).
[55] ibid.

to interact with the economic and social environment, as well as the legal rules and institutions in a particular jurisdiction.

Both sets of guidelines contain provisions that arguably mobilise and engage institutional investors. But there may be several advantages to putting the responsibility for the design of these best-practice guidelines into the hands of regulators.

Here it should be noted that in addition to economies of scale, the publicity of the drafting process reduces the information costs for potential users of the guidelines. Moreover, new networks are more likely to arise around public or country-based outputs. If we accept the idea that stewardship codes could create awareness and provide for more constructive and meaningful engagement, then a proliferation of codes is likely to further stimulate discussion and feedback, leading to the cross-fertilisation and refinement of the practice of 'stewardship engagement'.

V. Concluding Remarks

While a general consensus among policymakers and corporate governance experts suggests that improvements in corporate governance are necessary, widespread disagreement exists as to what good corporate governance entails, or how it might be achieved. Moreover, contemporary corporate governance frameworks that developed in the 2000s seemed to have little or no impact on the performance of listed companies during the last financial crisis, and the number, scale and effects of corporate scandals and economic failures do not appear to be diminishing. Recent corporate governance reforms generally recognise the shortcomings in the traditional debate and put greater emphasis on long-term value creation by attempting to improve board performance and create a stewardship culture.

And yet corporate governance reforms via new, revised or additional corporate governance rules, guidelines, principles or codes are often met with a mixture of indifference, scepticism and even hostility from management and governance experts working for listed companies. In practice, top-down corporate governance reform measures rarely, if ever, result in a genuine change in the governance and culture of firms.[56]

'Compliance fatigue' among corporate executives and other senior managers is a very common phenomenon that can be explained by several factors. First, corporate governance is an ongoing requirement that demands corporate executives' and compliance departments' almost constant attention and responsiveness to constant waves of corporate governance reform via new, revised or additional rules, guidelines, principles or codes.

In addition, corporate governance reform often takes place by repackaging old content with new or revised labels. For instance, the announcement of the Commonsense

---

[56] See S Turnbull, 'A Sustainable Future for Corporate Governance Theory & Practice' in S Boubaker et al (eds), *Corporate Governance: Recent Developments & New Trends* (Berlin, Springer, 2012) 347.

Principles of Corporate Governance[57] stated, with much fanfare, that wide disagreement exists regarding the parameters of high-quality or good corporate governance. Yet the Commonsense Principles of Corporate Governance do not seem to add very much that could genuinely be considered 'new'.

Corporate governance intermediaries often aim to satisfy corporate governance requirements through minimum compliance with the rules and regulations. Those intermediaries, such as lawyers, accountants, auditors, and other advisors and consultants, often have a conservative perspective when it comes to new corporate governance initiatives, and they attempt to use minimal efforts to achieve maximum compliance. In fact, compliance-based communications with shareholders often demonstrate such a 'tick-the-box' attitude, and contain bland, boilerplate or legalistic statements about corporate governance and the company's past performance and opportunities for future growth.

Moreover, corporate governance initiatives rarely work as expected by policymakers. While many obvious benefits derive from the adoption of stewardship codes, it is much less clear whether requiring shareholders to be more responsible can be a realistic, sensible or meaningful objective.

In fact, mobilising investors may actually lead managers to ask the wrong kind of questions about what needs to be done to ensure sustainable success. Rather than incentivising a focus on genuine innovation, such measures merely reinforce a centralised shareholder primacy view. Indeed, stewardship pressures can often expose companies to an unhealthy focus on short-term dividends and share buybacks that are designed to please the stock market.

Selected Further Reading

Bainbridge, S, *Corporate Governance After the Financial Crisis* (Oxford, Oxford University Press, 2016)

Bainbridge, S, *The New Corporate Governance in Theory and Practice* (Oxford, Oxford University Press, 2008)

Coase, RH, *The Firm, The Market, and The Law* (Chicago, IL, University of Chicago Press, 1990)

Easterbrook, F and Fischel, D, *The Economic Structure of Corporate Law* (Cambridge, MA, Harvard University Press, 1996)

Macey, JR, *Corporate Governance: Promises Kept, Promises Broken* (Princeton, NJ, Princeton University Press, 2008)

Romano, R, *The Foundations of Corporate Law*, 2nd edn (New York, Foundation Press, 2010)

---

[57] See www.governanceprinciples.org.

6

Corporate Criminal Law

I. Outline

Corporate criminal law and procedure refers to the body of legal norms—both substantive and procedural, domestic and international—that address socially undesirable business conduct through the application of criminal law to the corporation itself, rather than to the individual members of a corporation, such as the executives, directors, managers, employees or other stakeholders.

This chapter begins by suggesting that the reach of corporate criminal law has greatly expanded over the last three decades, particularly in the fields of market regulation, anti-corruption, anti-money laundering and securities laws. In addition to this expansion in the 'reach' of the substantive criminal law, various procedural innovations have also occurred, notably the expansion of pre-trial diversion in cases involving corporate suspects.

The result of these changes has been an enormous expansion in legal risk for corporations, and consequently businesses are now obliged to devote significant resources to 'compliance' in order to mitigate such risk.

Corporate criminal law embraces the legal fiction that a juristic person—ie a corporation—can commit a crime. This fiction is given legal effect via the doctrine of corporate criminal liability, which establishes a legal standard for determining the criminal liability of a business organisation.

Over the last three decades—but particularly post-2000—there have been a number of significant innovations in this field of law that will be reviewed in this chapter. As such, a new approach has emerged for responding to white-collar and corporate wrongdoing.

Somewhat unusually, corporate criminal law is defined by reference to a particular type of legal subject—the company—and cuts across a number of substantive fields of criminal law, notably anti-corruption laws, anti-money laundering laws and fraud laws, as well as the vast swathe of regulatory offences that are applied to businesses today. In addition, corporate criminal procedure law encompasses various procedural adaptations that have been adopted for dealing with corporate suspects and defendants.

As such, corporate criminal law is one of a number of responses available to nation states for dealing with socially undesirable corporate behaviour. The obvious alternatives are individual criminal liability, corporate civil liability, or some form of administrative liability, as well as more 'indirect' methods, such as securities laws or laws relating to a company's governance structures. Most states address corporate wrongdoing by adopting some combination or 'mix' of the aforementioned measures, and the challenge facing law makers and regulators is—in large part—to identify the most appropriate combination or 'cocktail' of strategies. Comparative institutional choice—ie identifying the 'value added' of a particular form of liability as opposed to the alternatives—becomes a crucial task in the normative justification of any particular form of liability. And given the fact that all forms of liability are imperfect in some way or other, the danger for policymakers is that they fall into an inefficient pattern of cycling in which they constantly shift between different flawed forms of liability.

The focus of this chapter will be examining these issues in the context of US federal and English law. The decision to focus on these jurisdictions can be justified by the extensive territorial reach of the new corporate criminal law in these two countries. Companies that issue securities in either the US or UK capital markets, or which—in the case of UK anti-corruption laws—even conduct a part of their business in the UK, may find themselves exposed to criminal liability. As such, Anglo-American corporate criminal law has taken on a transnational character that creates extensive legal risk for a wide range of firms that operate across national borders.

II. A History of Corporate Criminal Law

The historical position of all legal systems was that although individual members of a corporation could be criminally liable for offences committed in the course of their occupation, the corporation *itself* could not be liable. Criminal liability lay with members of the corporation—directors, managers or employees—but not with the corporation itself. A corporation fell beyond the domain of criminal liability. From the perspective of the criminal law, a corporation was an incorporeal entity that lacked the necessary degree of fault or blameworthiness that is a necessary condition for the imposition of criminal liability.

A. Origins

The legal basis of corporate criminal law—the legal doctrine of corporate criminal liability—can be traced back to developments in English law in the early decades of the nineteenth century.[1]

---

[1] For the early history of corporate criminal liability in English law, see especially C Wells, *Corporations and Criminal Responsibility* (Oxford, Oxford University Press, 2001). For the US experience, see especially W Laufer, *Corporate Bodies and Guilty Minds: The Failure of Corporate Criminal Liability* (Chicago, IL, University Chicago Press, 2006) ch 3.

In his *Commentaries*, for example, William Blackstone regarded it as self-evident that criminal liability was confined to natural persons and that any other approach would constitute an 'anthropomorphic error'. According to this view, a corporation is incapable of acting with the requisite moral fault necessary for the criminal law.[2] Moreover, Blackstone identified a number of practical difficulties that would arise in applying criminal law and procedure to corporations. In particular, a corporation cannot appear in court in person to offer a defence (resulting in a trial *in absentia*), a corporation cannot swear an oath, nor can a corporation be arrested, imprisoned or executed. For Blackstone, at least, it seemed fairly obvious that corporations were an impoverished legal subject and should not be subject to the discipline of the criminal law.

The origins of modern corporate criminal liability rules can be traced back to the early decades of the nineteenth century when, in the context of rapid industrialisation, corporations acquired a greater social presence as the scope and impact of their activities expanded dramatically.[3] In response to this socio-economic development, English law gradually extended the application of the criminal law to juristic persons, such as municipalities and then corporations.

This change initially occurred as a result of judicial rather than legislative action, and involved cases of criminal omission resulting in public nuisance. The scope of this new form of criminal liability gradually expanded, however, to include 'acts' as well as 'omissions', and finally to crimes requiring intent and not just absolute liability offences. Within half a century, Blackstone's concerns had been swept away by the pragmatic need to address the pressing social issue of misconduct by corporations. In this respect, the origins of corporate criminal law were a response to the harsh social realities of industrialisation and the resulting negative effects.

The emergence and development of corporate criminal liability in a US context was a similarly incremental process.[4] The early US history of corporate criminal liability, for instance, culminated in 1909 with the US Supreme Court decision in *New York Central & Hudson River Railroad v United States*.[5] Constitutional concerns about federal anti-trust legislation that explicitly imposed criminal liability on corporations were set aside in favour of the more pragmatic view that corporate criminal liability represented the 'only means' to 'control' errant corporations. The Court presented the issue as involving a stark choice between corporate criminal liability and blanket immunity for corporations, and suggested there was no strong reason to favour the latter.

By the early decades of the twentieth century, the idea of corporate criminal liability was well established in the main jurisdictions of the common law world. Nevertheless, for much of its history, corporate criminal law was marginalised from the mainstream of criminal justice, even in those jurisdictions that embraced the doctrine of corporate criminal liability. In practice, criminal prosecution of corporate suspects remained

---

[2] W Blackstone, *Commentaries on the Laws of England* (Chicago, IL, University of Chicago Press, 1979) 464.
[3] See, eg, Wells, n 1, ch 2.
[4] See, eg, T Bernard, 'The Historical Development of Corporate Criminal Liability' (1984) 22 *Criminology* 3.
[5] *New York Central & Hudson River Railroad v US*, 212 US 481 (1909).

something of an exception, perhaps reflecting both the economic importance of large corporations and a recognition on the part of the state that prosecuting such cases was difficult.

Interestingly, for most of the twentieth century most civilian jurisdictions rejected the doctrine of corporate criminal liability, preferring instead to concentrate attention on personal liability.[6] This approach reflected the prevailing view that the liability of legal persons, such as a corporation, is properly dealt with as part of public administrative law rather than the criminal law. Many countries in Europe (such as Germany, Italy and Spain) began to confront the growing power of business enterprises by introducing systems of administrative regulation, similar to public welfare offences in the US or regulatory offences in the UK. These infractions are enforced by administrative agencies and do not have the status of criminal offences. Moreover, they are usually thought to lack the element of condemnation and moral fault associated with criminal liability.

The consequence of these trends in both the common law and civilian worlds was that corporate criminal liability continued to occupy a marginal position in modern criminal justice.[7] As with white-collar offenders more generally, the early history of corporate criminal law is a familiar tale of economically powerful elites being shielded from the gaze of the criminal justice system.[8]

B. 'Net-widening'

Over the last three decades, however, this situation has changed considerably, and corporate criminal law has acquired a much greater significance in the 'mix' of regulatory strategies for responding to corporate wrongdoing, particularly in cases involving larger corporations.[9] Across multiple jurisdictions, a process of net-widening has occurred that has significantly expanded the scope of corporate criminal law.[10] Moreover, we have entered a new age of enforcement, as companies routinely find themselves facing the threat of investigation and indictment.

Although we should not be naive in underestimating the capacity of the business community—particularly large firms—to limit the degree of intrusion into their activities, an effect of this new emphasis on corporate criminal law is that business enterprises can no longer afford to ignore corporate criminal law, and they are now obliged to incorporate it into their decision-making processes, policies and practices, and their organisational structure.

---

[6] For a discussion of the principles underlying the traditional Continental European approach, see eg, L Leigh, 'The Criminal Liability of Corporations and Other Groups: A Comparative View' (1977) 9 *Ottawa Law Review* 247.

[7] See, eg, A Hamdani and A Klement, 'Corporate Crime and Deterrence' (2008) 61 *Stanford Law Review* 271; VS Khanna, 'Corporate Liability Standards: When Should Corporations Be Held Criminally Liable?' (2000) 37 *American Criminal Law Review* 1239.

[8] See, eg, E Sutherland, *White Collar Crime* (New York, Holt, Rinehart & Winston, 1949).

[9] See L Orland, 'The Transformation of Corporate Criminal Law' (2007) 1 *Brooklyn Journal of Corporate Finance & Commercial Law* 45.

[10] See S Cohen, *Visions of Social Control* (Cambridge, Polity, 1985).

This extension of the reach of criminal law to cover business, no doubt the result of multiple factors but including the prevalence of corporate scandals and the greater media attention (both old and new) given to the exposure of corporate misbehaviour, is a key element in this change. Business enterprises from across all sectors of the economy are, almost as a matter of routine, implicated in serious wrongdoing.

One consequence of this increased recognition of the problem of corporate wrong-doing is a belief that the legal system is failing. Public disappointment, frustration and—increasingly—anger have put pressure on policymakers around the world to engage in a re-evaluation of regulatory strategies for responding to corporate mis-conduct. Again, while we should not underestimate the capacity of powerful, well-organised and highly motivated corporate interests to resist state intrusion, this type of re-evaluation has resulted in significant amendments across multiple jurisdictions to corporate, criminal and other laws concerned with the organisation, financing and regulation of corporations and their business-related activities.

There are a number of different aspects to this process of net-widening. First, many civilian jurisdictions that did not previously have any provision for corporate criminal liability have now introduced it.[11] From the 1980s, the administrative law approach to corporate wrongdoing has gradually been supplemented by the introduction of corpo-rate criminal liability. In a European context, this seems largely to have been the result of pressure from regional and international organisations that identified a regulatory 'gap', which—it was believed—corporate criminal responsibility could fill.[12]

The second piece of evidence for net-widening in corporate criminal law has been the expansion in the scope of corporate criminal law and the creation of multiple new categories of criminal offence.[13] Even a cursory list of the main fields of contemporary corporate criminal law highlights the breadth of the law in this area: anti-corruption law, anti-money laundering law, fraud law (including investment fraud, securities fraud, government fraud, mortgage fraud, consumer fraud and false advertising), competition law, tax law (including off-shore tax evasion), accounting standards law, marketing law, export controls and sanctions law, labour law, health and safety law, and environmental law. Moreover, these are just the general fields of law; there are also many industry-specific laws that impact upon corporations operating in particular sec-tors of the economy. These are all areas that have significantly expanded over the last three decades.

A third trend is to apply corporate criminal law extra-territorially, or alternatively to apply it to the acts of foreign companies for acts committed in a third state, if such a company issues securities in the home state or conducts a significant part of its business in the home state. This issue will not be explored here, but—as mentioned in section I—the effect of this trend is to transform domestic criminal law into a form of

---

[11] See, eg, M Duber, 'The Comparative History and Theory of Corporate Criminal Liability' (2013) 16 *The New Criminal Law Review* 203; G Heine, 'New Developments in Corporate Criminal Liability in Europe: Can Europeans Learn from the American Experience—or Vice Versa?' (1998) 12 *St Louis-Warsaw Transnational Law Review* 173.

[12] See, eg, J Gobert and AM Pascal (eds), *European Developments in Corporate Criminal Liability* (London, Routledge, 2011).

[13] See, eg, J Braithwaite and P Drahos, *Global Business Regulation* (Cambridge, Cambridge University Press, 2000).

transnational law, as companies find themselves obliged to meet the legal requirements of multiple jurisdictions.[14]

Paralleling this expansion in the number of criminal offences and extended territorial reach has been a corresponding tendency to weaken the mens rea requirements for corporate crimes. The emergence and expansion of strict liability (ie no-fault or public welfare) offences is the most obvious example of this transformation. It is no coincidence that many strict liability offences are concerned with corporate activities, such as pollution and health and safety, where there is a clear public interest at stake in halting the proscribed acts. And yet there has also been a more general trend on the part of legislators to move from relatively high-level mens rea requirements, such as intent or knowledge, to relatively low-level requirements, such as recklessness and negligence. As with strict liability, this general trend has also been particularly important in the context of corporate regulation.

The final element in the widening of the criminal justice 'net' is a more aggressive attitude towards enforcement. Enforcement actions have increased substantially, particularly over the past decade. There is a great deal of discussion of a 'new era' of enforcement in multiple fields of corporate criminal law, notably anti-corruption law, anti-money laundering law, securities law and competition law.[15] There has also been a corresponding increase in the size of sanctions. Sentencing guidelines for organisations have been upwardly adjusted, and enforcement agencies are more aggressive in pursuing larger penalties.

The foregoing discussion has introduced the new corporate criminal law and suggested that a key feature of this rapidly developing field is that the criminal justice 'net' is widening. Significantly, this widening of the criminal justice net is paralleled by two other trends: first, the outer limits of criminal liability are becoming less certain; and, second, there are various uncertainties surrounding the doctrine of corporate criminal justice. The effect of these uncertainties is to obscure the underlying purpose of the law in this field and to raise doubts about the efficacy of the corporate criminal law as an response to corporate wrongdoing.

A key feature of contemporary corporate criminal law is the degree to which legal certainty has been compromised in this net-widening process. Two examples will be introduced to illustrate what is a more general trend to blur the lines of criminal liability by making the full scope or outer limits of the criminal offence unclear. The examples are taken from US federal criminal law but, given the territorial reach of these prohibitions, they impact business entities from multiple jurisdictions.

First, in the context of securities law, there has been a tendency to blur the lines of liability for insider trading. Insider trading law traditionally imposed liability on (i) corporate 'insiders', who traded on material non-public information in breach of a duty owed to their corporation, or (ii) corporate 'outsiders', who 'misappropriated' and traded on such information in breach of a duty owed to the *source* of the information.[16]

---

[14] See, eg, M Fenwick, 'The New Corporate Criminal Law and Transnational Legal Risk' in M Fenwick and S Wrbka (eds), *Flexibility in Modern Business Law: A Comparative Assessment* (Tokyo, Springer, 2016).

[15] See, eg, M Koehler, *The Foreign Corrupt Practices Act in a New Era* (London, Edward Elgar, 2014).

[16] See especially S Green, *Lying, Stealing and Cheating: A Moral Theory of White Collar Crime* (Oxford, Oxford University Press, 2007) ch 18.

Recently, however, the lines of liability have become increasingly uncertain and liability has been imposed on defendants where it is unclear whether they owe a duty to the corporation or the source of the information.[17] For example, there have been recent convictions where confidential information has been unwillingly thrust on a person, who then trades on that information; cases where the entity whose information was taken and used denied that it was owed a duty; and cases where a duty is found to have arisen where the insider and an inadvertent recipient of that information happen to be friends. In all such cases, neither of the traditional theories seems to apply, and the result of this more aggressive enforcement policy is to create ambiguities in the scope of the offence.

Moreover, post-2008 there has been the use of insider trading against hedge funds. For example, Steve A Cohen's SAC Capital Advisors was indicted in July 2013 for securities fraud, which led a number of investors to withdraw from the fund. Many in the financial services sector believe this to be highly controversial. The traders at SAC were not corporate insiders, nor were they outsiders seeking personal gain; rather they were investors looking for information about corporations whose shares they were thinking of buying, selling or shorting. Sceptics asked whether highly aggressive 'diligent' traders would be criminalised in this way? The activity of hedge funds helps speed the flow of information to financial markets, thus enabling more efficient and accurate pricing of the shares of corporations. Uncovering things about corporations that management would rather not disclose is something professional money managers are supposed to do. That is to say, hedge funds perform a valuable public interest function. The key point, however, is that such an enforcement policy seems to expand the scope of the offence to encompass (possible desirable) behaviour that was previously thought to fall outside the scope of the norm.

A second example of how uncertainties have been introduced into contemporary white-collar and corporate criminal law can be seen in anti-corruption law, particularly anti-corruption laws targeting corporate corruption conducted overseas, such as the US Foreign and Corrupt Practices Act (FCPA) (1977) or the more recent UK Bribery Act 2010.[18] Multiple uncertainties can be found in these instruments. The US law, for instance, prohibits a company or its agents paying or offering to pay money or anything of value to a foreign official to obtain or retain business. The statute defines a 'foreign official' in part as 'any officer or employee of a foreign government or any department, agency, or instrumentality thereof'.[19] However, uncertainty surrounds the interpretation of the term 'instrumentality', which is not defined in the statute. The Department of Justice (DOJ) and the Securities & Exchange Commission (SEC) have taken advantage of this uncertainty. To take one of a number of controversial cases, in an action against American construction company KBR, the DOJ and SEC alleged that KBR made improper payments to employees of Nigeria LNG Limited.[20]

---

[17] See, eg, S Crimmins, 'Insider Trading: Where is the Line?' (2013) 2 *Columbia Business Law Review* 330.
[18] See, eg, M Koehler, 'The Story of the Foreign Corrupt Practices Act' (2012) 5 *Ohio State Law Journal* 930. For the UK law, see E Engle, 'Understanding the UK Bribery Act by Reference to the OECD Convention and the Foreign and Corrupt Practices Act' (2011) 44 *The International Lawyer* 1173.
[19] 15 USC §§ 78dd-1(f)(1)(A).
[20] See D Juedes, 'Taming the FCPA Overreach Through an Adequate Procedures Defense' (2013) 4 *William & Mary Business Law Review* 37, 43–47.

The Government claimed that these employees were foreign officials under the FCPA, despite the fact that the only connection with the Nigerian Government was that the Nigerian Government held a minority ownership stake in LNG Limited. The case was settled by KBR to avoid the possibility of a damaging conviction.

Given an aggressive enforcement policy, on the one hand, and the uncertainty surrounding the scope of the law, on the other, it can be difficult for a company to decide ex ante whether a foreign partner is sufficiently state-owned or state-controlled to qualify as an instrumentality of a foreign official, that is to say whether the FCPA applies to a particular transaction or business relationship.

Both in the example from securities law and in anti-corruption law, therefore, the outer limits of the core offence—the boundary between permissible and impermissible conduct—seem to have become increasingly blurred as a result of a combination of executive (regulatory), legislative or judicial action.[21] The scope for aggressive enforcement is thus expanded, and the legal risk for any company concomitantly increases.

III. Justification and Rationale

A second set of issues surrounds the policy reasons for adopting corporate criminal liability in the first place. A great deal of ambiguity seems to surround the underlying purpose of corporate criminal liability and how—and whether—it might function to achieve such a purpose.

The normative justification for corporate criminal liability, in general, has conventionally been provided by arguments from deterrence and prevention, rather than retribution.[22] Although there is an academic literature defending retribution as a legitimate aim of corporate criminal law, the dominant approach amongst policymakers, judges and academics has been to focus on how corporate criminal liability contributes to the deterrence and prevention of corporate wrongdoing.[23]

This general unwillingness to advance versions of retribution as a justification for corporate criminal law can be explained by a reluctance to cause economic harm—by punishing a corporation—without some possibility of a clear countervailing social benefit (in the form of a reduction in future wrongdoing). Nevertheless, although retribution has not usually functioned as an independent justification for imposing criminal liability on corporations, it has served as a partial constraint upon the law in this area, in the sense that some blameworthiness on the part of the corporate defendant—in terms of either fault or harm—is required for many offences.

The main focus of the normative discussion, however, has been on the question of whether and how the goal of reducing corporate wrongdoing might be achieved.

---

[21] See also Orland, n 9.
[22] See especially VS Khanna, 'Corporate Criminal Liability' (1996) 199 *Harvard Law Review* 1477.
[23] See, eg, WS Laufer, 'Corporate Bodies and Guilty Minds' (1994) 43 *Emory Law Journal* 647.

In examining this issue, it is helpful to treat deterrence and prevention as separate justifications for corporate criminal liability.

In order to avoid terminological confusion, the process whereby a person desists from criminal conduct as a result of the threat of criminal sanction will be referred to as 'deterrence'. In contrast, the process whereby the threat of criminal sanction motivates persons to monitor other persons to ensure that crimes do not occur will be termed 'prevention'.

Taking deterrence first: imposing criminal liability on the corporation might seem incompatible with the aim of deterrence, because a corporation is a fictional legal entity that cannot itself be deterred in the way that a natural person can, ie a corporation cannot experience the feeling of being threatened, therefore it cannot be deterred. This means that corporate criminal liability really aims to deter the unlawful acts or omissions of a corporation's agents.

Although the criminal justice system could focus exclusively on deterring such wrongdoing via individual criminal liability, a system of purely personal criminal liability has various limitations from the viewpoint of deterrence. In particular, the state faces significant administrative costs in identifying individual offenders within large, complex organisations and proving, beyond a reasonable doubt, that criminal wrongdoing has, in fact, taken place. Such administrative costs greatly reduce the likelihood of detection—and hence the risks of crime for any prospective offender—and the resulting sense of security might embolden an individual contemplating wrongdoing. Holding the corporation liable therefore represents a cost-effective way to overcome the shortcomings of a system based purely on personal liability. The threat of corporate liability deters individual agents of the company from participating in wrongdoing because of the negative outcome an individual will suffer if the company is convicted and that individual is implicated in such wrongdoing.

In addition to deterring individual agents of the company from wrongdoing, advocates of corporate criminal liability also argue that is has the additional advantage of preventing wrongdoing by creating a strong incentive for all of the stakeholders within a company to monitor one another for wrongdoing and to correct any that is uncovered. In this way, corporate criminal liability motivates a company to reduce its liability exposure by assuming the task of policing the agents of that company.[24] Moreover, companies are particularly well placed to perform this monitoring function. At least, it can be convincingly argued that they are better placed than the state or other third parties negatively affected by corporate wrongdoing to engage in such monitoring. A company can thus introduce internal controls and ex ante measures for detecting agents contemplating wrongdoing. In addition, a company can react to wrongdoing by taking action against those involved in it, reporting them to the authorities or implementing reforms to ensure that there is no recurrence of the wrongdoing. In this way, corporate criminal liability can contribute to a reduction in corporate crime.

It is worth emphasising the differences between corporate and individual criminal liability on this point. When an individual is punished, or threatened with

---

[24] See, eg, S Simpson, *Corporate Crime, Law and Social Control* (Cambridge, Cambridge University Press, 2002).

punishment, the goal of that punishment or threat of punishment is to inhibit rather than to mobilise. As Brent Fisse has noted:

> The message conveyed [to the natural person by the criminal law] is 'refrain from committing that offence', rather than 'refrain from committing that offence and take such steps to improve your physiological and psychological capacity for self-control as are necessary to guard against repetition'. By contrast, when a corporate offender is punished or threatened with punishment, the message is catalytic as well as inhibitory. The message conveyed, for corporate offences of commission as well as for those of omission, is 'refrain from committing that offence and take such steps as are necessary organisationally to guard against repetition'.[25]

This reliance on both the 'inhibitory' (ie deterrence) and 'catalytic' (ie prevention) functions distinguishes corporate criminal liability from the criminal law as it is applied to natural persons. One of the central aims of the new corporate criminal law has been to bolster this catalytic function of corporate criminal liability and thereby promote internal efforts at ensuring compliance.

A key premise of both the deterrence and prevention justifications for corporate criminal liability is the claim that the threat of corporate criminal liability provides a strong behavioural incentive for all individuals either to desist from offending, or to monitor others and prevent them from offending. The belief that corporate criminal liability can have this kind of impact on individuals within business entities seems to be widespread among policymakers, judges, prosecutors, regulators and commentators. It is therefore important to look, in more detail, at the nature of the threat created by the existence of corporate criminal liability, and at some of the uncertainties that surround the assumption that this threat provides the necessary behavioural incentives.

Both the criminal justice system and society in general impose sanctions on any corporation found criminally liable: the criminal justice system sanctions via the formal penalty imposed (eg a fine); and society sanctions the company in the form of reputational damage caused by a conviction. Moreover, informal sanctions can arise from the fact of an indictment or criminal investigation, and are not necessarily contingent on a conviction. It is the combined threat of both types of sanction that deters wrongdoing and provides the incentive for corporations to engage in crime prevention. It is therefore worth considering the threat that these two types of sanctions pose.

The key question then becomes whether this threat is sufficiently severe and certain to have purchase over the behavioural incentives of those individuals contemplating wrongdoing or in a position to engage in crime prevention. In the following, it will be suggested that finding a clear answer to this question is not simple.

Taking formal sanctions first: judges and administrative agencies are empowered to impose a range of formal sanctions if a company is convicted, most obviously fines and loss of licence, although shaming penalties are increasingly used. Traditionally, fines are used as the primary sanction in the context of corporate crime.

The rationale for the fine seems fairly simple: the primary goal of all corporate activity is to make money, and corporations can thus be deterred from wrongdoing and motivated to invest in prevention by the threat of monetary sanctions that can directly impact upon the company's central purpose.

---

[25] B Fisse, 'Reconstructing Corporate Criminal Law' (1983) 56 *California Law Review* 1141, 1160.

Additional advantages of the fine as a sanction are that fines are cheap to administer and there is some (financial) benefit to the state. In general, fines do not extend to allow for compensation for victims, although this may be possible in some circumstances. Further advantages are that fines are flexible and can be calibrated to the specific facts of the case. Lastly, in extreme cases a fine can be imposed that is large enough to deprive a corporation of all of its assets and drive the company out of business (what can be thought of as a corporate death sentence).

However, many commentators have criticised fines as ineffective in either deterring or preventing corporate wrongdoing.[26] It is often suggested that fines have traditionally been set too low in the case of corporate crime and that, as a consequence, they are seen as the price to engage in criminal behaviour. It has also been suggested that fines are ineffective because the company may easily transfer the burden to innocent third parties, such as customers, shareholders or employees. If the effects of the fine can be ameliorated then the threat of the fine is significantly reduced; and increasing the level of fines would merely mean imposing a greater burden on these third parties.

The effect of this kind of consideration is to introduce significant doubts as to the scale of the threat posed by the fine and, as a consequence, to reduce the incentive to prevent wrongdoing. A common response to this argument is to suggest that the various third parties who ultimately bear the cost of the fines—eg shareholders or employees, perhaps even consumers—are not innocent parties since they will usually have benefited—either directly or indirectly—from the illegal activity in the form of higher share dividends, share price, wages or profits. Even though these parties may not be directly responsible for any illegality, it might seem fair to deprive them of these unlawfully obtained gains. It is precisely this possibility that is designed to motivate various third parties to engage in social enforcement.

The key issue is whether the loss of a job or a decrease in the value of an investment is proportionate given the lack of direct responsibility, and whether this possibility can actually be sufficiently powerful to incentivise these third parties to engage in social enforcement. Moreover, in the case of shareholders, the possibility of such harm may have a chilling effect on investment and reduce the capacity of companies to capitalise via securities markets. Either way, doubts seem to be cast over the capacity of the law to have a clear and predictable impact on behavioural incentives.

Of course, fines are not the only formal sanctions that are available in cases of corporate crime. Other sanctions can be imposed—such as loss of licence or shaming—and, depending on the nature of a corporation's business, these may be equally important—a conviction can have disastrous consequences for a company, even if only a small fine is imposed.[27]

A consensus amongst most commentators is that informal sanctions constitute a more significant threat to a company than formal sanctions.[28] The ability of any company to succeed is contingent on its having and maintaining a reputation for probity.

---

[26] See, eg, 'Fine and Punishment' (21 July 2012) *The Economist*, www.economist.com/node/21559315.

[27] PH Bucy, 'Civil Prosecution of Health Care Fraud' (1995) 30 *Wake Forest Law Review* 720, 693.

[28] See, eg, P Bharara, 'Corporations Cry Uncle and Their Employees Cry Foul: Rethinking Prosecutorial Pressure on Corporate Defendants' (2007) 44 *American Criminal Law Review* 53, 73 ('corporate defendants, subject as they are to market pressures, may not be able to survive indictment, much less conviction and sentencing').

Given the importance that the market attaches to corporate reputation, it is often suggested that large business entities will struggle to survive even an indictment, let alone a trial or conviction. This seems particularly true in some sectors, such as financial services. Even an investigation can be hugely damaging for any firm that depends on public trust as a key element of its business model.

Although it is difficult to verify empirically the claim that the threat to corporate reputation is the primary threat posed by corporate criminal liability, the behaviour of corporate executives in seeking to evade criminal investigation provides strong circumstantial evidence for the claim that executives place a premium on corporate reputation. Corporations that are under criminal investigation will often take drastic measures to avoid indictment, including waiving various legal professional privileges and disclosing the findings of any internal investigation, assisting in the investigation of individual employees and entering into pre-indictment agreements of various kinds (eg deferred prosecution agreements), many of which impose a significant and on-going burden on the company.

Business leaders clearly regard 'corporate reputation' as a valued asset of a company, which both improves profits and facilitates other objectives. The most obvious benefit of corporate reputation is the impact it has on customers. Consumer 'good will' is clearly connected to corporate profits.

But a positive corporate reputation has a number of other less obvious financial benefits. For example, banks will be more likely to offer credit during financial difficulties to companies with a positive reputation. The reputation of a company also affects the culture within an organisation, which has the potential to boost performance and facilitate attracting the best talent. A positive reputation may also bring benefits in dealings with public agencies and the state more generally. Lastly, a company with a positive reputation may enjoy more political influence when lobbying over state action likely to impact upon the company's sphere of business operations.

Adverse publicity may also trigger a variety of other non-financial bad effects for a corporation. Most significantly, a negative publicity spotlight may bring further unwanted attention to the corporation and trigger more government or media interest, and potentially private litigation (so-called 'spotlight syndrome').

Reputation thus helps a corporation to achieve a wide range of important corporate goals, and the threat posed by corporate criminal liability to that reputation has the potential to alter behavioural incentives in such a way as to deter and prevent corporate crime. However, all of the above seems to depend on various empirical claims and the particular circumstances of a particular company.

IV. Corporate Criminal Liability Doctrines

There are also a number of issues and controversies surrounding the legal doctrine that underlies *all* corporate criminal law, namely, the liability rules that comprise corporate criminal liability. It is worth noting from the outset that these uncertainties are not new; critics of corporate criminal liability have pointed to these issues for many years, but these concerns have taken on a greater significance as the scope of corporate criminal law has continued to expand and greater efforts are devoted to enforcement.

At least in the common law world, the traditional approach to corporate criminal liability has been some variation of 'imputation'.[29] Such an approach requires the identification of a single human offender whose crime is then imputed—ie attributed—to the company. An interesting contrast can be made, however, between the imputation approaches of the US federal courts and that employed in English law. In what follows, it will be suggested that both exhibit various problems, but that resolving these problems seems to have been accorded much less weight than the competing policy goal to establish a legal standard that can be utilised in effectively tackling corporate wrongdoing.

Since the early twentieth century, US federal courts have tended to adopt a broad vicarious liability standard, whereby the criminal act of any employee, 'regardless of rank', that occurs in 'the scope of employment' and which is intended, 'at least in part, to benefit the company', can be imputed to the company itself.[30] Moreover, a company can be convicted for any crime—including crimes of intent—based on this liability standard.

The rationale for this broad approach is that without the threat of criminal liability, there is little incentive for companies to curb illegal but profitable activities that place innocent parties at risk. However, the obvious difficulty with such a standard is that it seems unreasonable to expect a large corporation—particularly one operating transnationally—to take responsibility for the acts of *all* of its employees. This is particularly so if the consequences of a criminal conviction for the corporation may cause negative effects that extend to innocent third parties, such as other employees, investors and customers. And even if a particular company adopts all reasonable measures to prevent its staff from committing an offence, it could still be subjected to criminal sanctions under the vicarious liability standard. Stated bluntly, if the company faces the risk of conviction regardless of its actions, what incentive exists to invest heavily in preventive measures and compliance? The legal standard seems to be too open-ended, placing companies in a state of constant non-compliance.

The English approach, therefore, has been to ameliorate the extreme consequences of a vicarious liability standard by limiting the class of employees whose criminal acts can be imputed to the company.[31] This results in the so-called identification doctrine. Specifically, only those actions and thought patterns of certain high-ranking individuals within the company—the so-called 'directing mind' of the company—are regarded in criminal law as the acts of the company itself.

Criminal acts committed by those individuals are regarded as being committed by the company, ie their acts are 'identified' with the company. In the leading English case, the supermarket company, Tesco, was acquitted of falsely advertising prices on

---

[29] See, eg, E Lederman, 'Models for Imposing Corporate Criminal Liability' (2000) 4 *Buffalo Criminal Law Review* 641.

[30] See Leigh, n 6.

[31] Canada, Australia, Hong Kong and several US States also adopt variations on this approach.

the ground that the 'brains' of the company were unaware of the wrongdoing even though the store manager had the requisite degree of knowledge.[32] Under the US vicarious liability approach, the company would have been convicted in such a case.

The rationale for this more restrictive approach seems clear. It seems to acknowledge the limitations associated with the more expansive US approach highlighted above. Nevertheless, it has resulted in a number of difficulties. First, it has proved extremely difficult for English courts to arrive at a sufficiently clear and consistent definition of what—or who—actually constitutes the 'directing mind'. Similar difficulties seem to have occurred in Canada, Hong Kong and Australia in their use of identification standards as the basis of corporate criminal liability.[33]

Formalistic definitions of the 'directing mind' that focus on those individuals who occupy particular positions within a company—such as the board of directors or Chief Executive Officer (CEO)—often fail to capture the diverse realities of the distribution of power in complex modern organisations. Moreover, focusing on the title on the 'name card' or office door of a particular executive-manager-employee would seem to be easily circumvented by the delegation of criminal activities to lower-ranked employees or those holding no formal title within the organisation. On the other hand, however, a more substantive approach to defining the 'directing mind' has proved too vague in a criminal law context, as it requires the court to identify various functions or substantive powers—the power to direct company policy, for example—that are not amenable to such a precise identification and definition. The result is that both formalistic and substantive approaches to defining the directing mind of the company seem to be highly problematic in a criminal law context. Consequently, the core concept in the identification approach—the directing mind—is marked by serious difficulties.

In addition to the conceptual challenge of defining the directing mind, a further problem with identification doctrines is that it has been almost impossible for prosecutors to secure convictions against corporations because high-ranking managerial agents—however they are defined—are going to be relatively well placed to insulate themselves from criminal investigation (ie they are 'judgment proof').

In a UK context, for example, a series of high-profile acquittals due to failure to secure a conviction against senior management—most notably in the case against P&O concerning the sinking of the ferry, *The Herald of Free Enterprise*—reinforced public perceptions of injustice and fuelled a perception that identification doctrines are tantamount to immunity for corporations.[34] This perception of injustice has often been exacerbated when low-ranking employees are convicted for their role in the same incident.[35]

---

[32] *Tesco Supermarkets Ltd v Natrass* [1972] AC 153.

[33] See generally Department of Justice (Canada), 'Corporate Criminal Liability Discussion Paper' (2002); MJ Lau, 'Director's Criminal Liability in Hong Kong' (2003) 12 *Corporate Practice* 1. Australia is discussed later in this section.

[34] *P&O European Ferries Ltd* [1991] 93 Cr App Rep 72.

[35] *Attorney-General's Reference (No 2 of 1999)* [2000] QB 796. In this case, a rail company and the driver were both charged for offences connected to a serious rail accident near London. The driver was convicted, but the court dismissed the case against the rail company on the ground that there was no evidence that any corporate officers had engaged in any criminal act.

Judicial dissatisfaction with the identification standard can also be seen in a 1995 case, *Meridian Global Funds Management Asia Ltd v Securities Commission*, when Lord Hoffmann, in an important and influential judgment of the Privy Council, suggested that although there is a presumption in favour of identification in English law, vicarious liability 'may' be adopted if the purpose of a statute is better achieved by adopting the broader standard.[36]

The *Meridian* formula has been criticised on the grounds that the policy of a statute may be hard to find, and it is unlikely that the words of the relevant provisions will provide a clear answer as to *who* constitutes the company. As such, the new approach seems to introduce ambiguity into the liability standard.

Moreover, the more flexible *Meridian* approach does not really address certain fundamental problems with both forms of imputation. First, all imputation standards presume that a single person has committed a criminal offence, ie all elements of the offence have been committed by one person. In complex modern organisations, where corporate decisions and actions are the result of a combination of individual acts, this may be an unrealistic assumption. Second, by focusing on the criminal acts of only one person, the collective nature of corporate criminal liability is not captured. Stated bluntly, there is no idea of organisational fault associated with imputation doctrines. Criminal liability is derived from the criminal acts of a certain class of employees, and this seems a weak basis for the imposition of a criminal sanction against the organisation as a whole. Lastly, it can reasonably be suggested that corporate criminal liability for crimes of intent runs contrary to one of the basic principles of criminal law—punishment of the morally blameworthy—since it relies upon some variation of vicarious guilt rather than direct, personal fault.

A number of jurisdictions have therefore attempted to develop alternatives to imputation. A first alternative had already emerged in the US federal courts in the late 1980s, the so-called 'aggregation doctrine'. The need for aggregation arises when no one individual has committed an offence but the combined effect of several individual actions is criminal. The typically used example of this is the *Bank of New England* case from 1987, when a US bank was charged with knowingly violating the federal Currency Transaction Reporting Act.[37] This statute required financial institutions to report to the US Treasury all transactions in excess of $10,000. In this case, a customer of a bank withdrew cash from the same account but from three different branches of the bank. The total sum for the three transactions was greater than $10,000. The bank failed to report the transactions and was subsequently prosecuted. Under imputation doctrines the bank would have been acquitted, since no one individual employee had violated the rules. However, the court allowed the three acts to be aggregated in order to establish the corporation's guilt. The rationale behind a doctrine of this kind is clear: it prevents corporations evading criminal liability by compartmentalising their activities.

---

[36] *Meridian Global Funds Management Asia Ltd v Securities Commission* [1995] 3 All ER 918. *Meridian* involved the criminal acts of investment managers, therefore the broader US standard was required in order to ensure a conviction against the company.

[37] *United States v Bank of New England*, 821 F 2d 844 (1st Cir) (1987).

The principal difficulty with aggregation is that 'the total seems to exceed the sum of the parts'.[38] Two innocent states of mind are being added together to produce a guilty state of mind. Several non-culpable states (the acts of the individual bank tellers in the *Bank of New England* example) are combined to result in a culpable state. Again, this seems to run against basic notions of criminal responsibility. Of course, for those who favour aggregation, it is precisely the fact that the conviction of a company does not carry any implication that the workers are guilty of any offence that means this approach is preferable for grounding organisational fault.

However, there is something disturbing about the suggestion that the company committed a crime in the absence of any single criminal act.[39] Another difficulty lies in deciding which individual acts should be aggregated (any employees, or those identified with the company?) and justifying the distinction. As such, we arrive back at earlier debates about which employees are to be identified with the company and the attendant difficulties in such an approach.

Aware of many of the problems in this area, some jurisdictions have sought to develop new models that address the limited ability to stretch, in a fair and legitimate way, familiar criminal law categories (such as personal responsibility) to the very different context of organisational wrongdoing. However, these new approaches also suffer from various difficulties from the perspective of legal certainty.

One alternative, for example, is a so-called risk management model of corporate criminal liability. This can be found in the UK Corporate Manslaughter and Corporate Homicide Act 2007, as well as a 2001 reform in Italian law.[40] In both cases, the issue of criminal responsibility is framed in terms of whether the company's behaviour 'fell below what could reasonably have been expected in the circumstances'. That is to say, criminal liability is imposed on a company if there has been a corporate failure to manage risk in a reasonable manner. Unlike the imputation and aggregation doctrines, the company would be liable not for what its agents had done or thought, but for the organisation of its policies and practices pertaining to risk management.

A similar but even more radical example of attempting to rethink the legal basis of corporate criminal liability is found in the Australian Federal Criminal Code of 1995. Under this reform, liability is imposed on the corporation if 'a corporate culture existed within the body corporate that directed, encouraged, or tolerated' criminal acts.[41] The law goes on to define corporate culture expansively as 'an attitude, policy, rule, course of conduct, or practice existing within the body corporate'.[42] Companies are thus prevented from hiding behind codes of conduct or other policy statements if the reality of corporate practice is very different. This approach is not without difficulties. At the very least one is obliged to distort language in ascribing criminal guilt to

---

[38] J Gobert and M Punch, *Rethinking Corporate Crime* (London, Butterworths, 2004) 84 et seq. See also J Gobert, 'Four Models of Corporate Fault' (1994) 14 *Journal of Legal Studies* 393.

[39] It is on this basis that aggregation was rejected by English courts, see *Attorney-General's Reference (No 2 of 1999)* [2000] QB 796, 798.

[40] For an extensive discussion of both the English proposals and the Italian Law reform, see, eg, Gobert and Punch, n 38, ch 3.

[41] Australian Federal Criminal Code 1995, s 12(c)(2).

[42] ibid, s 12(c)(3).

a corporate body on the ground that it is responsible for the emergence of a morally blameworthy corporate culture.

Even the briefest overview of the liability standard of companies in a criminal law context reveals how various issues and controversies pervade the discussion, and how various competing policy interests need to be resolved in arriving at an appropriate standard.

In particular, there seems to be an inherent tension between, on the one hand, finding a fair and workable standard appropriate for dealing with large, complex business organisations that operate in multiple jurisdictions and, on the other hand, finding a standard that is sufficiently compatible with fundamental principles of criminal law, such as legal certainty and procedural fairness. Against this background, it is perhaps not surprising that concerns of legal certainty have often taken second place to a more pragmatic desire to find a standard that is going to be workable in complex cases involving highly-motivated and well-resourced corporate suspects and defendants.

V. Post-2000 Procedural Innovation

Post-2000, a number of new and controversial legal mechanisms have been used by regulators against corporations suspected of criminal wrongdoing. Notable amongst these are so-called deferred prosecution agreements (DPAs).[43] These are an example of pre-trial diversion, in that a corporate suspect avoids prosecution in exchange for fulfilling various obligations contained in an agreement negotiated between the company and prosecutor-regulators.

The increased use of this type of instrument since 2000 represents a significant change in how law enforcement deals with corporate crime. The emergence and expansion of DPAs is widely seen as a response to the bankruptcy of Arthur Andersen in 2002, after the firm was convicted of obstruction of justice in the context of the shredding of documents relevant to the Enron investigation. Although the conviction was subsequently overturned by the US Supreme Court, the firm closed down, causing many innocent employees to lose their jobs and the market to lose a valuable service provider.

In order to avoid so-called collateral damage of this kind, the US Government began to look for alternatives, notably some form of pre-trial diversion that sanctions a company whilst seeking to ensure that it is not driven out of business and is able to continue operations, albeit in a reformed state.

---

[43] See, eg, BL Garrett, *Too Big to Jail: How Prosecutors Compromise with Corporations* (New York, Belknap, 2014); IE Gilbert, *Corporate Crime and the Use of Deferred and Non-Prosecution Agreements* (New York, Nova, 2010); W Kaal, 'The Effect of Deferred and Non-Prosecution Agreements on Corporate Governance' (2014) 70 *Business Lawyer* 1.

In a typical DPA, a criminal charge is filed against a corporation, and the corporation acknowledges and accepts responsibility for the criminal wrongdoing. The prosecution is deferred for a period of time—usually from one to two years—provided the corporation fulfils the terms of the DPA and does not engage in further misconduct. If the company fulfils all obligations under the agreement then the charge is withdrawn. If there is a failure to comply with the terms of the agreement then the charge can be activated and the case will proceed to trial.

The kind of obligations that are imposed on a company as part of these agreements include the following: the immediate payment of a 'fine' agreed between the prosecutor and the company; cooperation with any ongoing investigations; waivers of various trial rights and privileges—such as attorney–client privilege, the work product doctrine and statute of limitation defences; implementation of and compliance with corporate governance reform measures (a so-called 'Compliance and Ethics Program'); and consent to oversight by an 'independent' monitor approved by the Government.

The specific terms are negotiated between the Government and the particular company. Such agreements have a number of advantages, at least from the perspective of regulators. With a DPA, the company admits to culpability, a change in the company is assured, monitors are placed in the company to avoid future problems and the cooperation of the company is assured. Moreover, the company is forced to pay a 'fine'. Lastly, the company is allowed to continue operating without the possible negative collateral consequences of prosecution—eg suspension or debarment from contracting with government entities, liquidation of the company, loss of jobs for employees not involved in the misconduct and loss of beneficial products or services in the marketplace.

On the other hand, if the case goes to trial, there is the risk of a costly not guilty verdict (and this risk is significant given a jury system and the complex law and facts that characterise most corporate crime cases). And even if the company is convicted, it will have cost the taxpayer a significant amount of money for the prosecution, and the net result will be payment of a fine by the company. Since a 'fine' is guaranteed under a DPA, along with other benefits that would not occur if the case went to trial, the 'value added' of going to trial is not always clear. Moreover, in the event of a conviction there is a risk of the kind of collateral damage associated with the fate of Arthur Andersen.

Nevertheless, the increased use of settlement agreements in cases of corporate crime has been criticised. First, there are separation-of-powers and rule-of-law concerns. Should prosecutors have this kind of discretionary power? Surely it is for a court ultimately to determine the sanction to be imposed for criminal conduct? In the UK version of the scheme, this criticism was acknowledged and a much greater role for the judiciary was required in permitting the negotiation of a DPA, monitoring such negotiations and approving the terms of any agreement.[44]

---

[44] Freshfields Bruckhaus Deringer, 'Deferred Prosecution Agreements: What you Really Need to Know' (2013).

The second related set of concerns involve the lack of uniformity, transparency and accountability. Until 2007, there were no governing standards or guidance to US attorneys on whether to adopt pre-trial diversion in a particular case. Since 2007, a series of guidelines has been issued, but these afford enormous discretion to the prosecutor. As a result, uncertainty surrounds both whether a particular firm will be offered the opportunity to enter into such an agreement and the terms of any such agreement.

Lastly, there are concerns about the capacity of prosecutor-regulators to be making this kind of agreement. The 'value added' of such agreements is that a corporation emerges from the DPA with reformed governance. Nevertheless, it does seem reasonable to ask whether prosecutor-regulators have the necessary skills and resources to be making this kind of judgement, and whether such governance reform results in a genuine change within the company and does not simply constitute a box-ticking or window-dressing exercise.

VI. New Legal Risk

One important effect of the expansion of the new corporate criminal law is to greatly expand the legal risk facing companies. Managing this new legal risk therefore obliges companies—particularly larger companies—to invest heavily in meaningful, flexible and adaptable compliance mechanisms within organisational governance, which aim at minimising the liability exposure that has been created by uncertainties as to the scope of the law and liability.

Such internal governance mechanisms can be characterised as a form of 'social enforcement'. It seems clear that corporate adoption of social enforcement is a response, at least in part, to the new legal risk that such developments have created.

Social enforcement aims at ensuring that meaningful self-regulatory capacities—a culture of compliance—become firmly embedded in the structure and culture of an organisation. In this context, a culture of compliance can be characterised by a generalised awareness of relevant legal obligations, putting in place incentive structures that encourage compliance with those obligations, and establishing institutionalised control mechanisms for monitoring corporate conduct and implementing corrective action in the event of non-compliance.

In this way, the new corporate criminal law transfers much of the responsibility and many of the functions and administrative costs associated with 'policing' compliance from the state to private actors. This approach can be justified on the grounds that the corporation is best placed to monitor for, and, when necessary, self-correct corporate wrongdoing at the lowest cost to society. Public enforcement—in the form of indictment, trial and possible conviction—is regarded as a measure of last resort, to be employed in the event of a breakdown or failure of social enforcement mechanisms.

A key organising principle of the corporate criminal law seems to be to provide corporations with incentives to engage in social enforcement. This is not to suggest that other principles more traditionally associated with criminal justice, such as punishment or deterrence, are irrelevant in the context of the new corporate criminal law. Modern legal systems have a complex character, in the sense that they can simultaneously embed multiple, possibly competing, principles and objectives. Nevertheless, the contemporary emphasis on social enforcement gives the new corporate criminal law a distinctive character, and this type of account offers a better interpretive and explanatory 'fit' with a wide range of recent developments than the more traditional justifications for imposing criminal liability. The point to be emphasised in this context is that the legal risk facing a company functions as a powerful incentive for that company to bolster social enforcement procedures. In this way, uncertainty might be said to contribute to achieving a socially desirable policy objective.

Corporate compliance can be understood as the most important institutional means adopted by firms to achieve the goal of social enforcement.[45] Stand-alone compliance departments developed in the early 1960s, initially in the US. Prior to that time, the legal department would take responsibility for compliance functions. However, the legal risks associated with the new corporate criminal law, as well as the proliferation of regulation more generally, have triggered a greatly expanded role for the discourse and practice of compliance in contemporary business.

Significantly, many legal systems increasingly offer incentives to implement effective compliance programs. That is to say, the criminal justice system offers 'rewards' for implementing compliance structures in the event that wrongdoing does occur, ie in the event of a breakdown in social enforcement, companies will be 'rewarded' for having had compliance mechanisms in place at the time any offending occurred.

Modern corporate criminal law therefore seems to be predicated on a recognition that perfect compliance is impossible and that demands for perfection may be counterproductive. Such an expectation has a potential 'chilling effect' on a firm's willingness to invest in what will often be regarded as a non revenue-generating activity.

There are a number of examples of legal measures designed to 'reward' compliance. First, compliance can function as a justification, that is to say, a full defence against criminal liability. A company that can show it had adequate compliance procedures in place at the time an offence occurred is not criminally liable. The UK Bribery Act, for example, offers a full defence to the payment of bribes, if—at the time the offence occurred—the corporation had 'adequate' compliance mechanisms in place. Second, compliance can provide mitigation at the sentencing phase.[46] The US Sentencing Guidelines for Organizations include compliance as a key factor in the reduction of sentence. Lastly, compliance can provide a company with leverage in any settlement negotiations that take place prior to indictment.

In each of these different ways, therefore, the legal system offers clear and additional incentives for a corporation to implement compliance processes and procedures aimed at social enforcement.

---

[45] See Gobert and Punch, n 38, ch 10.
[46] For a comparative perspective on the compliance defence in different jurisdictions, see Koehler, n 15.

VII. Concluding Remarks

Modern corporate criminal law seems to be characterised by simultaneous processes of net-widening (ie more offences applied to companies, often with lower *mens rea* requirements) and diminishing legal certainty (ie ambiguity as to the outer limits of these offences). In addition, various controversies surround the legal doctrine that forms the basis of this whole field of law, namely, corporate criminal liability.

This chapter has suggested that one important effect of this change has been to contribute to a significant expansion in the legal risk facing companies, obliging them to invest in meaningful and flexible compliance mechanisms within organisational governance that aim at managing this new legal risk. This trend towards social enforcement—ie transferring much of the responsibility and many of the functions and administrative costs associated with policing compliance from the state to private actors—seems to be a distinctive feature of the contemporary corporate criminal law. It seems to be closely connected to the difficult and on-going task of managing the complex profile of legal risk that has emerged in recent years.

Selected Further Reading

Braithwaite, J and Drahos, P, *Global Business Regulation* (Cambridge, Cambridge University Press, 2000)

Garrett, B, *Too Big to Jail: How Prosecutors Compromise with Corporations* (New York, Belknap, 2014)

Gobert, J and Punch, J, *Rethinking Corporate Crime* (London, Butterworths, 2004)

Laufer, W, *Corporate Bodies and Guilty Minds: The Failure of Corporate Criminal Liability* (Chicago, IL, University Chicago Press, 2006)

Simpson, S, *Corporate Crime, Law and Social Control* (Cambridge, Cambridge University Press, 2002)

Wells, C, *Corporations and Criminal Responsibility* (Oxford, Oxford University Press, 2001)

7

E-Commerce Law

I. Outline

Electronic commerce law (e-commerce law) is an increasingly important area of law. Until the late twentieth century, face-to-face transactions dominated the landscape. The rise of the Internet in particular, however, opened new marketing and sales channels that have incrementally been simplifying distance selling. Over time, concluding commercial contracts has become easier, cheaper and faster. Nowadays, ordering goods and services can be realised in cyberspace with only a few mouse-clicks or touches of virtual buttons. More than that, given the availability of Internet access, one can place orders from basically anywhere in the world. Looking at modern electronic commercial transactions, it is justified to suggest that trade has become more and more borderless, in the sense that—compared with conventional transaction methods—parties can interact with each other regardless of their places of residence or location. In a seminal statement on e-commerce, the European Commission, for example, referred to it as being of an 'essentially transnational nature'.[1] It is this borderlessness that, in combination with two other factors—John Dickie refers to them as the 'transience' (ie the risk of untraceability of electronic messages and data) and the 'size' of the e-commerce market—makes e-commerce an interesting and highly relevant area of legal discourse in practice.[2]

Looking at e-commerce from a legal perspective, it should be noted that its regulatory and substantive framework is highly complex. The rise of e-commerce has undeniably accelerated over time. In some cases, it has created (new) legal challenges that regulators and stakeholders have to take into consideration when discussing ways to strengthen the electronic commercial market. Although it is virtually impossible to define and delineate the terms 'e-commerce' and 'e-commerce law', it is widely agreed that they touch upon various legal fields. Some of the key questions revolve

---

[1] European Commission, A European Initiative in Electronic Commerce, 16 April 1997, COM(97) 157 final, 4.
[2] J Dickie, *Producers and Consumers in EU E-Commerce Law* (Oxford, Hart Publishing, 2005) 7–9.

around issues relating to advertising, contracting, the choice of law, jurisdiction and enforcement, intellectual property, cybercrime, privacy and data protection, as well as taxation.[3]

It is not the purpose of this chapter to discuss existing e-commerce regimes exhaustively and conclusively. Given the comprehensiveness of the topic, even pertinent e-commerce literature must give up on this idea—in particular when it comes to a truly global perspective.[4] Instead of daring the impossible, this chapter aims to convey a basic understanding of some of the underlying developments and future challenges with respect to selected aspects of (particularly transnational) e-commerce law. The emphasis is on questions of the harmonisation and divergence of selected legal frameworks and instruments, national and international endeavours to facilitate electronic transactions, and the considerably wide and diverse group of involved regulators. It should further be noted that e-commerce is also discussed in some other chapters of this book, in particular within the frameworks of alternative dispute resolution (Chapter 4) (in particular in the context of online dispute resolution) and consumer law (Chapter 1).

This chapter starts with a brief overview of the history and development of e-commerce in general, before looking at some jurisdictional examples of how legislative regulators have attempted to answer selected issues. In this context, we shall encounter some national as well as international endeavours. The outline will commence with a look at non-legislative actors and be rounded off with a brief presentation of some—we believe—pressing issues that will (or at least should) be addressed in the future.

II. The Development of E-Commerce

E-commerce can be broadly defined as any form of commercial activity that involves electronic means. The term would normally be used in the context of commercial transactions that are concluded in cyberspace, usually via the Internet or with the help of emails. The good or service that builds the basis for such a transaction can be, but does not need to be, of a digital nature. Subsequently, the e-commerce literature traditionally classifies relevant transactions into one of two categories: (i) commercial activities with respect to/commercial contracts concluded with the

---

[3] In a comparable vein are, eg, the listings in SE Blythe, *The E-Commerce Law Trilogy*, vol 1: *E-Commerce Law around the World* (Bloomington, IN, Xlibris, 2011) 19; S Spindler and F Börner (eds), *E-Commerce Law in Europe and the USA* (Berlin, Springer, 2002).

[4] For a non-conclusive list of pertinent literature, see the 'Selected Further Reading' section at the end of this chapter.

help of an electronic medium; and/or (ii) the electronic fulfilment of a contract.[5] Because of conceptual differences in the underlying legal concepts, further differentiations are occasionally made with respect to the parties involved. The two categories most often found are business-to-business (B2B) and business-to-consumer (B2C) transactions.[6]

In particular since the late twentieth century, e-commerce has become an area of increasing regulatory interest. As will be shown in the course of this chapter, many governments, international and non-governmental organisations, as well as private actors, have expressed their interest in shaping the e-commerce environment.

The phenomenon of electronic transactions can be traced back to the early second half of the twentieth century, when technological developments paved the way for the electronic exchange of messages. In the early beginnings, the commercial impact of electronic data exchanges and communication was, however, relatively low. It was not before the last decade of the twentieth century that e-commerce—largely as a consequence of the rise of the Internet—saw its first peak, when an increasing number of private users began to access the Internet.[7] In the 1990s, a number of domestic, international and non-governmental stakeholders crafted the first, mostly sectoral pieces of legal regulation. Although the scope of the initiatives differed, the underlying ideas were basically the same. They all aimed to address possible legal obstacles to e-commerce, to broaden and simplify access to the electronic commercial market for both business and consumers. In the aforementioned 1997 e-commerce Initiative,[8] the Commission for example, expressed the view that intensifying attempts to support e-commerce would help to stimulate economic growth. In the words of the Commission, 'The aim of this European Initiative is to encourage the vigorous growth of electronic commerce in Europe. A fast-moving sector, electronic commerce will have a considerable impact on Europe's competitiveness in global markets.'[9] The Organization for Economic Cooperation and Development (OECD) took an even broader approach, linking the potential benefits of a strengthened electronic commercial market to societal advantages more generally. In its 1998 Action Plan on 'A Borderless World: Realising the Potential of Global Electronic Commerce' (OECD E-Commerce Action Plan), the OECD called e-commerce 'a central element in the OECD's vision for economic growth, jobs and improved social conditions'.[10]

---

[5] See, eg, FF Wang, *Law of Electronic Commercial Transactions: Contemporary Issues in the EU, US and China*, 2nd edn (Abingdon, Routledge, 2014) 8, where the author uses the terms 'electronic ordering of tangible goods' and 'online delivery of intangibles' to differentiate between the two categories. Andrew Murray adds a third category—'the trade in telecommunication and Internet services'—see A Murray, 'E-commerce' in P Cane and J Conaghan (eds), *The New Oxford Companion to Law* (Oxford University Press, 2008) 354, 354. For the sake of concentrating on key questions, however, we limit the e-commerce discussion to issues (i) and (ii).

[6] See, eg, LE Gillies, *Electronic Commerce and International Private Law: A Study of Electronic Consumer Contracts* (Aldershot, Ashgate, 2008) 26; Wang, n 5, 8.

[7] A Davidson, *Social Media and Electronic Commerce Law*, 2nd edn (Oxford, Oxford University Press, 2016) 5.

[8] Above n 1.

[9] ibid, 4.

[10] OECD, 'A Borderless World: Realising the Potential of Global Electronic Commerce' (1998) 3, SG/EC(98)9/FINAL.

The following section will highlight the development of e-commerce law at various levels and with respect to different stakeholders. We shall touch upon national, regional, supranational and international regulation, and discuss the impact of state, non-state private actors in attempts to support electronic transactions.

III. E-Commerce and the Law

A. E-Commerce Law in the US

In the relevant literature, there is a general consensus that electronic commerce emerged in the US, facilitated by its early lead in information and communication technology (ICT). Unsurprisingly, the first transactions concluded via the Internet were reported from the US. Common examples include the launch of a US pizza delivery service and the online sale of Sting's album 'Ten Summoner's Tales'.[11] Both transactions took place in US States in 1994.

In the early days of commercial ICT, the US was also remarkably active when it came to legislation on e-commerce. In the context of his global analysis of e-commerce law, Stephen Errol Blythe explains that Utah was the first jurisdiction to pass a law on this issue—its electronic signature law in 1995.[12] The early emergence of e-commerce laws at the US State level might be considered one reason why electronic commerce appeared on the US federal political agenda relatively soon after the commercial introduction of the Internet. Early State laws, the often borderless character of electronic transactions and the scattered framework of e-commerce-relevant areas of law (as a result of autonomous State legislation) gave rise to the need for a more comprehensive discussion in the US. As a consequence, several influential US institutions began to draft principles, model and uniform rules to simplify and align the legal embeddings for electronic transactions. Calling the US 'a leader in developing e-commerce law policy since the Internet's inception', Michael Geist explains that the American Bar Association (ABA), for example, was one of the first institutions worldwide to launch a project on electronic signatures.[13] Crafted as early as 1992, the resulting drafts served

---

[11] On the former, see 'Pizza Hut Celebrates 20th Anniversary of World's First Online Purchase With 50 Percent Off Online Deal for Hut Lovers Members' (2 January 2014) *PR Newswire*, www.prnewswire. com/news-releases/pizza-hut-celebrates-20th-anniversary-of-worlds-first-online-purchase-with-50-percent-off-online-deal-for-hut-lovers-members-238428021.html. On the latter, see M Grothhaus, 'You'll Never Guess What the First Thing Ever Sold on the Internet Was' (26 November 2015) *Fast Company*, www. fastcompany.com/3054025/youll-never-guess-what-the-first-thing-ever-sold-on-the-internet-was.

[12] Blythe, n 3, 17 and 66, with reference to the Utah Digital Signature Act (Utah Code §§ 46-3-101 to 46-3-504, 1995).

[13] M Geist, 'A Guide to Global E-Commerce Law', www.itu.int/ITU-T/special-projects/ip-policy/final/Attach04.doc, 10.

as blueprints for some subsequent State legislation (including Utah's Digital Signature Act) and resulted in ABA model rules in 1996.[14]

Geist adds a number of further US institutions that have played a significant role in the development of US e-commerce law. Most notably they include the Department of Commerce and the Federal Communications Commission (as monitoring institutions over the Internet on the one hand and functioning as a coordinator of the communications infrastructure more generally), the Federal Trade Commission and the Department of Justice (with respect to consumer and privacy law issues and competition law respectively), the State Department (as the representative at the Hague Conference on Private International Law) and the National Conference of Commissioners on Uniform State Law (NCCUSL).[15]

It was the last of these that—supported by the ABA and its model rule experience—presented the Uniform Electronic Transaction Act (UETA). Published in 1999, it was one of the first (and remains one of the) core pieces of US e-commerce regulation. The UETA has been welcomed by a large majority of US jurisdictions. As of mid-2017, it had already been implemented in 47 US States, the District of Columbia and the US Virgin Islands. Only Washington, Illinois and New York are still pending.[16]

The main purpose of the UETA was to align State regimes on electronic transactions with respect to digital signatures, and to introduce the respective rules in those jurisdictions that had not yet introduced any. The NCCUSL was convinced that 'relying on paper for the memorialization of transactions and upon manual signatures for verifying them are most likely to impede electronic transactions, adding to their costs'.[17] Hence, improving the validity and recognition level of electronic communication and signatures was the top priority for the NCCUSL.

The central provision of the UETA is its Section 7, which comprises the following four subsections:

(a) A record or signature may not be denied legal effect or enforceability solely because it is in electronic form.
(b) A contract may not be denied legal effect or enforceability solely because an electronic record was used in its formation.
(c) If a law requires a record to be in writing, an electronic record satisfies the law.
(d) If a law requires a signature, an electronic signature satisfies the law.

Parallels can be drawn with the (later to be discussed) UNCITRAL Model Law on Electronic Commerce of 1996. The Model Law's Article 5 on the legal recognition of data messages (relating to the UETA's 'records'), Article 6 on requiring information to be in writing (cf the UETA's 'in writing') and Article 7 on signatures (cf the UETA's 'signature') obviously served as a prominent source for Section 7 of the UETA.

---

[14] American Bar Association, 'Digital Signature Guidelines: Legal Infrastructre for Certification Authorities and Secure Electronic Commerce' (1996), apps.americanbar.org/dch/thedl.cfm?filename=/ST230002/otherlinks_files/dsg.pdf.

[15] Geist, n 13, 10.

[16] For the status of enactment, see the Enactment Status Map at uniformlaws.org/Act.aspx?title=Electronic%20Transactions%20Act.

[17] National Conference of Commissioners on Uniform State Law, 'Electronic Transactions Act Summary', uniformlaws.org/ActSummary.aspx?title=Electronic%20Transactions%20Act.

The UETA undoubtedly succeeded in introducing widely harmonised rules on the validity of electronic records and signatures. However, it is relatively narrow in terms of scope, leaving other important e-commerce issues untouched. This is not to say that e-commerce did not enjoy broader attention when it came to the crafting of US model and uniform laws. One complicating factor in achieving results similar to the UETA, however, has been the challenging task of balancing State, federal, business, consumer and academic interests in establishing rules that would encompass electronic transactions in a more comprehensive way.

Two examples to illustrate this relate to the attempt to introduce aligned rules for computer information transactions that would have gone beyond the mere regulation of the validity and recognition of electronic records and signatures. In 2000, shortly after the presentation of the UETA, the NCCUSL issued a second uniform law—the Uniform Computer Information Transactions Act (UCITA). It aimed to introduce a uniform commercial code in the form of a model law for 'computer information transactions'.[18] A comparably broad project was completed in 2009, when the American Law Institute presented its Principles of the Law of Software Contracts (PLSC).[19] Both instruments—the UCITA and the PLSC—included a comprehensive set of legal rules that were specifically and comprehensively designed, ranging from rules on the conclusion of relevant contracts to performance-related issues, as well as remedies for bad or non-fulfilment of contractual obligations. The echo, however, was not as positive as in the case of the UETA. Neither the UCITA nor the PLSC has reached a comparable level of significance. As of mid-2017, the UCITA, for example, had been enacted in only two US States—Virginia and Maryland. The PLSC has not seen any significant implementation either. The strong opposition, in particular by consumer representative groups and by States with a comparatively high level of protection, might be explained by the alleged low level of consumer protection offered by the UCITA and the PLSC, as well as by the States' general wish to maintain their own regimes.[20]

Looking at the US e-commerce framework from a legislative perspective, it is possible to note that, overall, consumer issues play a less prominent role in (federal or uniform) US legislation compared with the situation in the European Union (EU), as discussed in section III.B. One notable exception (in addition to the UETA) is to be found in the Electronic Signatures in Global and National Commerce Act of 2000 (E-Sign Act).[21] The E-Sign Act aims to protect buyers in electronic transactions to some degree, by allowing the delivery of consumer notices via email (only) if the buyer

---

[18] s 103(a) UCITA.

[19] American Law Institute, *Principles of the Law, Software Contracts* (Philadelphia, PA, The American Law Institute, 2010).

[20] For a broader discussion of the instruments from the perspective of fairness, public interest and consumer protection criticism see J Braucher 'New Basics: Twelve Principles for Fair Commerce in Mass-Market Software and Other Digital Products' in JK Winn (ed), *Consumer Protection in the Age of the 'Information Economy'* (Aldershot, Ashgate, 2006) 177; RA Epstein, 'Contract, not Regulation: UCITA and High-Tech Consumers Meet Their Consumer Protection Critics' in Winn (ed), *Consumer Protection in the Age of the 'Information Economy'* 205.

[21] 15 U.S.C. c 96.

consents. Nevertheless, while the US continues to take a leading role in raising ICT to the next level, in terms of contributing to the development of transnational rules on e-commerce, other stakeholders have turned out to be more active. This—as will be seen in some of the following subsections—can be explained either by the legislative competencies (and actual capabilities) of the involved actors, or, at least, by the focus of their operations.

B.   E-Commerce Law in the EU

The EU first considered e-commerce in the late 1990s. The foundations for a pan-EU regulation of e-commerce were laid in 1997 with the 1997 e-commerce Initiative and a number of e-commerce workshops and conferences that followed. At a Ministerial Conference, one of the organising members, for example, expressed the need to intensify efforts in regulating pan-EU e-commerce as follows, when he explained the origins of the idea to host the event:

> First, I wanted to give a clear signal that we in Europe are prepared and determined to be a leading player in the world league as we enter the global information age. We need to raise the level of awareness in our countries of the enormous potential of this development—not only in politics, but also in business, in the groups in society and amongst the public at large. That is where we are still lagging far behind.[22]

Compared with the US initiatives, the European e-commerce debate started relatively comprehensively. The EU, in particular the Commission, did not restrict its focus to questions of validity and recognition of electronic records and signatures. Policymakers took a broader approach that encompassed additional issues, which were all connected by the idea of trust-building. In particular because of the special, supranational legislative competencies of the EU legislator, the EU constitutes a paramount example for transnational e-commerce law that sets it apart from the majority of other regional regimes, eg the Association of Southeast Asian Nations (ASEAN).

With its 1997 e-commerce Initiative, the Commission introduced four targets it considered as key to a common electronic commercial market. The first of these four—'the need for global consensus'[23]—can be understood as a commitment to international cooperation. Target 2 asked for a stronger contribution to the development of ICT. Target 4 aimed to foster the stakeholders'—primarily business and consumers—ICT and e-commerce awareness. It was, however, Target 3 that formed the basis for the first concrete legislative plans: the Commission was convinced that a strong, harmonised regulatory framework was needed to build 'trust and confidence' to support the e-commerce market.[24]

---

[22] Transcript of Günter Rexrodt's opening speech in European Ministerial Conference, 'Global Information Networks: Realising the Potential' (1997), publications.europa.eu/en/publication-detail/-/publication/f829ad7a-63f0-4f2e-90b2-d5b95bd38d83, 3.

[23] European Commission, n 1, 7.

[24] ibid, 12.

Just one year later, the Commission presented its Proposal for a Directive on certain legal aspects of electronic commerce in the internal market (1998 E-Commerce Directive Proposal).[25] Compared with, for example, the abovementioned first US initiatives, it differed in terms of scope and comprehensiveness. Although the 1998 E-Commerce Directive Proposal did not touch upon electronic signatures—they were regulated separately in the Electronic Signatures Directive[26]—the Proposal was very broad. The core rules covered the following aspects: questions relating to the establishment of 'Information Society service providers'[27] and rules on their transparency; rules on 'commercial communications'[28] and 'commercial contracts';[29] (broad limitations of) the liability of intermediaries;[30] and (basic rules on) fostering compliance and simplifying redress procedures.[31]

In 2000, the EU legislator passed the E-Commerce Directive,[32] which, in principle, followed the structure of the Proposal and incorporated the same focus points. Because of its broad material scope the E-Commerce Directive is arguably the key e-commerce instrument in the EU.[33] In line with the call for clearer rules on electronic transactions, the Directive establishes a framework that covers all stages of contracting. Looking at e-commerce from a lifecycle perspective, the regulatory regime of the Directive starts with rules on enhancing the introduction of cyberspace platforms by limiting Member States' authorisation competencies with regard to (information society) service providers.[34] This is followed by requiring Member States to enact rules, in particular to increase the quality and visibility of information that is transmitted via commercial communications.[35] Rules on treating electronic contracts in the same way as ordinary contracts in terms of their validity and binding character follow as a third step.[36] With rules on limiting the possible liability of intermediary service providers, the Directive aims to motivate third parties to install e-commerce platforms.[37] Encouraging the use of codes of conduct and the call for appropriate in- and out-of-court dispute resolution schemes complete the package.[38]

---

[25] Proposal for a Directive on certain legal aspects of electronic commerce in the internal market, 18 November 1998, COM(1998) 586 final.

[26] Directive 1999/93/EC, [2000] OJ L13/12.

[27] 1998 E-Commerce Directive Proposal, c II, s 1. For a definition of the terms 'Information Society service' and 'service provider', see Arts 2(a) and 2(b) of the Proposal.

[28] 1998 E-Commerce Directive Proposal, c II, s 2.

[29] 1998 E-Commerce Directive Proposal, c II, s 3.

[30] 1998 E-Commerce Directive Proposal, c II, s 4.

[31] See, in particular, Arts 16 (Codes of conduct), 17 (Out-of-court dispute settlement) and 18 (Court actions) 1998 E-Commerce Directive Proposal.

[32] Directive 2000/31/EC, [2000] OJ L178/1.

[33] Its comprehensiveness and progressiveness might have partly been why the vast majority of Member States failed to meet the implementation deadline of 17 January 2002. Lodder points out that only three of (at that time 15) Member States managed to follow the schedule—see AR Lodder, 'Directive 2000/31/EC on Certain Aspects of Information Society Services, in Particular Electronic Commerce, in the Internal Market' in AR Lodder and AD Murray (eds), *EU Regulation of E-Commerce: A Commentary* (Cheltenham, Edward Elgar Publishing, 2017) 15, 16.

[34] Art 4 E-Commerce Directive.

[35] Arts 5–8 E-Commerce Directive.

[36] s 3 E-Commerce Directive.

[37] s 4 E-Commerce Directive.

[38] Arts 16 (on codes of conduct) and 17–18 (on dispute resolution) E-Commerce Directive.

Over the years, the E-Commerce Directive and the earlier Electronic Signatures Directive were followed by a number of complementary instruments that aimed to create a level playing field for e-commerce, in particular at a transnational level within the EU. As is the case with e-commerce law in general, there is no consensus regarding the exact scope of EU e-commerce law. Nevertheless, the following initiatives can—in chronological order—be considered as forming its backbone:[39]

— the 1999 Electronic Signatures Directive,
— the 2000 E-Commerce Directive,
— the 2001 Copyright Directive (also known as the InfoSoc Directive),[40]
— the 2002 Privacy and Electronic Communications Directive,[41]
— the 2004 Intellectual Property Enforcement Directive,[42]
— the 2006 Service Directive,[43]
— the 2009 Electronic Money Directive,[44]
— the 2011 Consumer Rights Directive,[45]
— the 2013 Alternative Dispute Resolution Directive (ADR Directive),[46]
— the 2013 Online Dispute Resolution Regulation (ODR Regulation),[47]
— the 2014 Collective Management of Copyright Directive,[48]
— the 2014 Electronic Identification and Trust Services Regulation,[49]
— the 2015 Electronic Payments Directive,[50]
— the 2016 General Data Protection Regulation,[51]
— the 2016 Data Protection and Crime Prevention Directive,[52]
— the 2016 Network and Information Systems Security Directive.[53]

Many of these instruments take a comparably broad approach. The 2001 Copyright Directive, for example, deals with copyright issues without concentrating on specific works or performances. It was the answer to two earlier initiatives of the World Intellectual Property Organization (WIPO) to align national copyright rules—the WIPO Copyright Treaty and the WIPO Performances and Phonograms Treaty. Harmonising copyright rules at the EU level ranked high on the list of priorities, because cyberspace allowed for easier digital processing of information and data.

The EU copyright regime is a good example illustrating one practical challenge for regulating e-commerce in the EU. Largely as a consequence of the often difficult

---

[39] One has to note, however, that the list is not conclusive and will very likely further increase over the years.
[40] Directive 2001/29/EC, [2001] OJ L167/10.
[41] Directive 2002/58/EC, [2002] OJ L201/37.
[42] Directive 2004/48/EC, [2004] OJ L157/45.
[43] Directive 2006/123/EC, [2006] OJ L376/36.
[44] Directive 2009/110/EC, [2009] OJ L267/7.
[45] Directive 2011/83/EU, [2011] OJ L304/64.
[46] Directive 2013/11/EU, [2013] OJ L165/63.
[47] Regulation (EU) 524/2013, [2013] OJ L165/1.
[48] Directive 2014/26/EU, [2014] OJ L84/72.
[49] Regulation (EU) 910/2014, [2014] OJ L257/73.
[50] Directive 2015/2366/EU, [2015] OJ L337/35.
[51] Regulation (EU) 679/2016, [2016] OJ L119/1.
[52] Directive 2016/680/EU, [2016] OJ L119/89.
[53] Directive 2016/1148/EU, [2016] OJ L194/1.

and time-consuming compromise- and law-making processes, the 2001 Copyright Directive has survived its first 16 years without revision. To compensate for the lack of swiftness of law-making in this regard, the European Court of Justice (ECJ; now the Court of Justice of the European Union, CJEU) has played an important role in further developing pertinent rules. It was not before 2016 that the Commission finally succeeded in intensifying efforts to improve the transparency of the legal situation by adapting the Copyright Directive regime with its Proposal for a Directive on copyright in the Digital Single Market in 2016.[54] As this example shows, it is not only the remarkable number of EU directives and regulations that address electronic transactions, but also the additional work of the Court of Justice that makes e-commerce an increasingly complex area in the EU.

The European initiatives launched thus far have to be considered a significant step forward for transnational e-commerce law making. Nonetheless, these steps are not the end of the road. Rather they have induced a regulatory discussion that aims to further align and standardise European e-commerce parameters. Technical developments, in particular, call for further advances. Lodder, for example, argues that advancements in ICT, which include the rise of social networks and apps, demand additional steps. The projects realised thus far, according to Lodder, have not been able to address such issues adequately.[55]

In the framework of the Digital Single Market initiative, the most recent e-commerce policy project at the EU level, the Commission presented its Digital Single Market Strategy (DSM Strategy). It pointed out that the regulatory e-commerce standards should be raised further to achieve the following goals:

(1) better access for consumers and businesses to digital goods and services across Europe; (2) creating the right conditions and a level playing field for digital networks and innovative services to flourish; (3) maximising the growth potential of the digital economy.[56]

The DSM Strategy specifies these three undertakings in more detail by introducing 16 'key actions'. At first sight the majority of the mechanisms indicate that the Commission sees the main stimulating factor as enhancing ICT. But a closer look reveals that the plans are much more complex and permeate several core legal concepts. Some of the key actions build upon existing instruments. These include the areas of contract law and consumer protection for online sales in general; law enforcement in a broader sense (including the regimes introduced by the Consumer Protection Cooperation Regulation[57] and antitrust legislation); data protection and privacy; as well as rules on copyright.

The 16 DSM Strategy key actions go beyond the existing frameworks, however, and require stronger examination and regulation of questions that previously had been widely neglected. Some of them address practical concerns in fulfilling contractual obligations. Parcel delivery issues (which include excessive costs and unreliable

---

[54] Proposal for a Directive on copyright in the Digital Single Market, 14 September 2016, COM(2016) 593 final.

[55] Lodder, n 33, 58.

[56] European Commission, A Digital Single Market for Europe: Commission sets out 16 initiatives to make it happen, 6 May 2015, IP/15/4919.

[57] Regulation (EC) 2006/2004, [2004] OJ L364/1.

services) might be highlighted in this respect. Others—they form the biggest key action group—involve the consequence of technical developments. Cloud computing, the rise of social networking and modernised Internet connectivity standards fall into this category.

Overall, one can conclude that the EU efforts to stimulate e-commerce by aiming to establish a truly borderless environment for commercial online transactions have undeniably seen remarkable process over the years. In terms of transnational significance, EU e-commerce law is arguably one of the most pivotal regimes of the early twenty-first century. This is largely due to the merits of its supranational embedding, which allows for directly harmonising national laws. However, two decades after the emergence of EU e-commerce law, the regime is still far from being complete. At the time of writing, more than a dozen sectoral proposals relating to e-commerce are pending. These projects include possible refinements of, for example, the contracts, copyright and e-privacy frameworks, as well as more recent initiatives to tackle practical issues revolving around geo-blocking and parcel delivery.[58] But even this significant number of proposals cannot hide the fact that some underlying concerns have yet to be discussed more broadly, as commentators repeatedly point out. Challenges posed by differences in language and buying behaviour need to be pointed out in this respect.[59]

C. E-Commerce Law in Asia, South America and Africa

The development of e-commerce regulation has been slightly different in many other parts of the world, in particular in most of Asia, South America and Africa.[60] This is largely due to the fact that ICT, particularly in the context of electronic commercial transactions, developed comparatively late in those regions. From a regulatory perspective, the still widely unexploited potential of the electronic commercial markets in Asia, South America and Africa constitutes an attractive challenge.

---

[58] For details, see the respective lists in the Commission's Work Programme of 2017, Annex 3, Points 5–12. The proposal for a new e-privacy directive—COM(2017) 10 final—was not yet included in those lists.

[59] See, eg, AR Lodder and AD Murray, 'The European Union and E-Commerce' in Lodder and Murray (eds), n 33, 6. With respect to geo-blocking, one should note a gradual relaxation that aims at an enhanced borderless market. More recent examples include the 2016 Roaming Regulation (Regulation (EU) 2016/2286, [2016] OJ L344/46), which simplifies the use of mobile phones throughout the EU regardless of the actual location of a phone's use, and the 2017 Online Content Portability Regulation (Regulation (EU) 2017/1128, [2017] OJ L168/1). The latter Regulation—pursuant to its Art 1(1)—aims to ensure 'that subscribers to portable online content services which are lawfully provided in their Member State of residence can access and use those services when temporarily present in a Member State other than their Member State of residence'. Further initiatives are still pending. Most notably this includes strategies to comprehensively end 'unjustified geoblocking' to ensure a genuinely Digital Single Market in the areas of 'the sale of goods without physical delivery', 'the sale of electronically supplied services' and 'the sale of services provided in a specific physical location'—for details see European Commission, 'Digital Single Market: EU negotiators agreed to end unjustified geoblocking' (20 November 2017), available at europa.eu/rapid/press-release_IP-17-4781_en.htm.

[60] Initiatives taken by developed regions other than the US and the EU Member States will—due to the lack of space—not be the subject of comment. For information on, eg, Australia, see in particular Davidson, n 2. For comments on the Canadian situation, see, eg, the contributions by Michael Geist—for information see www.michaelgeist.ca.

Regulatory endeavours have clearly benefitted from the US and European role models outlined earlier, as well as from the work carried out by international organisations discussed later in this chapter.[61] Nevertheless, in particular initially, the discussions revolved to a great extent around technological issues, as the transnational example of the ASEAN shows. In efforts to catch up with leading e-commerce jurisdictions, the 10 ASEAN Member States concluded the e-ASEAN Framework Agreement in 2000, at a time when e-commerce discussions had commenced in the first few ASEAN states. As indicated in its preamble, the e-ASEAN Framework Agreement expressed the hope for 'opportunities offered by the revolution in information and communications technology (ICT) and electronic commerce'.[62]

The starting point for the ASEAN e-commerce debate was the perceived need to introduce and utilise ICT on a broad scale in the ASEAN Member States. The majority of the 15 articles of the Framework Agreement addressed the widely insufficient state of ICT. To lay the foundations for subsequent legislative measures, the signatories affirmed their intention to work jointly on a stable and broadly accessible ICT environment. In this sense one can understand, for example, Article 4(1), which provides that the 'Member States shall enhance the design and standards of their national information infrastructure with a view to facilitating interconnectivity and ensuring technical inter-operability between each other's information infrastructure'.

The e-ASEAN Framework Agreement further addressed certain legal issues. Its Article 7(1), for example, asked for the conclusion of bilateral and multilateral 'Mutual Recognition Arrangements (MRA) … [to] align national standards to relevant international standards'. To a certain extent, cooperation was facilitated by the widespread willingness to introduce first national e-commerce laws based on the UNCITRAL E-Commerce Model Law. Brunei and the Philippines took the lead in 2000.[63] Five more ASEAN Member States followed. As of mid-2017, only three—Cambodia, Indonesia and Myanmar—had not yet done so. The clearest call for legislative measures was, however, provided by Article 5 of the Framework Agreement. Building upon earlier, Western initiatives, it (rudimentarily) encouraged the ASEAN Member States to work on measures with respect to the possible introduction and mutual recognition of e-signature regimes, electronic payment mechanisms and IP protection, as well as data protection/consumer privacy and ADR.

A couple of further initiatives have followed over the years. Most recently, ASEAN adopted three actions plans in 2015 that all (to a greater or lesser extent) addressed electronic transactions. The ASEAN ICT Masterplan 2020, the most comprehensive of the three, largely built on the e-ASEAN Framework Agreement.[64] It reaffirmed the need to foster the use of ICT throughout the Association. One can see, however, that the ASEAN Member States further expressed their awareness of more recent phenomena, such as cloud computing and social media services. The ASEAN ICT Masterplan 2020 linked technological advancements to legal challenges that might

---

[61] For details see Blythe, n 3; SE Blythe, *The E-Commerce Law Trilogy*, vol 2: *An E-Commerce Law for the World: The Model Electronic Transactions Act* (Bloomington, IN, Xlibris, 2012).

[62] ASEAN, '2000 e-ASEAN Framework Agreement' (24 November 2000) Preamble.

[63] www.uncitral.org/uncitral/en/uncitral_texts/electronic_commerce/1996Model_status.html.

[64] ASEAN, 'The ASEAN ICT Masterplan 2020' (2015).

become highly significant with a further rise in ICT. Questions related to data security and data protection are good examples in this respect.

The other two 2015 initiatives—the ASEAN Economic Community Blueprint 2025 (AECB) and the ASEAN Strategic Action Plan for Consumer Protection 2016–2025 (ASAPCP)—complemented the Masterplan with more general issues.[65] The AECB stressed that e-commerce was one of the main reasons why 'governments [were asked] to find innovative ways of protecting and promoting the interests of consumers'.[66] In a comparatively short chapter, it asked for closer cooperation to achieve the following for the sake of improved transnational confidence in e-commerce:

i.   Harmonised consumer rights and protection laws;
ii.   Harmonised legal framework for online dispute resolution, taking into account available international standards;
iii.   Inter-operable, mutually recognised, secure, reliable and user-friendly e-identification and authorisation (electronic signature) schemes; and
iv.   Coherent and comprehensive framework for personal data protection.[67]

Overall, the AECB, in general, repeated the ideas first voiced in 2000 by the e-ASEAN Framework Agreement, without going into more detail. The main reason for this may be rooted in the plan to convince those states which had yet to introduce modern e-commerce frameworks—most notably the three jurisdictions listed above—of the importance of taking appropriate action.

The ASAPCP suggested that a common modernisation process was needed to achieve acceptable consumer protection standards. Areas that were considered still under-developed in large regions of the ASEAN related to unfair contract terms, product liability, data protection and e-commerce in general.[68] Concrete results are still pending.

From a developmental perspective, the situation in most African and South American is even further behind the times. The UNCITRAL E-Commerce Model Law, for example, has not yet obtained a degree of acceptance that would be comparable to that in most ASEAN Member States. As of 2017, Argentina, Brazil and Chile, for example, were still pending in this respect. The picture is not much better in Africa. In particular with respect to transnational issues, the gap is significant, as a 2016 study by Sonia Rolland shows, for example. The number of African jurisdictions to have concluded bilateral or multilateral agreements that contain provisions on e-commerce is considerably lower than in other parts of the world.[69] Things might change in the future as electronic commercial transactions attain truly global popularity. This would necessitate policymakers' intensifying discussions, followed by legislative steps.

---

[65] ASEAN, 'ASEAN Economic Community Blueprint 2025' (2015); ASEAN 'The ASEAN Strategic Action Plan for Consumer Protection 2016-2025: Meeting the Challenges of a People-Centered ASEAN beyond 2015' (2015).
[66] ASEAN, 'ASEAN Economic Community Blueprint 2025', Recital 26.
[67] ibid, Recital 53.
[68] ASEAN, 'The ASEAN Strategic Action Plan for Consumer Protection 2016–2015', 4. 2013 data on the regulatory landscape confirmed that a considerable number of ASEAN jurisdictions had yet to adopt pertinent legislation—see U Beranada, 'E-commerce and Development: An ASEAN Perspective' (2016) 8, www.wto.org/english/tratop_e/ecom_e/s3usanabernanda_asean.pdf.
[69] SE Rolland, 'Consumer Protection Issues in Cross-Border Ecommerce' in JA Rothchild (ed), *Research Handbook on Electronic Commerce Law* (Cheltenham, Edward Elgar, 2016) 365, 374.

D. E-Commerce Law and UNCITRAL

The United Nations Commission on International Trade Law (UNCITRAL) was established in 1966 as the central UN body to develop international trade rules. It is strongly involved in the drafting and negotiating of conventions and model laws to enhance transnational trade. The 1980 Convention on Contracts for the International Sale of Goods (Vienna Convention; CISG) is one of the earlier and arguably best-known examples in this respect.

The operational work of UNCITRAL is (currently) shared by six working groups. Since 1997, Working Group IV has been covering the area of e-commerce exclusively. But already prior to that, UNCITRAL had discussed e-commerce-related topics. From 1992 to 1996, for example, Working Group IV crafted rules on Electronic Data Interchange (EDI), which paved the way for subsequent works on e-commerce model rules.

Arguably the first time, however, that UNCITRAL expressly considered the importance of ICT in the context of transnational trade was as early as in 1985, when it issued a Recommendation on the legal value of computer records.[70] With this Recommendation UNCITRAL expressed the view that 'automatic data processing (ADP) [was] about to become firmly established throughout the world in many phases of domestic and international trade', and that legislators should work on the recognition and validity of ADP documents.

In the mid-1990s and early 2000s, UNCITRAL intensified its efforts to design a legal framework for e-commerce that could be used as a basis for national legislation. One year before tasking Working Group IV with regulatory deliberations on e-commerce, UNCITRAL issued the pioneering 1996 Model Law on Electronic Commerce (UNICTRAL E-Commerce Model Law).[71] Five years later, a second set of rules followed—the 2001 Model Law on Electronic Signatures (UNCITRAL E-Signatures Model Law).[72]

The UNCITRAL E-Commerce Model Law, in particular, has enjoyed significant acceptance around the globe. As of mid-2017, 69 states had adopted national legislation based on it. Although most jurisdictions did so around the beginning of the new millennium, and fewer states more recently, the UNCITRAL E-Commerce Model Law should be considered the core regulatory e-commerce product of global elaborations.

Comprising 17 articles, the UNCITRAL E-Commerce Model Law aims to cover 'any kind of information in the form of a data message used in the context of commercial activities'.[73] With the exception of Articles 16 and 17 (which introduce

---

[70] UNCITRAL, 'Recommendations to Governments and international organizations concerning the legal value of computer records' (1985).

[71] See UNCITRAL, 'Model Law on Electronic Commerce with Guide to Enactment 1996 with additional article 5 bis as adopted in 1998' (1999) for the text of the UNCITRAL E-Commerce Model Law and supplementary information.

[72] See UNCITRAL, 'Model Law on Electronic Signatures with Guide to Enactment 2001' (2002) for the text of the UNCITRAL E-Signatures Model Law and supplementary information.

[73] Art 1 UNCITRAL E-Commerce Model Law.

complementary rules for carriage of goods contracts), the model rules are broad in scope and apply, in principle, to any type of electronic commercial activity. The UNCITRAL E-Commerce Model Law contains a variety of provisions that aim to foster the use of data messages for trade purposes. The framework addresses and discusses issues such as the significance of data messages when concluding contracts (eg rules on the acceptance and the time and place of dispatch and receipt of data messages), or the overall attributability of data messages to a particular sender/ originator of a data message. In line with the view earlier expressed that electronic messages and signatures should be subject to the same treatment as conventional messaging, Article 5 of the UNCITRAL E-Commerce Model Law enshrines a key demand. It requires legislators to guarantee that '[i]nformation shall not be denied legal effect, validity or enforceability solely on the grounds that it is in the form of a data message'.

Although the value of the UNCITRAL E-Commerce Model Law for promoting e-commerce law must not be underestimated, compared with the aforementioned EU initiatives in particular, it should be noted that most of its subject matter is relatively narrow. It focuses, in general, on the validity and recognition of data messages in the context of commercial activities.

One of the issues that required further regulation was the question of defining electronic signatures (a term that was only rudimentarily addressed by Article 7 UNCITRAL E-Commerce Model Law). To guide national legislators, UNCITRAL worked on supplementary rules. The result, the UNCITRAL E-Signatures Model Law followed in 2001. Although not being of the same practical significance—as of mid-2017, 'merely' 32 states, mostly developing countries, had introduced legislation based on it—the 2001 Model Law still deserves its place on the list of important international e-commerce regimes. It clearly served to help promote the introduction of e-signature laws in jurisdictions that might not have reacted in the absence of the Model Law.

UNICTRAL, more precisely its Working Group IV, is still strongly involved in shaping the regulation of electronic transactions. Since the completion of the two e-commerce Model Laws in 1996 and 2001, a number of further initiatives have followed. In 2005, for example, the United Nations Convention on the Use of Electronic Communications in International Contracts was adopted. A couple of years later UNICTRAL presented the results of a Working Group IV study on electronic signatures and authentication methods.[74] The report confirmed what had already been generally assumed: the key to enhancing electronic commercial transaction markets would be the further strengthening of trust in e-commerce. It will have to be seen to what extent UNCITRAL will continue to play a decisive role in the further shaping and development of transnational e-commerce law. Projects already realised by other UNCITRAL Working Groups, such as research carried out by Working Group III on Online Dispute Resolution from 2010 to 2016, might indicate and give hope that UNCITRAL will broaden its e-commerce focus in the future.

---

[74] UNCITRAL, 'Promoting confidence in electronic commerce: legal issues on international use of electronic authentication and signature methods' (2009).

E. E-Commerce Law and the OECD

The OECD is an important intergovernmental stakeholder in international trade policymaking by leading industries. In 1998, the OECD adopted its Action Plan for Electronic Commerce (OECD E-Commerce Action Plan) to take policy action in response to the growth in cross-border e-commerce and the first national and international initiatives to regulate it.[75] Designed as 'a complement to the proposed work plans of other international organisations and the ongoing efforts of the private sector', the action plan aimed to pave the way for a possible global e-commerce regime.[76] The OECD members were convinced that coordinated, common initiatives would be best suited to realising the full potential of the transnational electronic commercial market.

The OECD E-Commerce Action Plan specified four principal themes:

A.   building trust for users and consumers;
B.   establishing ground rules for the digital marketplace;
C.   enhancing the information infrastructure for electronic commerce;
D.   maximising the benefits of electronic commerce.[77]

Unlike UNICTRAL, the OECD did not (at least not primarily) focus on the use and legal classification/treatment of data messages. The topics discussed in the Action Plan were broader, and furthermore included questions relating to privacy and data protection, consumer protection in general or taxation. Some of the issues had already been addressed by earlier OECD initiatives. With respect to data security, for example, the OECD issued Guidelines on Cryptography Policy in 1997.[78]

Overall, the OECD is quite actively involved in developing e-commerce guidelines and conducting e-commerce research. Its Directorate for Science, Technology and Innovation, in particular, takes a leading role in this respect, benefitting from the expertise of its sub-committees, which specialise in different areas. Data safety, for example, is considerably covered by the Internet Economy group, whereas consumer protection is dealt with by the Consumer Policy division. Over the years, additional themes, including copy control, digital rights management, Internet fraud, mobile and online payments, as well as dispute resolution, have been added to the list of OECD e-commerce focus points, making the organisation one of the key players when it comes to the comprehensive discussion of e-commerce policies, in particular in the context of B2C transactions. Since 1999, the OECD has issued several guidelines and recommendations in this respect.[79] In one of its most recent instruments, the 2016 Recommendation on Consumer Protection in E-Commerce (2016 OECD E-Commerce Recommendation), the OECD re-emphasised the importance of trust building and suggested a bundle of strategies that—according to the OECD—would

---

[75] OECD, 'OECD Action Plan for Electronic Commerce' (1998).
[76] ibid, 3.
[77] ibid.
[78] See the Annex 'Guidelines on Cryptography Policy' in OECD, 'Recommendation of the Council concerning Guidelines for Cryptographic Policy' (1997).
[79] See www.oecd.org/sti/consumer/consumersinthedigitaleconomy.htm for an overview.

complement one another in this endeavour.[80] The framework is comparatively broad, encompassing 54 suggestions ('principles') divided into three main categories: general principles; implementation principles; and global cooperation principles. With 52 principles, the first category is by far the most comprehensive.

It is not only its comprehensive nature that might explain the practical relevance of the 2016 OECD E-Commerce Recommendation. The Recommendation tries to take an interdisciplinary approach, in the sense that it covers e-commerce issues regardless of whether they are predominantly of legal significance or not. Entitled 'Education, Awareness and Digital Competence', Principles 50 to 52, for example, address pressing questions that the regulation of 'purely' legal issues might be ill-equipped to answer. Of central concern are two considerations. First, developing legal rules further is not absolutely helpful if their content is not communicated sufficiently well. Raising awareness with respect to rights and obligations, coupled with the introduction of institutions that can assist without being slowed down by complex or expensive intermediary steps, could be one of the most effective strategies to foster confidence in e-commerce. Second, ICT competence, ie the actual capability of stakeholders to access, understand and make use of electronic commercial markets, creates an additional challenge. Here the central question is how to react to diverse levels of knowledge and experience in using electronic platforms. Some groups might need to catch up if a generally and easily acceptable market is to be guaranteed. This would be particularly the case, in the opinion of the OECD's, as a consequence of differences in 'age, income, and literacy'.[81]

It is still too early to tell whether these endeavours will result in sustainable success. In any event, a genuinely borderless electronic commercial market—if understood in a global sense—would require the greater involvement of (or at least support for) those developing countries which still lag far behind in terms of ICT availability, infrastructure and use. The OECD's broad e-commerce initiatives raise hope. But effective projects are still (generally) pending.

F. E-Commerce Law and the WTO

The World Trade Organization (WTO) has its headquarters in Geneva and was formed as an intergovernmental organisation in 1995 to succeed the General Agreement on Tariffs and Trade (GATT). With more than 160 Member States (as of 2017), it is the largest international economic organisation worldwide. Generally speaking, the main function of the WTO is to facilitate trade between its Member States by providing an environment for the negotiation and supervision of trade agreements, as well as for simplified dispute resolution.

In 1998, two years after UNCITRAL had presented its E-Commerce Model Law, the Ministerial Conference, the highest decision-making body of the WTO, adopted

---

[80] OECD, 'Consumer Protection in E-Commerce: OECD Recommendation' (2016).
[81] ibid, 18 (Principle 51).

the Declaration on Global Electronic Commerce.[82] The WTO's key operational body—the General Council—was asked to 'establish a comprehensive work programme to examine all trade-related issues relating to global electronic commerce'.[83] The subsequent 1998 Work Programme on electronic commerce (WTO E-Commerce Work Programme) laid the foundations for a broad analysis, mandating the General Council's subsidiary bodies to undertake evaluation tasks.[84]

The WTO E-Commerce Work Programme has served as the basis for extensive discussions at the level of the General Council (supported by the subsidiary bodies) and the Ministerial Conferences. Overall, there is a broad consensus on adhering to the basic WTO principles, most notably non-discrimination, transparency and predictability, when discussing the possible future of e-commerce. The biggest merit of the WTO's being involved in the e-commerce discussions might be viewed as its offering a platform for comprehensive negotiations and policy discussions at the highest level. However, unlike some other initiatives outlined in this chapter, the efforts taken by the WTO have not yet led to comparable, concrete outcomes as to how to enhance the e-commerce market.

G. E-Commerce Law and WIPO

The World Intellectual Property Organization (WIPO) sits at the junction of IP and ICT. Technical advancements in digital communication have significantly simplified the process for exchanging IP information. Works of intellectual property can be transmitted over the Internet with unparalleled speed at minimum cost. The steady rise in ICT, however, has also created challenges in working towards effective IP protection.

WIPO tried to answer this with its 1999 Digital Agenda, which followed two treaties concluded in 1996: the WIPO Copyright Treaty (WCT); and the WIPO Performances and Phonograms Treaty (WPPT). These constituted the first relevant IP framework that aimed to complement the Berne Convention on the Protection of Literary and Artistic Works of 1886 (Berne Convention). In the absence of suitable Berne Convention provisions, the WCT and the WPPT introduced special rules on copyright that take account of new (information) technologies. Most notably, the WCT clarifies that computer programs can be considered as literary works, and that the arrangement and selection of database material fall under the protective WIPO regime.[85]

The Digital Agenda followed in 1999 as the result of the WIPO-hosted International Conference on Electronic Commerce and Intellectual Property held in Geneva in late 1999. It aimed in particular at discussing ways to facilitate e-commerce by promoting and refining the rules under the two earlier treaties. Ever since, WIPO has

---

[82] Ministeral Conference of the WTO, Delaraction on Global Electronic Commerce, 20 May 1998, WT/MIN(98)/DEC/2.

[83] ibid.

[84] For details, see General Council of the WTO, 'Work Programme on Electronic Commerce' (1998).

[85] See Arts 4 (on computer programs) and 5 (on databases) WCT. See, additionally, the references to the 'digital environment' and 'digital forms' in the WPPT.

re-emphasised its role as a provider of IP-related national and transnational e-commerce information, which can be accessed free of charge on its website.[86]

H. E-Commerce Law and ICANN

The Internet Corporation for Assigned Names and Numbers (ICANN) was founded amidst the first national and international attempts to regulate e-commerce in 1998.[87] The rise in commercial Internet activity called for a better-organised regulatory cyberspace regime. ICANN has been strongly involved in regulating domain names and developing operational frameworks for the commercial use of the Internet. As a non-profit public-benefit corporation, it aims to represent the interests of stakeholders involved in such Internet activities.

ICANN does not comprehensively cover nor does it directly address e-commerce issues in their conventional meaning, but it performs maintenance and developmental functions with respect to the operability of the Internet. For example, ICANN is the key organisation when it comes to managing and further developing Internet Protocols and the Domain Name System. At the centre of its activities stand strategies to ensure a safe Internet environment and the smooth functioning of cyberspace.

Since its launch in 1998 ICANN's role has nevertheless been disputed. Criticism that ICANN is ill-equipped to serve its Internet governance role remains strong.[88] However, in the absence of a better-qualified alternative and consensus to establish an advanced, more sophisticated and truly independent regime, ICANN will—for the time being—remain the key player in the technical stabilisation of the e-commerce environment.

I. E-Commerce Law and the Hague Conference on Private International Law

The Hague Conference on Private International Law (HCCH) has its origins in the late nineteenth century. It has been playing an active role in the exchange of academic expertise and in the drafting of model rules with respect to private law at an international level.

The HCCH has provided a platform for academic debates regarding and exchanges on electronic transactions since the early days of e-commerce discussions. It has

---

[86] www.wipo.int/sme/en/e_commerce/index.htm. See also the events in the context of the annual World Intellectual Property Day (26 April), which serve as forums for pertinent discussions (www.wipo.int/ip-outreach/en/ipday/).

[87] For detailed information on ICANN, see www.icann.org.

[88] See, eg, J Malcolm, *Multi-Stakeholder Governance and the Internet Governance Forum* (Wembley, Terminus Press, 2008) s 2.1.3 with further references; 'Ralph Nader renews criticism of ICANN' (2 January 2002) *cnet*, www.cnet.com/news/ralph-nader-renews-criticism-of-icann/.

repeatedly co-hosted international workshops to outline the regulatory framework, to pave the way for possible projects that could add substance to other initiatives by some of the aforementioned bodies. Topics discussed at the HCCH level range from questions of the general law of obligations to choices of forum and law, from data protection to dispute resolution.[89] One of those conferences, the 1999 Geneva Round Table on Electronic Commerce and Private International Law (Geneva Round Table), led to a number of recommendations, which the participants hoped would help to create a stable, clear and transparent e-commerce environment. These recommendations included the following points:

— Exercising restraint when it comes to the introduction of new/additional rules and norms. Rather, existing frameworks (introduced by other transnational stakeholders) should be carefully exercised and evaluated.
— Generally equal legal treatment of e-commerce-related technologies.
— General emphasis on party autonomy, with likely restrictions in B2C situations to protect consumers.
— Differentiating between online and offline performances of contracts in the context of determining the competent jurisdiction and applicable law. While the place of performance should be the deciding connecting factor with regard to offline performance, the location of the parties should be decisive for disputes arising from online performance.
— Collecting information on data protection regimes and aligning diverging data protection rules (if identified as significant).
— Enhancing dispute resolution, with a focus on online dispute resolution.[90]

The HCCH has not yet crafted any specific e-commerce framework in the form of model rules or concrete legislative suggestions. It has, however, regularly discussed the significance of electronic transactions in the context of more general HCCH initiatives. Arguably, the most prominent example relates to the 2005 Hague Choice of Court Convention. As early as its first draft, the 1999 Draft Choice of Court Convention, for example, explained that choice-of-court agreements in electronically concluded contracts should be considered valid if such non-paper-based communication 'renders information accessible so as to be usable for subsequent reference'.[91] This idea was incorporated verbatim into the final 2005 Convention by Article 3(c)(ii). It should be noted, however, that the scope of the Convention eventually turned out to be comparatively narrow. In particular, B2C contracts were excluded from the potential applicability of the regime.[92] The practical significance of the Convention is further limited by the fact that, as of 2017, only three parties—Mexico, Singapore and the EU, with effect for all Member States with the exception of Denmark—had ratified it.

---

[89] Some contributions were subsequently published. See, eg, K Boele-Woelki and C Kessedjian (eds), *Internet: Which Court Decides? Which Law Applies? Quel tribunal décide, quel droit s'applique?* (The Hague, Kuwer Law International, 1998); A Schulz (ed), *Legal Aspects of an E-Commerce Transaction* (Munich, Sellier, 2006).
[90] For details, see Hague Convention, 'Les échanges de données informatisées, internet et le commerce électronique/Electronic Data Interchange, Internet and Electronic Commerce' (2000).
[91] Art 4(2)(b) 1999 Draft Choice of Court Convention.
[92] Art 2(1)(a) 2005 Hague Choice of Court Convention.

J. Additional E-Commerce Law Initiatives

The abundance of regulatory initiatives that have been launched since the 1990s makes it physically impossible to give a conclusive overview of transnational e-commerce law. Nevertheless, some additional projects should be briefly discussed in this subsection. The focus will be put on non-governmental actors and contributions from legal academia.

Since the early years of e-commerce, non-state parties have shown a particular interest not only in utilising ICT, but also in shaping the normative framework to govern electronic transactions. The underlying rationale behind this has been primarily twofold. E-commerce represented a new distribution channel, which was widely considered un(der)regulated. Business stakeholders in particular were convinced that active contribution to the regulatory debates could give them an edge over competitors, who would miss the chance to build a relationship of trust with possible customers. Second, some stakeholders saw regulating e-commerce itself as a chance for commercial growth. A good example is companies with an interest in upholding cyber privacy and safety. For the sake of simplicity, we shall refer to them as 'e-commerce facilitating companies'.

As a consequence of these trends, several interest groups have emerged over the years (e-commerce interest groups). Early examples, which represent businesses on a global scale, include the Internet Law & Policy Forum (ILPF, founded in 1995) and the Global Business Dialogue on e-Society (GBDe, which followed in 1999).[93] A more regional, yet notably large and active, contributor to regulatory debates is Ecommerce Europe, an EU-wide network with (as of 2017) 20 domestic associations representing more than 25,000 businesses in policy-making and non-governmental e-commerce projects.[94] Most of the e-commerce interest groups take a dual approach. First, they provide state policymakers and law makers with data and feedback with regard to e-commerce usage, and represent the interests of their members in legislative deliberations. By doing so, the groups complement the research conducted by individual states and international/intergovernmental organisations.

Second, e-commerce interest groups are heavily involved in (private) self-regulation. Two strategies should be pointed out in this regard. The most genuine form of self-regulation is involvement in the crafting and publication of e-commerce codes of conduct. These instruments aim to introduce common yet basically voluntary regulatory standards, by laying down best practices guidelines and establishing legal compliance frameworks.[95] Although codes of conduct (even if followed by their addressees) do not guarantee that consumers (and customers in general) necessarily enjoy a high level of protection, regulatory competition to achieve the highest possible level of trust might arguably create sustainable customer satisfaction and confidence. This would

---

[93] www.ilpf.org and www.gbd-e.org/.
[94] www.ecommerce-europe.eu/.
[95] ME Price and SG Verhulst, *Self-Regulation in the Internet* (Alphen aan den Rijn, Kluwer Law International, 2004) 163–72 (App 1. Model Code: A Toolkit for Planning), where the authors discuss these issues at a more general (Internet-based) level.

be the case in particular where companies accept codes that go beyond the standards enshrined in conventional legislation. Examples include longer withdrawal periods and simplified return procedures.

The phenomenon of e-commerce codes of conduct is complemented by a more visible development. Based on the belief that the most direct way of conveying a feeling of trust lies in the visualisation of trustworthiness, e-commerce interest groups (often supported by e-commerce facilitating companies) began to introduce e-commerce trustmarks. These trustmarks aimed at convincing possible customers that e-commerce shops were safe and prevented e-commerce cybercrimes. Specific examples include rather technical issues, such as data and payment safety. Trustmarks offered by relevant stakeholders might include phrases such as 'approved by ...' or '... certified'. In particular those trustmark providers that reach a common level of recognisability arguably add significant value to e-commerce shops. A different group of trustmarks addresses reliability on an even broader scale. Relevant trustmarks would confirm not just technical reliability in terms of data and payment safety, but also the overall level of customer orientation. This could include, for example, questions relating to contractual performance and customer service standards. The trustmark market has become particularly competitive in this context. Leading initiatives (that to a large extent were founded on the initiative of private actors) include the following projects: The Global Trustmark Alliance (GTA), the Asia-Pacific Trustmark Alliance (ATA)/ World Trustmark Alliance (WTA), EMOTA European Trustmark, the Euro-Label and TRUSTe. They all have in common the aim to introduce standards fulfilment of which would lead to their being given the right to display specific trustmarks.

A number of studies have arrived at the conclusion that trustmarks do indeed add value in terms of communicating reliability.[96] Two things should be noted, however. First, the extent to which increased trust is directly attributable to trustmarks (and not to the recognisability of a brand or an e-commerce actor) remains unclear. Second, the abundance of trustmark initiatives and the lack of transparency on the accreditation system make it difficult for potential e-commerce customers to understand the true value of trustmarks: some rely on stricter criteria than others. The average customer (very likely) does not have sufficient information to allow for the objective comparison and interpretation of trustmarks. Nevertheless, the overall value of trustmarks should not be underestimated.

One of the most comprehensive global e-commerce law studies thus far was conducted by Blythe and published in three volumes as *The E-Commerce Trilogy*, from 2011 to 2013.[97] Volumes 1 and 3 focus on national legislation—Volume 1 on national

---

[96] J Trzaskowski, 'E-Commerce Trustmarks in Europe: An overview and comparison of trustmarks in European Union, Iceland and Norway' (2006), dokumenter.forbrug.dk/forbrugereuropa/e-commerce-trustmarks-in-europe/helepubl.htm; P Balboni, *Trustmarks in E-Commerce: The Value of Web Seals and the Liability of their Providers* (The Hague, TMC Asser Press, 2009); TNO and Intrasoft International, 'EU Online Trustmarks—Building Digital Confidence in Europe' (2012), ec.europa.eu/newsroom/dae/document.cfm?doc_id=1815.

[97] Blythe, n 3; Blythe, *The Model Electronic Transactions Act*, n 61; SE Blythe, *The E-Commerce Law Trilogy*, vol 3: *Certification Authority Law around the World* (Bloomington, IN, Xlibris, 2013).

e-commerce laws in general, Volume 3 on national certification authority laws. Volume 2 adds a transnational perspective by introducing a comparatively broad model law—the 'Model Electronic Transactions Act'—as an alternative to earlier initiatives. It is based on an evaluation and comparison of more than 120 national regimes and comprises 148 articles, going far beyond, for example, UNCITRAL's E-Commerce Model Law (17 articles) and its E-Signatures Model Law (12 articles). Blythe explains the rationale behind his ambitious project as follows: 'There is a need for a new world theory of E-commerce Law. The E-commerce laws of the world suffer from a lack of uniformity, an unfortunate situation since E-Commerce transactions are often carried out by citizens of different nations.'[98]

In addition to the 'popular' issues of validity and recognition of electronic records and signatures, the Model Electronic Transactions Act discusses a number of further topics. They range from electronic contract rules to consumer and data protection. Further areas covered are Internet crimes, e-commerce courts, domain name registration and intermediary liability, as well as extensive rules on certification authorities to monitor, enhance and safeguard the e-commerce market. Whether Blythe's initiative will be taken into account by policymakers in future endeavours to regulate the electronic commercial market is anyone's guess. However, the study adds enhanced value to the e-commerce discussions, in particular because it offers comprehensive national data and an unparalleled analysis of commonalities and differences in domestic e-commerce law.

Two other, and arguably more discussed, authors on transnational law take a different approach from Blythe (who focuses on state regulation). With their 'Rough Consensus and Running Code' (RCRC) concept, Gralf-Peter Calliess and Peer Zumbansen present an innovative approach that aims to provide a mixed solution for transnational legal scenarios in general. Cross-border electronic B2C transactions form a large part of their endeavour, which looks at different norm creators—states, the international community and the private sector. Calliess and Zumbansen argue that their concept of 'a mixed, public-private, dynamic norm creation process' expresses 'a form of law-making, which does not replace but complements existing modes of norm-creation, either on the nation-state or international level'.[99] In this sense one can say that—with respect to e-commerce transactions—the RCRC merges some of the initiatives outlined earlier into a holistic, integral regime of e-commerce law. Of central concern are transnational consumer contracts, which Calliess and Zumbansen use as the prime example of an area that benefits from trust making.

The authors outline four private ordering initiatives that have predominantly been applied to support conventional, state-based e-commerce norm making.[100] Their first pillar, online reputation, might be seen as the most genuine form of transaction feedback. Online reputation can relate to products and services offered online, as well as to e-commerce stakeholders—most commonly sellers. Resting on the fact that the lack

---

[98] See, eg, Blythe, *The Model Electronic Transactions Act*, n 61, 25.

[99] G-P Calliess and P Zumbansen, *Rough Consensus and Running Code—A Theory of Transnational Private Law* (Oxford, Hart Publishing, 2010) 10.

[100] ibid, 154–63.

of physical interaction is a notable characteristic of electronic transactions, feedback mechanisms, according to Calliess and Zumbansen, would be used to (partially) compensate for this deficiency. Potential buyers could benefit from rating systems and user comments, because they add information that goes beyond prices and delivery conditions.

Trustmarks and codes of conduct could—as discussed already—add convincing arguments in the decision-making process. Trustmarks, in particular, might constitute more objectivity than user feedback, if they are issued by neutral and competent third parties.

Online dispute resolution (ODR) represents Calliess and Zumbansen's third group of private ordering initiatives with the potential to boost e-commerce confidence. As has been explained in more detail earlier in this book, ODR has (in particular in more recent years) been subject to intensified state regulation.[101] Its origins, however, are closely linked to private initiatives. It aims to offer an attractive alternative to conventional dispute resolution, because it can be accessed from anywhere in the world and operates comparatively quickly and at low cost.

Payment and credit security initiatives round off Calliess and Zumbansen's private ordering observations. This pillar refers to payment intermediaries, such as credit card companies and online payment providers, which try to support users with 'trusted third parties' commitments. Enhanced charge-back procedures, in particular, might, according to the authors, serve as a stabiliser in e-commerce transactions.

The stance taken by Calliess and Zumbansen is indeed an interesting one, because it goes beyond the unilateral description of sectoral mechanisms. In the context of electronic transactions, the RCRC primarily asks for two things. First, the use of the instruments outlined needs to be encouraged further; they need to be interlinked and put into mutual competition to maximise the level of contractual compliance and fairness. This—as a consequence—could strengthen party trust in the electronic commercial market.

Without clear strategies, however, regulatory private competition would not necessarily accomplish the goal of trust building. This is where some further criteria— transparency, objectivity and minimum standards—come into play. Calliess and Zumbansen address them under the term 'hybrid order'.[102] The starting point for this second argument is the observation that pertinent transnational private-ordering schemes have become considerably distinct and autonomous. The authors regroup the four private ordering initiatives in (again) four bigger groups: 'private rule-making (codes of conduct), ... online dispute resolution procedures (ODR), mechanisms of socio-economic sanctioning (reputation, loss of trustmark, exclusion), and private enforcement (money-back guarantee, charge-back)'.[103] Despite the perceived competitive benefits of private ordering, state- or non-private-originating norm making still plays an important role. Such rules would, according to Calliess and Zumbansen,

---

[101] See the comments on ODR in ch 4, 'Compensatory Collective Redress and Alternative Dispute Resolution'.
[102] Calliess and Zumbansen, n 99, 166–78.
[103] ibid, 168.

be necessary to prevent the legal exploitation of weaker parties. The authors frame this argument as follows:

> [S]tate-backed regulation disappears on the substantive level of the primary contract law rules, but should reappear on the meta-level of the secondary rules which ensure that the competition of consumer-protecting transnational law regimes will not lead to a so-called 'race to the bottom' in terms of substantive consumer rights.[104]

This constitutes a strong call for interaction between private and non-private ordering mechanisms to increase the overall level of trust in the e-commerce market.

Calliess and Zumbansen give two examples to justify their suggestion. 'Reflexive trademarks' can be seen as highlighting the merits of private/non-private interaction with regard to substantive law protection. One of the key purposes of trademarks is to attest to the trustworthiness of goods and service providers, and to stakeholder compliance with codes of conduct. The private/non-private interaction strategy can help to increase the transparency and objectivity of trademarks by adding 'secondary trustmarks'.[105] These could illuminate the exchange between private and non-private norm creators and (where applicable) monitoring and supervision by the latter. The authors offer the aforementioned Global Trustmark Alliance as an example, and argue that this initiative benefits from the exchange of experience with the OECD.[106]

Online dispute resolution adds (in particular) a procedural law perspective to their argumentation.[107] It has become increasingly popular, in particular with respect to disputes arising from electronic transactions. With the rise in general attention to ODR, stakeholders have had to address some of the early concerns about it, which traditionally included an alleged lack of transparency and an insufficient commitment to objectively fair substantive and procedural standards. Individual ODR providers have aim at establishing their own rules to address these issues. But ongoing criticism has led to requests for initiatives to create a commonly acceptable ODR environment. As the more recent example of the interlinked ADR Directive and ODR Regulation regime shows, the interaction between private and non-private stakeholders has led to a significant enhancement of ODR in this respect, in particular from a trust perspective.

Calliess and Zumbansen conclude their observations on the legal B2C e-commerce market with a broadly positive evaluation. The authors suggest that more recently, e-commerce has been experiencing comparatively active regulatory competition between different state and non-state stakeholders, with the overall aim of establishing reasonable minimum standards of substantive and procedural protection. Although this trend should generally be considered positive, the authors have to admit that one complicating factor might be the relatively short history of hybrid order regulation. Only time will tell what mixture of state and private regulatory ingredients offers the objectively best solution.[108]

---

[104] ibid.
[105] ibid, 169.
[106] ibid, 173–74.
[107] ibid, 174–78.
[108] ibid, 180.

IV. Concluding Remarks on Pending Issues and Challenges for E-Commerce Law

E-commerce is arguably the fastest-growing commercial environment with regard to B2B and B2C transactions. This is to a large extent the consequence of attempts to broaden distribution channels, in particular with the help of cyberspace and facilitated by constant advancements in ICT.

It should be noted, however, that technological developments and the rise in e-commerce create legal challenges to which policymakers need to respond. The present chapter has illustrated the variety of initiatives launched at different levels and with different scopes—domestically and internationally, by private and public actors, sectorally and comprehensively. Of central concern in most of these endeavours is the question of how to strengthen trust in the e-commerce market most effectively and efficiently. The absence of face-to-face interaction, coupled with the often significant distance between the parties, constitutes psychological barriers and creates practical challenges when negotiating, concluding and fulfilling contractual obligations.

From a legal perspective, endeavours to put electronic signatures and online contracts on an equal footing with paper-based signatures and contracts have dominated the discussions, especially in the early years of e-commerce. UNCITRAL in particular, with its two model laws on electronic transactions, has played a leading role in attempts to lead national jurisdictions towards a significantly standardised transnational regime.[109]

More recently, the focus began to shift away from relatively narrow approaches towards a more comprehensive discussion of key issues. The OECD, with its broad catalogue of guiding principles, most recently updated by the 2016 OECD E-Commerce Recommendation, is a good example in this context.[110] It adds further fields of legal interest, which e-commerce regulators are advised to take into consideration when crafting specific rules. These include questions relating to IP, privacy, redress and cybercrime. Looking at the examples given in this chapter, it should be noted, however, that despite the abundant number of e-commerce initiatives launched since the mid-1990s, e-commerce law is still in its infancy, in particular in a transnational context.[111]

The regulatory challenges remain stark and—most notably in a cross-border context—do not comprise only predominantly legal issues. In their 2017 commentary on EU e-commerce law, Arno Lodder and Andrew Murray identified three concerns

---

[109] See section III.D, 'E-Commerce Law and UNCITRAL', and the references to the UNCITRAL E-Commerce Model Law and the UNICTRAL E-Signatures Model Law in the context of national projects.
[110] OECD, n 80.
[111] In a similar vein see, eg, Dickie, n 2, 145.

that might be of the utmost importance in an attempt to realise a sustainable and truly borderless e-commerce market in this regard: recognition, language and transactional costs. Recognition refers to the parties' actual knowledge and awareness with respect to non domestic e commerce actors. As is the case with conventional, offline shopping, customers might be more used to—and hence confident regarding—shops where they usually make their purchases.[112] From a business perspective, finding appropriate marketing strategies to build a universally known brand might be a top priority to increase the recognition level.

Linguistic barriers create a second, not necessarily legal obstacle. Differences in language can be considered a practical barrier to the transnational e-commerce market, even if parties recognise the actors. Foreign language capacity clearly helps to broaden commercial opportunities. But unless transactions can be made entirely in a language that both parties understand, the threshold for entering into negotiations might simply be too high to overcome. Translating services could be of further assistance to unlock the potential of the e-commerce market. Automated translation services have begun to support stakeholders in this respect.

Transactional costs create a third hurdle. In particular in cases that involve exchange fees, the actual costs might be negatively affected. Postal fees (where applicable) might contribute further to an increase. Distributors who offer to bear the return costs might have to calculate the risk when determining prices. Likewise in cases where buyers have to bear the costs, these additional (possible) costs could have a deterrent effect.

In any event, e-commerce ranks high on the list of transnational law themes. Arguably, it constitutes a 'playground' for further activities to vie with more conventional law making. In this regard Lodder and Murray conclude their 2017 observation with the following statement:

> As with all Internet law-related topics global regulations are ideal, but difficult to realize. This may change over time as more digital natives take positions in law-making and regulatory enforcement bodies. This though is still some way off ..., but maybe one day the classic approach to state sovereignty and jurisdiction in relation to e-commerce will be replaced by a globally oriented approach.[113]

One of the biggest challenges for any attempt to regulate the e-commerce market can be seen in the speed at which ICT develops. Regulatory initiatives, in particular in a transnational context, where the rule-making process is slowed down by the necessity for complex compromise-making, have thus far not necessarily proved to be fast enough to keep up with relevant ICT advancements.

One of the most frequently discussed examples to illustrate this in recent times has been the phenomenon of cryptocurrencies. Based on cryptographically secured chains of blocks—commonly referred to as 'blockchain'—inventors first succeeded in crafting digital currencies as an alternative to conventional payment methods

---

[112] Lodder and Murray's recognition criterion is arguably of less relevance with regard to goods and services people only rarely consume. Here, possible customers might not possess the same degree of purchase experience when deciding on a particular seller. Nevertheless, the visibility and general level of recognition of e-commerce actors is an important factor when it comes to making purchase decisions.

[113] Lodder and Murray, n 59, 14.

around 2008/09, when the 'bitcoin' project was introduced. Bitcoin has experienced a remarkable rise in popularity, dissemination and use, particularly in cyberspace. This trend creates significant regulatory challenges for states and international actors.

Overall, cryptocurrencies have received mixed reactions. The biggest achievement of digital currencies might be their universality. As a basic principle, they can genuinely be used across borders. Despite controversies regarding the use and lawfulness of cryptocurrencies, their digital acceptance has grown. Studies show that bitcoin, the leading cryptocurrency at the time of writing this book, passed the acceptance mark of 100,000 traders as early as 2015.[114] In 2017, a study conducted by Cambridge University revealed that at least 2.9 million unique users used digital currencies.[115]

Cryptocurrencies have triggered academic interest. A significant number of pertinent books and journal articles have increasingly been published over the last decade. Some of them focus exclusively on digital currencies. *Ledge*, for example, was the first such journal, hitting the market in 2015. Furthermore, a number of international conferences chose cryptocurrencies as their underlying theme.[116]

Some countries have already taken steps to legalise and promote the use of digital currencies. With effect from April 2017, Japan, for example, adopted a law to, in principle, recognise cryptocurrencies as a legal payment option.[117] Generally speaking, however, comprehensive regulatory mechanisms are still pending in most jurisdictions. The exact general legal status of digital currencies, in particular regarding their classification either as currency equivalent or as a commodity, as well as the taxability of cryptocurrencies, remains widely unclarified. Additionally, there is more underlying concern regarding possible legal circumvention caused by digital currencies. Particular criticism voices objections as a result of fears of money-laundering and the difficulties involved in physically controlling the flow of digital currencies. Considering these reservations and their technical distinctiveness, it remains unclear whether digital currencies have the potential to become a truly widespread alternative method of payment, even if they were to be commonly accepted by the law. For the time being, it remains questionable whether the average consumer will become familiar enough with cryptocurrencies to make them an everyday payment method.

It seems clear that the rise in e-commerce is set to continue. The near and mid-term future of legal policymaking might be significantly characterised by a pooling of further initiatives to take electronic transactions to the next level. As was highlighted

---

[114] A Cuthbertson, 'Bitcoin now accepted by 100,000 merchants worldwide' (4 February 2015) *International Business Times*, www.ibtimes.co.uk/bitcoin-now-accepted-by-100000-merchants-worldwide-1486613.

[115] G Hileman and M Rauchs, 'Global Cryptocurrency Benchmarking Study' (2017), www.jbs.cam.ac.uk/fileadmin/user_upload/research/centres/alternative-finance/downloads/2017-global-cryptocurrency-benchmarking-study.pdf.

[116] See, eg, the 'Blockchain & Bitcoin Conference' series (kiev.bc.events/en) with reference to past and upcoming events, or the cryptocurrency conferences listed at bitcoin.org/en/events.

[117] Act on Settlement of Funds as amended on 25 May 2016. For details, see K Shiba, 'Enforcement of Japanese Law on Crypto Currency and Future Issues' (2017), www.iima.or.jp/Docs/column/2017/0410_e.pdf.

in the present chapter, this undeniably requires an intensified transnational exchange of expertise, and eventually the willingness to take common steps to unlock the full potential of the electronic commercial market.

Selected Further Reading

Blythe, SE, *The E-Commerce Law Trilogy*, vol 1: *E-Commerce Law around the World* (Bloomington, IN, Xlibris, 2011)

Blythe, SE, *The E-Commerce Law Trilogy*, vol 2: *An E-Commerce Law for the World: The Model Electronic Transactions Act* (Bloomington, IN, Xlibris, 2012)

Chissick, M and Kelman, A, *Electronic Commerce*, 3rd edn (London, Sweet & Maxwell, 2001)

Coteanu, C, *Cyber Consumer Law and Unfair Trading Practices* (Farnham, Ashgate, 2005)

Davidson, A, *Social Media and Electronic Commerce Law*, 2nd edn (Oxford, Oxford University Press, 2016)

Dickie, J, *Internet and Electronic Commerce Law in the European Union* (Oxford, Hart Publishing, 1999)

Dickie, J, *Producers and Consumers in EU E-Commerce Law* (Oxford, Hart Publishing, 2005)

Edwards, L (ed), *The New Legal Framework for E-Commerce in Europe* (Oxford, Hart Publishing, 2005)

Gillies, LE, *Electronic Commerce and International Private Law: A Study of Electronic Consumer Contracts* (Aldershot, Ashgate, 2008)

Lodder, AR and Murray, AD (eds), *EU Regulation of E-Commerce: A Commentary* (Cheltenham, Edward Elgar Publishing, 2017)

Mann, RJ (ed), *Electronic Commerce*, 4th edn (New York, Aspen, 2011)

Riefa, C, *Consumer Protection and Online Auction Platforms: Towards a Safer Legal Framework* (Farnham, Ashgate, 2015)

Rothchild, JA (ed), *Research Handbook on Electronic Commerce Law* (Cheltenham, Edward Elgar Publishing, 2016)

Schulz, A (ed), *Legal Aspects of an E-Commerce Transaction* (Munich, Sellier, 2006)

Spindler, S and Börner, F (eds), *E-Commerce Law in Europe and the USA* (Berlin, Springer, 2002)

Stokes, S and Robert, C, *Encyclopedia of E-Commerce Law* (London, Sweet & Maxwell, 2003)

Tang, ZS, *Electronic Consumer Contracts in the Conflict of Laws*, 2nd edn (Oxford, Hart Publishing, 2015)

Todd, P and Craig, W, *E-Commerce Law*, 2nd edn (London, Routledge, 2017)

von dem Bussche, A and Klein, D, *E-Commerce Law in Germany* (Munich, CH Beck, 2015)

Walden, I and Hörnle, J (eds), *E-Commerce Law and Practice in Europe* (Abingdon, Woodhead Publishing, 2001)

Wang, FF, *Law of Electronic Commercial Transactions: Contemporary Issues in the EU, US and China*, 2nd edn (Abingdon, Routledge, 2014)

Winn, JK (ed), *Consumer Protection in the Age of the 'Information Economy'* (Aldershot, Ashgate, 2006)

Yuthayotin, S, *Access to Justice in Transnational B2C E-Commerce: A Multidimensional Analysis of Consumer Protection Mechanisms* (Heidelberg, Springer, 2015)

Conclusion: The Future of Business Law?

I. Outline

Over the last half century, the 'digital revolution' has had a profound effect on all aspects of social and economic life. This transformation has been driven by a series of technological developments, most significantly: (i) cheaper and smaller digital hardware (initially PCs and, more recently, smart phones); (ii) global communication networks and mass connectivity; (iii) cloud-based data storage and automated algorithms; and (iv) emerging technologies (eg robots/automation, artificial intelligence and blockchain).

These overlapping developments have provided the foundation and basic infrastructure for an on-going process of 'digitalisation'. The social, economic and cultural impact of these changes are so significant that many commentators now speak of a new 'digital world'.

As discussed in the previous chapter, this change has had a profound effect on how businesses operate, but also on business regulation. This concluding chapter develops this discussion by outlining the main features of our 'near-future' digital world, and offers a more general review of the impact of these developments on business and business regulation.

II. A New Digital World

The following is a brief overview of some of the main features of the 'digital world' that has emerged as a result of the shift from 'analogue' to new digital 'technologies'.

A. A World of 'Ubiquitous Computing'

The social effect of technological advances is that we now all live in a world of 'ubiquitous computing'.[1] Computing is embedded in all aspects of our everyday lives. Computer code provides the unseen and unnoticed 'architecture' structuring our existence.[2] Consider work, recreation, communication, consumption, travel or education/research. All areas of life are now organised by and around digital technologies.

Think about how much of our lives is spent interacting with devices that are, at a deep level, running digital code. Such interaction can be direct and proximate—using a smart phone or computer, for instance—or more distant—travelling to work on a subway system that is automated in various ways. In both cases, it is code that makes the experience possible and code that, ultimately, provides the structure and choice associated with that experience. It is this 'code-based' character of social reality that justifies characterising the present as a digital age.

B. A World of 'Unmediated' Communication

An important manifestation of digital technologies has been the growth of the Internet and social media. The result? Networked digital technologies have transformed *how* we communicate. A more open culture of transparency and sharing has emerged, which facilitates learning, discovery and innovation, and has disrupted traditional forms of communication.[3]

In particular, new technologies facilitate less 'mediated' dissemination of information and more direct forms of communication between 'sender-producer' and 'recipient-audience'. Social media operate at a personal level, but also at an institutional level. Individuals can communicate directly with their 'audience' (family, friends, social/professional networks), but so can companies and other organisations.

New forms of communication have transformed our information culture and disrupted settled concepts of privacy and the established media (newspapers, TV, etc) and advertising industries.

---

[1] This term was first coined by Mark Weiser in around 1988 during his tenure as Chief Technologist at Xerox, but has since been widely adopted. See U Hansmann, *Pervasive Computing: The Mobile World* (London, Springer, 2003); S Poslad, *Ubiquitous Computing, Smart Devices, Smart Environments and Smart Interaction* (London, Wiley, 2009).

[2] See W Mitchell, *City of Bits, Space, Place and the Infobahn* (Cambridge, MA, MIT Press, 1996). In a legal context, the best discussion remains L Lessig, *The Code: and Other Laws of Cyberspace, Version 2* (New York, Basic Books, 2006).

[3] See R Mansell, *Imagining the Internet: Communication, Innovation & Governance* (Oxford, Oxford University Press, 2012).

C. A World of Freedom and Opportunity

Traditional status hierarchies and the social roles associated with such hierarchies become much less important in a networked, digital age.[4] The younger generation, for example, no longer aspire to a stable, long-term 'career' in a high-status profession, for example, but instead desire a meaningful and fulfilling working experience that facilitates opportunities for personal expression and growth.

New digital technologies have created a world of freedom and opportunity, where talent, imagination and drive matter much more than status, background or experience.

This claim is not meant to suggest that social exclusion has disappeared, but to highlight how digital culture has disrupted traditional concepts of status and created new forms of exclusion, as well as new opportunities.

D. A World of Risk and Uncertainty

A paradox of digital technologies is that they make our lives easier, but they also make the world harder—perhaps even impossible—to understand. The digital world is a world of *risk*—of identifiable and measurable dangers—but, more significantly, it is also a world of radical *uncertainty*.[5] Our relationship with new technology is often characterised by uncertainty, in the sense that 'all we know is that there are many things that we do not know' about a technology and its effects.

Any list of potential outcomes—positive or negative—created by new technologies is always going to be incomplete. As such, the digital world is a world where 'reality' and 'truth' regarding new technologies are uncertain, unsettled and constantly being contested.

In part, this is simply a function of the ever-quickening speed of technological change. As soon as we believe that we have a clear understanding, a new development has already occurred that renders any existing understanding obsolete. But something else is also going on. 'Understanding' of complex man-made systems is now increasingly 'beyond' human comprehension.[6] For the first time in history, we live in a world where more and more technologies are simply beyond human understanding.

E. A World Where Creativity Matters More than Experience or Status

In a fast-changing world, 'experience'—understood as accumulated practical wisdom—can no longer provide clear guidance in the way that it once did. In the past,

---

[4] For a more sceptical view on this line of thinking, see N Ferguson, *The Square & the Tower, Networks and Power, from the Freemasons to Facebook* (London, Penguin, 2018).

[5] See U Beck, *Risk Society: Towards a New Modernity* (London, Sage, 1992).

[6] See S Arbesman, *Overcomplicated: Technology at the Limits of Comprehension* (New York, Current, 2016).

problem solving and decision making could rely on the application of pre-existing templates to any 'new' situation. But, in a world of constant change there is no longer any 'last time' that can provide clear and reliable guidance.

In a digital world, the capacities to be creative and to tell a story that can persuade others have replaced experience as *the* core competencies in effective decision making. A willingness to be open to the possibilities and potential of the 'new' has become critical.

F. A World of 'Influencers' and 'Co-creators'

Many traditional roles are disrupted in a digital world, and this has had an effect on conceptions of good leadership. In this new world, relatively settled leadership roles— think 'executives', 'politicians' or 'teachers'—are being replaced by a more complex mix of 'influencers', 'co-creators' and 'collaborators'.

Most significantly, the digital world is a 'flatter' world in which the 'influencer' is a more modest figure that seeks to inspire, to motivate and to nudge a 'team', rather than dictate or control 'subordinates'. Team building and teamwork are key, and the 'influencer' of today understands that team members are on a shared journey of constant learning and that they do not have all of the answers.

G. A 'Global' World

'Globalisation'—broadly defined as the emergence of global supply chains and the opening up of national markets—has greatly accelerated the proliferation of digital technologies. By 2020, more than 80 per cent of the world's adults are expected to have a smart phone and there will be over 25 billion networked devices. The digitalisation of reality is a global event that impacts everyone.

Similarly, digital culture is now a global phenomenon that co-exists with other forms of culture. Moreover, emerging technologies are less centred than ever before on specific places, and important technological innovations can happen almost anywhere.

H. A World of Technological Innovation

Commentators on previous modern technological revolutions—for example the water-powered spinning wheel, the steam engine, electrical lighting, the mass-produced automobile, improvements in oil-refining technology—have identified three 'phases' in the dissemination of a new technology.[7]

---

[7] See C Perez, *Technological Revolutions & Financial Capital: The Dynamics of Bubbles and Golden Ages* (London, Edward Elgar, 2003).

First, there is an 'Installation phase', in which the core applications of a new technology are discovered, developed and scaled. Interestingly, however, after 'Installation', all previous modern technological revolutions seem to have experienced a 'Crisis phase' around 20–30 years later. As expectations overtook the capacities of a new technology, a 'bubble' was created that eventually burst, requiring a painful process of 'collapse and re-adjustment'.

Crucially, with previous technological revolutions, government and business leaders would then work together in a third phase, to ensure 'Deployment', ie the state-managed control of new technology that would ensure mass dissemination under safe conditions. Such 'deployment' involved a reactive process of 'fact-finding' (gathering all relevant information/evidence regarding a new technology), 'understanding' (identifying and evaluating the risks) and 'regulation' (the imposition of a legal framework that would control how a new technology could be legitimately used).

In a digital age, this process of 'Deployment' seems much more problematic. Most obviously, the speed, persistence and diversity (both geographically and technologically) of technological advances, as well as the uncertainties surrounding such technologies, means that any kind of reactive learning and fact-based regulation is extremely difficult. The result? The 'deployment' of new technology is much more difficult and less controlled than in previous technological revolutions. On the one hand, the capacity of governments to regulate new technologies is diminishing, and on the other, the growth of new technologies is rapidly accelerating. As a consequence, there is an ever-increasing 'gap' between regulation and technology.

III. Doing Business in a Digital Age

Organisations—particularly businesses—have been transformed, as a result of these technological changes and related social processes. For a start, every organisation is now obliged to engage with new technologies in all aspects of their operations. Moreover, visionary entrepreneurs have quickly recognised the commercial possibilities of digital technologies. The new businesses that they have created offer new consumer experiences. Think Amazon, Apple, Facebook, Google or Microsoft.

Significantly, however, this success has also been achieved by changing *how* businesses are organised and operate. In particular, the most successful businesses today organise themselves as more open and inclusive 'ecosystems'. Whereas, in the past, businesses were organised as closed hierarchies, the most successful businesses today embrace 'flatter', de-centralised and more open structures.[8]

---

[8] See M Fenwick and EPM Vermeulen, 'The New Firm: Staying Relevant, Unique and Competitive' (2015) 16 *European Business Organization Law Review* 595.

Older, more established companies, as well as other organisations, such as governments, recognise the new opportunities in a digital world, but they often struggle to implement these types of more open governance structures. All too often, existing organisational culture and deeply entrenched patterns of working mean that organisations find it difficult to adapt and, as a result, are less effective than they could or should be.

There is a broad consensus that the interconnected processes of globalisation and rapid technological change—particularly the emergence of technologies related to networked computers—have profoundly disrupted traditional forms of corporate organisation and created new business models, as well as opportunities. A great deal of energy—both in traditional media outlets and online—has been devoted to understanding these trends.

A recurring theme in this discussion is the suggestion that an important recent development is a contraction in the size of business enterprises and a concomitant reliance on an extended 'network' that is facilitated by new computer technologies. Smaller, more agile firms—think Uber or AirBnB—now employ software platforms to provide a global service that eliminates the need for many jobs. In this way, these new companies have been extremely successful in disrupting traditional business models.

This trend has been explained by employing a perspective derived from Ronald Coase's famous account of the origins of the firm.[9] Coase's central insight was that firms exist because repeatedly going back to the market imposes high transaction costs. In the absence of a firm, workers need to be hired, prices need to be negotiated and contracts enforced, and this whole process needs to be constantly repeated. Such repeat transactions can be enormously costly, and the firm—by stabilising relationships over time—offers a simple and effective way of circumventing this 'failure' in the ability of the market to deliver a less expensive alternative.

A corollary of this claim about the origins of the firm is the idea that if the transaction costs of exchanging value in the market are significantly reduced, the rationale for the firm disappears and the size of firms will shrink. Firms do not keep getting bigger forever; they create transaction costs of their own, which tend to rise as they grow in size. If it makes no economic sense to maintain stable, long-term relationships within the framework of a firm—ie if transactions outside the firm become cheaper—then firms will inevitably start to contract.

It is this aspect of Coase's story that is interesting today. The suggestion is that new technologies—and particularly network-based technologies—have disrupted markets by facilitating a significant reduction in transaction costs across multiple sectors of the economy. As such, we are entering a world of smaller, leaner firms that build their business model on a combination of software 'platform', network technologies and market-based transactions outside the conventional framework of the firm. In consequence, traditional firms are being driven into extinction by the emergence of more agile competitors that take advantage of these low-cost opportunities.

A simple example of this reconfiguration in firm structure would be on-line retailers, who have adopted a 'platform-plus-network' business model in order to

---

[9] RH Coase, *The Firm, the Market, and the Law* (Chicago, IL, University of Chicago Press, 1990).

challenge traditional retailers. A company like Amazon, for example, utilises a technology platform to remove the need for (i) physical stores and the associated costs of maintaining those stores (instead, everything is done online), (ii) 'knowledgeable' sales staff to help customers identify the best product for their needs (instead, a sophisticated search engine helps customers find what they want and accessible customer reviews establish which products are 'best') and (iii) cashiers to process payments (instead, the software allows payments to be made autonomously by the customer). In each case, network technologies facilitate a significant reduction in the size of the firm. Amazon then employs local delivery companies to distribute the goods quickly and more cheaply.

Other, often quoted examples of a similar phenomenon include Uber, Lyft or AirBnB. In each case, a traditional business model (be it taxi companies, minicabs or travel agents) has been disrupted by a small-firm-plus-extensive-network model.

This narrative of how traditional business models have been destabilised by new computer network-based technologies offers a powerful framework for understanding a number of interesting and important trends in contemporary business organisation.

IV. Regulating Business in a Digital Age

Designing a regulatory framework that is appropriate for the new realities of a digital age is by no means easy. Particularly when such a framework needs to ensure the safety of consumers and the public, whilst facilitating the commercial use and consumer enjoyment of disruptive innovation.[10] This is especially true in contemporary settings, where innovation is quicker and the global dissemination of new technology is much faster.[11]

In such circumstances, regulators can often struggle to keep up. Many commentators have commented on the 'pacing problem' that such a situation has created:

> Moore's Law notoriously states that the 'functional capacity of ICT products roughly doubles every 18 months', with the same dynamics manifesting in biotechnology, and namely in sequencing human genome. As a result, regulating innovation involves what is called a 'pacing problem' in the academic literature from the US, or the 'challenge of regulatory connection' or 'regulatory disconnection' in European-based scholarship.[12]

---

[10] See GE Marchant et al (eds), *The Growing Gap Between Emerging Technologies and Legal-Ethical Oversight: The Pacing Problem* (New York, Springer, 2011); A Butenko and P Larouche, 'Regulation for Innovativeness or Regulation of Innovation?' (2015) 7 *Law, Innovation & Technology* 52.

[11] R McGrath, 'The Pace of Technology Adoption is Speeding Up' (2013) *Harvard Business Review*, perma.cc/DA8M-7QQV/.

[12] BR Allenby, 'Governance and Technology Systems: The Challenge of Emerging Technologies' in Marchant et al (eds), n 10, 3.

The 'pacing problem' refers to a situation when technology develops faster than the corresponding regulation, the latter hopelessly falling behind:

> The 'pacing problem' is an attempt to understand the struggle to 'keep up' with technology. There is more than one way to describe the 'pacing problem'. One can look at the types of legal and regulatory problems that arise as a result of technological change including the need to manage new negative impacts and risks, the need to manage uncertainty in the application of existing laws, the need to adapt regulatory regimes that may be over-inclusive or under-inclusive when applied in the new context and the need to manage obsolescence. Alternatively, Brownsword distinguishes between descriptive and normative disconnection, and between productive and unproductive disconnection. These line-up to some extent, although there are differences in emphasis. On a simplistic level, numerous scholars point to hare and tortoise metaphors to explain the difficulties faced by 'law' when interacting with 'technology.' On a deeper level, new technologies can force us to question our commitment to and interpretation of important concepts and values, such as democracy.[13]

This metaphor of 'the hare and the tortoise' is frequently used to describe this situation. As summed up by Marchant and Wallach, 'at the rapid rate of change, emerging technologies leave behind traditional governmental regulatory models and approaches which are plodding along slower today than ever before'.[14]

The last two decades offer multiple examples of such regulatory struggles:

> Emerging technologies such as nanotechnology, biotechnology, personalized medicine, synthetic biology, applied neuroscience, geoengineering, social media, surveillance technologies, regenerative medicine, robotics and artificial intelligence present complex governance and oversight challenges. These technologies are characterized by a rapid pace of development, a multitude of applications, manifestations and actors, pervasive uncertainties about risks, benefits and future directions, and demands for oversight ranging from potential health and environmental risks to broader social and ethical concerns. Given this complexity, no single regulatory agency, or even group of agencies, can regulate any of these emerging technologies effectively and comprehensively.[15]

To take a simple, but nevertheless relevant example: current rules in many jurisdictions do not allow self-driving cars on the roads. Making this change is relatively simple. For example, the 1968 Vienna Convention on Road Traffic, to which 72 countries are party, was amended in March 2014 to take such new technologies into consideration.

However, there are many other more complex regulatory issues that will need to be addressed. The driverless car will generate an enormous amount of data for possible alternative usage, which is likely to create new issues related to data security and privacy:

> The self-driving car from Google already is a true data creator. With all the sensors to enable the car to drive without a driver, it generates nearly 1 Gigabyte every second. It uses all that

---

[13] L Bennett Moses, 'How to Think About Law, Regulation and Technology: Problems with 'Technology' as a Regulatory Target' (2013) 5 *Law, Innovation & Technology* 5, 7.

[14] Butenko and Larouche, n 10, 66.

[15] GE Marchant and W Wallach (2013) 'Governing the Governance of Emerging Technologies' in GE Marchant et al (eds), *Innovative Governance Models for Emerging Technologies* (London, Edward Elgar 2013) 136.

data to know where to drive and how fast to drive. It can even detect a new cigarette butt thrown on the ground and it then knows that a person might appear all of a sudden from behind a corner or car. 1 Gigabyte per second, imagine the amount of data that will create every year: On average, Americans drive 600 hours per year in their car. That equals 2,160,000 seconds or approximately 2 petabytes of data per car per year. With the number of cars worldwide to surpass one billion, it is almost unimaginable how much data will be created when Google's self-driving car will become more common on the streets.[16]

In a tort context, questions will need to be resolved as to who is at fault in the event of an accident involving driverless cars:

> Living in fear of hypothetical worst-case scenarios and basing policy on them will mean that the best-case scenarios associated with intelligent vehicles will never come about. Thus, patience and regulatory forbearance are generally the wise policy dispositions at this time, bearing in mind that the tort system will continue to evolve to address harms caused by intelligent-vehicle systems.[17]

Moreover, driverless cars will need to communicate both among themselves and with the transport infrastructure to be the most effective in their operation. To facilitate this, regulators will need to safeguard telecommunication frequencies and protect against security threats, most obviously the possibility of 'car-hacking'.

The regulatory dilemma created by a digital society seems fairly clear and obvious. But a less-documented aspect of this issue concerns what we might think of as the basis or foundation of any regulation, namely some empirical 'facts' about a piece of new technology and its likely social, economic or health effects. In this respect, regulation is always premised on a selection of information—what we shall refer to as the facts—about a particular technology. Crucially, the selected facts are those that are seen as more relevant by the regulators in determining for *what*, *when* and *how* they should make a regulatory intervention.

The '*what* question' concerns identifying the disruptive technology that must be regulated or which requires regulatory reform. Demarcating the scope of a technology may not always be self-evident. For example, when should a car be thought of as autonomous, rather than merely as providing driver-assistance (as many cars already do)? 'Facts' about a particular technology are crucial for this kind of definitional judgement, and normative issues inevitably intrude on such judgements.

The '*when* question' concerns the timing of any regulatory intervention. This entails ensuring that regulation is not adopted too soon, stifling or distorting a particular path of technological development, nor so late that problems arise as a result of the absence of effective regulation:

> The urge for legal change in response to technological change has a greater sense of timing: laws regulating railroads are only needed after track is laid; uncertainties relating to the split of genetic and gestational motherhood need only be resolved in response to the availability

---

[16] M Van Rijmenam 'Self-Driving Cars Will Create 2 Petabytes of Data, What are the Big Data Opportunities for the Car Industry?', datafloq.com/read/self-driving-cars-create-2-petabytes-data-annually/172/.

[17] A Thierer and R Hagemann, 'Removing Roadblocks to Intelligent Vehicles and Driverless Cars' (2015) 5 *Wake Forest Journal of Law & Policy* 339, 340.

of in vitro fertilization. There is no doubt that legal change may be demanded as a result of changes in our collective knowledge and beliefs, or social change more broadly, but differences in how such changes are timed and perceived (as well as limitations of space) explain why this article focuses only on part of the story (which is not to say that it might not, in some places, have a broader resonance).[18]

Lastly, the '*how* question' concerns the form and substance of the regulation. Should the technological innovation be encouraged, prohibited or restricted in some way? What substantive rules or principles should be adopted to achieve this regulatory goal? And what form should any regulatory intervention take? A 'hard' legal rule or some 'softer' alternative?

In each case, these policy judgements have traditionally been made by a combination of politicians and bureaucrats, based—in large part—on facts provided by expert scientists. The delegation of regulatory decisions to such a combination of democratically chosen politicians, professional bureaucrats and scientific experts is one way of conceptualising the distinctiveness of policymaking in political modernity.

In this context, however, we are most interested in the identification of the relevant facts as a crucial step in regulatory design. Some of the relevant facts may be obvious. The fact that drones may interfere with low-flying planes or inadvertently land on innocent bystanders, for example, makes establishing reliable information on the likelihood of such occurrences a vital precondition of any responsible policy intervention.

However, there are various potential problems with this fact-identification exercise. Some facts may be difficult to empirically establish or contest, even amongst experts in that field. The task of establishing facts about new technology may be made difficult by the lack of an adequate sample or other reliable data on the effects of new technology. Uncertainties surrounding an emerging technology's future development and possible risks mean that there will be limitations in how specific a regulatory framework can be developed, particularly early in the life of a new technology.

Identification of relevant or irrelevant facts may also be 'distorted' or otherwise influenced by the concerns of entrenched interests about new (and commercially threatening) technologies.

Lastly, other facts may simply be 'unknown unknowns'. We simply lack the information, experience or imagination to predict what negative possibilities may be associated with a piece of new technology.[19]

In this respect, the 'relevant facts' that form the basis of any regulation are never going to be obvious or settled. The regulation of any disruptive new technology is always going to be reactive and based on an uncertain and politicised (to some degree) factual basis.

We need to be careful not to overstate the newness of this issue. To some extent, these difficulties have always been around, at least since the rise of industrial capitalism and the acceleration in technological advancement that it facilitated.

---

[18] L Bennett Moses, 'Agents of Change: How the Law 'Copes' with Technological Change (2011) 20 *Griffith Law Review* 763, 768.
[19] See, generally, WA Kaal, 'Dynamic Regulation of the Financial Services Industry' (2013) 48 *Wake Forest Law Review* 791.

Schumpeter, for example, famously described, as early as the 1940s, the 'gales of creative destruction', unleashed by technology, that periodically sweep through industries and sink weak and outdated firms. For Schumpeter, this process was at the core of capitalism:

> The opening up of new markets, foreign or domestic, and the organizational development from the craft shop and factory to such concerns as US Steel illustrate the process of industrial mutation that incessantly revolutionizes the economic structure from within, incessantly destroying the old one, incessantly creating a new one. This process of Creative Destruction is the essential fact about capitalism. It is what capitalism consists in and what every capitalist concern has got to live in. … Every piece of business strategy acquires its true significance only against the background of that process and within the situation created by it. It must be seen in its role in the perennial gale of creative destruction; it cannot be understood irrespective of it or, in fact, on the hypothesis that there is a perennial lull.[20]

An obvious solution to the uncertainties of this on-going process of disruption and the resulting regulatory dilemma might be to engage in some form of policy experimentation, testing different regulatory schemes and then comparing the results. But such experimentation also poses a problem for regulators. Too often, 'success' for regulators is defined in negative terms as the avoidance of catastrophe. Avoiding grounds for criticism inevitably results in an overly cautious approach (the 'precautionary principle').[21]

From the perspective of entrepreneurs and consumers, such caution can be a 'disaster', or at least less preferable than a more open approach. The result is that, all too often, there is a disconnect between regulation and commercial and consumer access to that innovation.

In spite of these problems, a fact-based approach to regulation may have worked relatively well in the past when innovation cycles were longer and the pace of disruptive innovation occurred over decades. Regulators had the time necessary to get their facts in order before making a regulatory intervention:

> We see a growing divergence between time cycles of government and those of technology development. Quite simply, this presents government operations with a Hobson's choice: Either live within a shorter response time and run the concomitant risk of ill-considered actions (or inactions) or see government input become less relevant and assume reduced stature … The risk of insufficient access to information is large. This goes beyond the problem of gaining awareness of and collating relevant data series. A related and in many ways more problematic issue is that of managing and accounting for data and other knowledge resources. There is then, of course, the central task of analyzing and providing an interpretation of the data. These issues are already of concern and will increase in time.[22]

---

[20] JA Schumpeter, *Capitalism, Socialism, and Democracy* (New York, Harper, 1962) 83–84.

[21] See, generally, E Fisher et al (eds), *Implementing the Precautionary Principle: Perspectives and Prospects* (London, Edward Elgar, 2006).

[22] SW Popper, 'Technological Change and the Challenges for 21st Century Governance' in AH Teich et al (eds), *AAAS Science and Technology Policy Yearbook 2003* (Washington, DC, American Academy for the Advancement Science, 2003) 86.

In this respect, it is again instructive to consider the origins of the modern automobile industry. Karl Benz was awarded a patent for the internal combustion engine in 1879, and started producing automobiles in the mid-1880s.[23] But Benz's engine did not disrupt the horse and carriage industry or bring the automobile into the mainstream of everyday life. This only occurred much later, in 1908, when Henry Ford started to mass produce the Model T.[24]

The slower pace of technological disruption explains why, until relatively recently, the public were happy to delegate regulatory decisions about new technology to policymakers relying on the scientific advice of experts.[25] There was a relatively high degree of trust in both the political process and the scientific/expert method.

In today's world, however, the incessant speed of technological change means that this kind of approach faces insurmountable challenges. The pressure of time means that the facts surrounding a piece of new technology or other innovation may not be there, or the regulators may simply select the 'wrong'—or at least contested or otherwise irrelevant—facts as the basis of regulation. The lack of time means that establishing facts or negotiating with entrenched interests becomes much more difficult.

Moreover, there is a much greater degree of scepticism about the policymakers and scientists.[26] Most people may not be familiar with terms such as 'agency capture' or 'minoritarian bias',[27] but they are acutely aware of the way in which political and scientific processes have been distorted by vested interests and lobbying on the part of well-organised interest groups.[28]

Take AirBnB, for example. Regulators in some countries have become concerned that individuals looking to get rich from renting out properties via AirBnB are buying housing in desirable urban residential areas, thus distorting property prices and—potentially—creating housing shortages in such areas. The solution? A rule that requires that those renting out accommodation via AirBnB to be actually living in the property when it is being used.

Of course, the selection of the 'relevant facts' in this case and the resulting rule benefits certain vested interests, most obviously the hotel industry, which stands to lose out from the new competition from AirBnB. But are the selected facts in this case relevant, or even correct? A possible effect of a rule requiring residency in rented accommodation is that it may limit AirBnB in certain markets, so it is clearly important to get this right.

---

[23] See, generally, J Coad, *Finding and Using Oil* (New York, Heinemann, 2008).

[24] A Axelrod and C Phillips, *What Every American Should Know About American History* (New York, Adams Media, 2008) 210.

[25] M Callon et al, *Acting in an Uncertain World: An Essay on Technical Democracy* (Cambridge, MA, MIT Press, 2009).

[26] See RM Bratspies, 'Regulatory Trust' (2009) 51 *Arizona Law Review* 575.

[27] See NK Komesar, 'A Job for the Judges: The Judiciary and the Constitution in a Massive and Complex Society' (1988) 86 *Michigan Law Review* 657.

[28] JC Coffee, 'The Political Economy of Dodd-Frank: Why Financial Reform Tends to be Frustrated and Systemic Risk Perpetuated' (2012) 97 *Cornell Law Review* 1019, 1036.

Are the people intending to offer AirBnB accommodation really only in it for the money? In many cases, renting out accommodation may be about connecting with people from other cultures, or offering a welcoming experience for tourists visiting a new city. The 'factual' premise or basis of the regulation—ie individuals looking to make easy money from residential properties—may simply be incorrect. The selected facts may not even be facts, or at least the most relevant facts about a particular innovation.

As a second example, consider Uber or similar 'taxi-like' car-sharing services.[29] There is no doubt that services like Uber are disrupting the taxi industry. The effect is that regulatory debates around Uber are currently dominated by an unfair competition argument: (i) Trustworthy and reliable taxi companies are facing unfair competition from Uber, and this kind of unlicensed activity poses enormous risks for consumers. (ii) US start-up companies, in particular, do not respect the legal order that protects the European labour market. These 'facts' are then used to justify regulatory intervention that effectively attempts to kill Uber in certain markets.

But as with the AirBnB case, are these 'facts' really facts? Or at least, are they the most relevant facts? Do taxis really offer a better service than Uber? Is Uber any less safe than a licensed taxi? And is a lack of respect for labour laws a pertinent factor motivating companies like AirBnB?

The two-way rating system (drivers rate customers and customers rate drivers) and an algorithm-based system for matching up drivers and customers appear to offer an effective means of policing Uber drivers and ensuring a safe ride for customers. And is most people's experience of licensed taxis really so great, at least when compared with Uber? Most consumers simply want a reliable, clean and respectful service, but all too often incumbent taxi companies offer a substandard service. There is a disconnect between the facts that regulators identify as important and the expectations and experience of most consumers.

None of this is necessarily to blame the regulators. Agency capture, in which entrenched interests distort regulatory decisions, has always posed some risk, but the acceleration in innovation cycles means that even in the best conditions and with the best of intentions, selecting relevant facts is a difficult task. And the option of simply waiting seems likely to result in further complications and criticism.

In an age of constant, complex and disruptive technological innovation, knowing *what for*, *when* and *how* to structure regulatory interventions has become much more difficult. Regulators can find themselves in a situation where they believe they must opt either for reckless action (regulation without sufficient facts) or for paralysis (doing nothing). Inevitably in such a case, caution tends to be over risk. The precautionary principle becomes the default position. But such caution merely functions to reinforce the status quo, and the result is that new technologies struggle to reach the market in a timely or efficient manner.

How, then, should regulators respond to this unprecedented situation? Two ideas that may be of interest in the context are dynamic regulation and regulatory sandboxes. First, the idea of dynamic regulation aims to improve the ability to respond to

---

[29] See B Rogers, 'The Social Costs of Uber' (2015) 82 *University of Chicago Law Review* 85.

changing industry practices and the ability to improve relationships between regula-tors and regulated companies. Dynamic regulation can respond to changing industry practices through feedback effects and enhanced information for regulation.

In this context, regulatory decisions should not be thought of as 'final events' (to be made for all time and from which we 'all move on'). Rather, we should think of them as 'measured decision making', ie regulatory choices that are open-ended and highly contingent choices, forming one stage in a longer process and not the 'final word' on a particular issue. Regulators need to abandon a fixation on finality and legal certainty and embrace contingency, flexibility and an openness to the new.

This shift in perspective affects how we regulate disruptive technologies. Rather than approaching decisions as final events, Michel Callon has proposed the alterna-tive notion of 'measured action', or measured decision making, where 'you do not decide an outcome, you take measures' that are based on inclusive processes involving both experts and the public. Any regulatory 'choice' ultimately remains open-ended, leaving space to incorporate new knowledge, discoveries and claims. The need for finality, Callon argues, is usually overstated, more the product of expediency and habit than actual necessity. The antidote to the dichotomy of recklessness versus paralysis is a willingness to remove the temporal horizon that currently defines decision making, while at the same time creating new mechanisms for consistent citizen involvement in the ongoing process of determining measured action.[30]

A second idea is that of so-called 'regulatory sandboxes'. The Financial Conduct Authority (FCA), the financial regulatory body in the UK, is widely credited with this approach. In April 2016, the FCA broke new ground by announcing the introduction of a regulatory sandbox, which allows both start-up and established companies to test new ideas, products and business models in the area of Fintech (ie new technologies aimed at making financial services, ranging from online lending to digital currencies, more efficient). The aim of such approach is to create

> a 'safe space' in which businesses can test innovative products, services, business models and delivery mechanisms without immediately incurring all the normal regulatory consequences of engaging in the activity in question.[31]

The idea behind the sandbox is to provide a firm-specific, de-regulated space for the testing of innovative products and services, without the firm being forced to comply with the applicable set of rules and regulations.[32] With the sandbox, the regulator aims to foster innovation by lowering regulatory barriers and costs for testing disruptive innovative technologies, while ensuring that consumers will not be negatively affected. The three key questions that were investigated by the FCA on the sandbox proposal concerned 'regulatory barriers' (how and to what extent can they be lowered?), 'safe-guards' (what protector measures should be in place to ensure safety?) and 'legal framework' (what regulatory arrangement are mandated by EU law?).

---

[30] Callon et al, n 25.
[31] Financial Conduct Authority, 'Regulatory Sandbox' (2015), www.fca.org.uk/publication/research/regulatory-sandbox.pdf/.
[32] ibid.

What is perhaps most interesting about the sandbox is that new ideas, products and services can be tested in a 'live' environment. Firms will be given authorisation to test their products or strategies without being subjected to existing regulatory requirements and their associated compliance costs. In order to create this environment, the FCA has defined a set of default parameters that can be altered on a case-by-case basis, depending on the needs of a particular firm. These parameters include:

(1) *Duration*. As a default, the FCA considers three to six months to be an appropriate length of time to 'test' a particular innovation.
(2) *Scale*. The number of customers should be big enough to generate statistically relevant data and information on the product or service. This means that customers should be selected based on certain criteria that are appropriate for the product and service. Clearly, pre-agreed safeguards and protections should be in place to protect consumers.
(3) *Prior Disclosure*. Customers should be accurately informed about the test and any available compensation (if needed). Moreover, indicators, parameters and milestones that are used during the testing phase should be clearly set out from the outset.

What makes the regulatory sandbox so attractive is that, in so far as technology has consequences that flow into everyday lives, such technology will be open to discussion and democratic supervision and control. In this way, public entitlement to participate in regulatory debates can help to create a renewed sense of legitimacy that justifies the regulation.

It comes as no surprise that 'regulatory sandboxes' are being adopted by other regulators, such as the Australian Securities and Investment Commission, Singapore's Monetary Authority and Abu Dhabi's Financial Services Regulatory Authority.

V. Concluding Remarks

Designing a regulatory framework that ensures the safety of users and the public, whilst facilitating the commercial use and consumer enjoyment of disruptive innovation, is by no means easy. This is particularly true in contemporary settings, where innovation is quicker and the global dissemination of that technology is much faster.

We need to build on current understandings of best practice and identify principles that are important for corporate success, and which can provide the basis for new rules appropriate for a digital age. In particular, there is a need to focus on the centrality of value creation and the cultivation of sustained relevancy. Business regulation needs to do more to accommodate companies that are built around individuals who are there for the experience, the skills, the image and the sense of participation. In so doing, the value creation possibilities of the new-style firm can be fully enhanced.

Crucially important in this regard is the need to develop new metrics of success that acknowledge the less tangible values that are so vital for the long-term growth of a company in a digital age. From the perspective of policymakers, this entails an imaginative design of rules that can utilise these new metrics. In this way, regulators can work in partnership with companies to provide them with the best opportunity to succeed.

Index